JOURNALISM:
DATELINE, THE WORLD

JOURNALISM:
DATELINE, THE WORLD

by

Carl H. Giles

RICHARDS ROSEN PRESS, NEW YORK, N.Y. 10010

Standard Book Number: 8239–0269-2

Library of Congress Catalog Card Number: 73–76364
Dewey Decimal Classification: 371.897

Published in 1973 by Richards Rosen Press, Inc.
29 East 21st Street, New York City, N.Y. 10010

First Edition

Manufactured in the United States of America

23437

DEDICATION

This one is for Sheldon
out of love and for all
those who want/ need
the best basic journalism
education out of labor . . .
to all those who truly communicate. . . .

About the Author

CARL H. GILES is a professor of Journalism at the University of Tennessee at Martin and a widely known free-lance writer. He has written more than 350 stories and articles for national magazines and the general editorial market, including *Holiday, Resources, Progressive Farmer, Southern Living, Grit, Collegiate Journalist,* numerous men's magazines, and King Features Syndicate.

Among his books are *1927: The Picture Story of a Wonderful Year,* a Book Club selection; *Writing Right—To Sell* and *Advising Advisers,* widely used textbooks; and *The Student Journalist and Feature Writing,* a volume in the Student Journalist Series published by Richards Rosen Press.

Professor Giles is a native of Big Stone Gap, Virginia. He holds degrees of Bachelor of Science in Journalism from West Virginia University. Before joining the faculty of the University of Tennessee in 1965, he taught high school in Jacksonville, Florida. Among his awards and honors, he is a Kentucky Colonel, a Tennessee Squire, and the recipient of several writing awards. He is a member of KTA, the honorary journalism society.

Contents

Acknowledgments

The author appreciates the cooperation, contributions and courtesies extended to him for his work by the following:
Publisher Amon C. Evans and editorial cartoonist Charles Bissell of *The Nashville Tennessean;* Editor Gordon Hanna, Managing Editor William Sorrels, and editorial cartoonist Draper Hill of *The Commercial Appeal,* Memphis; Editor John F. Bridge, Managing Editor, *The National Observer;* Mr. John Herchenroeder, Assistant to the Executive Editor, *Courier-Journal* and *Louisville Times;* Editor Jerome H. Walker of *Editor and Publisher;* Professor LaRue W. Gilleland of the Journalism Department of the University of Nevada and editor of *Journalism Educator;* Professor Douglas P. Starr of Florida State University; Adviser Judith Funk and the *Tiger Hi-Line* of Cedar Falls (Iowa) High School; Brother David Cosgrove, adviser, and *The Crusader* of Salpointe High School, Nashville, Tennessee; Mrs. Douglas Roberts, Jr., adviser, and *The Pony Express* of David Lipscomb High School, Nashville, Tennessee; Adviser Mary Benedict and *The Lancer* of Arlington High School, Indianapolis, Indiana; Adviser James "Rusty" Farrell and *The Oak Leaf* of Oak Ridge (Tenn.) High School; Adviser C. Barton and *The Flame* of Brick Township High School, Bricktown, New Jersey; Adviser Pamela F. Caulley and *The Axe* of Eugene High School, Eugene, Oregon; Adviser John W. Wheeler and *The Lion* of Lyons Township High School, LaGrange and Western Springs, Illinois; Adviser Darrel Emerson and *Arthur Hill News* of Arthur Hill High School, Saginaw, Michigan; English Department Secretary Gertrude Myrick of The University of Tennessee at Martin; Adviser Louise Crawford and *The Broadcaster* of Whitehaven High School, Memphis, Tennessee; Adviser Georgia Moore and *Mustang Roundup* of East High School, Memphis; Adviser Pam Rieke and *The First Edition* of Memphis Catholic High School; Adviser Marlene Schultz and the *Elmhurst Advance,* Elmhurst High School, Fort Wayne, Indiana; Professor Neil R. McFadgen, Journalism Department, Dickinson State College in North Dakota; King Features Syndicate; The Associated Press; United Press International; Adviser Jean Dugat of *The Trojan,* Jones High School, Beeville, Texas; *Southern Living Magazine* and Editor John Logue.

Special thanks are due to the following:

Dr. Lawrence R. Campbell, Director of Quill and Scroll Studies of the School of Education, Florida State University, who contributed some outstanding information from his writings and research studies. He is the foremost authority on all aspects of secondary journalism.

Dr. Lester G. Benz, Executive Secretary of the Quill and Scroll Society of the School of Journalism, State University of Iowa, Iowa City, who is responsible for my obtaining some of Dr. Campbell's work and research. He is an acclaimed educator and authority on the secondary press. He and Dr. Campbell are among the elite of professional journalists, noted for their work with the high-school press and the journalism profession.

Professor Paul A. Atkins of the School of Journalism, West Virginia University, one of the best copy editors in the nation. His advice and editing of the copy-editing chapter are very much appreciated, as are his "tours" of SDX convention cities.

My secretary, Pat Elmore, for her dedication to the monumental task of typing this work.

*   *   *

Parts of the chapters on advertising and editorials in this book are based on materials from *Advising Advisers: The High School Press* by this author, which was published by the University of Tennessee, Department of Correspondence, Division of Continuing Education.

Introduction

EDUCATION, U.S.A.—January-December, is the most important dateline of the news media. Directly and indirectly, all news and progress come from here.

Education is the womb of logic and intelligence. Every citizen must undergo the educational process. High-school students represent one of the nation's largest population groups. They are physically and mentally involved with all that constitutes life.

Economically, they make one of the largest contributions to the financial system. Millions of students are part of the nation's work force. They labor at part-time jobs and positions daily. Many more are employed full time during summers. They constitute one of the largest segments of the buying public. They put hundreds of millions of dollars into the economy with the goods and services they buy. Politically, they are concerned with the mechanics of democracy. Some are able to exercise their obligation to vote before they graduate.

Students make good, bad, lucky, and unlucky news and features daily, as does any other major group in society. Teachers and other educational personnel are also news makers. Some students will win awards and prizes of significant news value. Others will be arrested as lawbreakers. Some will be acclaimed for heroic acts. Some will die in accidents.

Students live and cope with life like everyone else. No major portion of the people can be compartmentalized. Millions must act and react with millions. And—all are individuals. News relates the activities of man. Feature writers put those activities in perspective. Editorials offer explanations, alternatives, and guidance.

Words and pictures are the raw materials of education and of the mass media. Man needs them to communicate. His survival and progress depend on his ability to send and receive messages. And one reads, listens, and looks virtually all the time. The mass media have three functions. They inform, entertain, and influence. Each function may operate more or less separately, but generally all three are involved to varying extents with most stories, whether printed, visual, or oral. People are in virtually constant contact with one or more of the mass media from birth until death.

Many people assume that they are authorities on journalism because they consume so much of it daily. But they are just that, consumers. Absorbing something and being technically expert on it are different realities. Journalism laces the universe together. Wires, waves, and words carry a constant flow of information and entertainment to people. The scope is overwhelming, and it continues to increase in the technical drama of the communications revolution.

CARL H. GILES

CHAPTER I

The Scope of Mass Media

Journalism is a synonym for mass communications and mass media. The *press* is another all-encompassing term. *News media* is a little more restrictive, more or less excluding two mediums. The six that make up the mass media are three printed mediums—newspapers, magazines, and books—and three electronic mediums—radio, television, and motion pictures.

Daily newspapers in America total approximately 1,750. Over half of them are published in towns with less than 25,000 population. Most are in the 10,000 circulation level. Only 125 or so newspapers in the nation have circulations of over 100,000.

There are 334 morning and 1,429 evening newspapers. Cartoons to the contrary notwithstanding, most people do not have a morning newspaper with their breakfast. The total daily newspaper circulation is over 62,000,000.

Why do only 586 of the newspapers publish on Sundays? The sabbath edition is a unique package. It has more pages and sections than its weekday counterparts. Economics is the primary answer. Small towns cannot compete with the major metropolitan papers. The latter have more money, larger staffs, and the facilities to amass the necessary copy. Some people subscribe only to the Sunday issue; some subscribe only on weekdays. The total Sunday circulation is almost as large as the total daily circulation, some 50,000,000 copies.

Small-town newspapers average 8 to 16 pages per day, whereas metro dailies average 47 pages per day. Sunday issues average 145 pages. The content of the dailies averages over 60 percent advertising and less than 40 percent news, features, and editorials. Advertising is virtually the sole source of revenue for all the mass media, except books. It costs more to print a newspaper or magazine than the public pays for it in cover price.

The average amount of time a person devotes to daily newspaper reading ranges from 20 to 35 minutes, depending on the source of the estimate.

The following chart from the American Newspaper Publishers As-

15

sociation analyzes daily newspaper readership as to age, education, and income.

DAILY NEWSPAPER LEADERSHIP

Daily Newspaper Readership for 1970 (For 18 years and older)

		Readers Projected to the U.S. Population
Total Adults	78%	(98,183,000)
Males	78	(46,659,000)
Females	78	(51,524,000)

Percent Coverage of Weekday Newspaper Audience by Age

by Age:	Total Adults	Male	Female
18–19	72%	74%	71%
20–24	73	73	74
25–34	77	76	78
35–49	82	83	82
50–64	79	78	80
65 or older	72	72	72

Percent Coverage of Weekday Newspaper Audience by Education

by Education	Total Adults	Male	Female
College Graduate	87%	88%	85%
1–3 years College	87	87	86
High-School Graduate	83	82	83
1–3 years High School	75	75	75
No High School	64	63	64

Percent Coverage of Weekday Newspaper Audience by Household Income

by Household Income:	Total Adults	Male	Female
$25,000 and Over	86%	88%	83%
$15,000–$24,999	88	88	88
$10,000–$14,999	86	85	86
$ 8,000–$ 9,999	82	83	81
$ 5,000–$ 7,999	75	74	76
Less than $5,000	64	60	67

Source: American Newspaper Publishers Association

Some people assume that everyone reads every column inch of a newspaper. According to the Continuing Study of Newspaper Reading, conducted for eleven years by the Advertising Research Foundation, no story has ever claimed more than 90 percent readership. The study found that men read 14 percent of the total newspaper each day, and women score 3 percent less. As the chart indicates, women do represent a higher percentage of readership in some education and income brackets than do men.

A daily newspaper is like a variety store. One shops through it looking only at the items that he feels for some reason he must and at others that attract his attention or interest. Most people read and scan the front page as a matter of patriotic duty. It is the obligation of the intelligent citizen today to stay informed. One feels ostracized from society if he is unaware of significant or human interest current news. Often one cannot participate in a conversation unless he has read the newspaper that day.

Weekly newspapers are the essence of "community journalism." The term has poor connotations for most journalists. Small-town and village coverage can be done well, but that happens with very few of the 9,400 weeklies in the nation. Fewer than one fourth of them use editorials. Of course, some small-town dailies lack the courage or the conviction to publish editorials.

There is little news in a weekly. When something of major news value occurs in a rural area, almost all of the population learns about it by word of mouth. Except for late-breaking news, the best a weekly can do with its news diet is to run week-old news to clarify and correct rumors. Features and news features must be emphasized to keep decent quality in a weekly. Most weeklies are deplorable in almost every editorial respect. They rarely cover the news well, too often are crudely written, and often ignore—or are not aware of—the basic guidelines of good newspaper journalism.

Seven out of ten people read one or more magazines regularly, devoting from a few minutes to over an hour to each issue. Only 600 or so of these publications are considered general consumer magazines. Fewer than 100 of them have 1,000,000 or more circulation. *Reader's Digest* has a circulation of over 15,000,000, and *Good Housekeeping* and *McCall's* are among those with over 5,000,000 circulation. The major groups are: comics, confessions, fact-crime, farm, general interest, juvenile, literary or "quality," men's adventures, men's slicks, regional, religious, sport and outdoor, teen, theater, movie, TV, and entertainment, travel, and women's magazines.

Some 10,000 magazines are published by businesses for their employees and customers. These publications are called house organs, business magazines, and industrial publications. Every sizable firm publishes one or more. Some are in newspaper rather than magazine format. The automotive house organs such as *Ford Times,* Chevrolet's *Friends, Dodge News,* and Lincoln's *Continental* have circulations in the millions. House organs, unlike any other publications, are given away. They are a part of the public-relations and labor-relations programs of business.

Trade magazines add 2,500 to the total. Virtually every trade and profession has one or more magazines edited for it. Increasing profits and efficiency are their primary objectives. Service is their reason for being. There are magazines for journalists such as *Editor & Publisher,*

Quill, Writer's Digest, and *The Writer.* Brick-manufacturing executives have the *Brick & Clay Record.*

Religious journals add 1,500 more, bringing the figure to approximately 14,000 magazines. Of all of them, 5,000 or more depend to some degree on free-lance writers for their articles and stories. The others are staff-written.

Of some 1,500 book publishers, only 100 or so are considered major firms. Big houses publish hundreds of books per year, while some small firms publish fewer than a dozen. One out of four people reads a book each month. Less than one third of the population reads books at all. It is estimated that over 1,000,000 paperback books are sold each day.

Magazines and books have the advantage of time and space over newspapers. The daily press must publish the gamut of occurrences. It cannot devote too much time or too many column inches to any one story. Magazines and books can and do publish exposés and comments on major news events. On occasion they make news with their publication of news.

Television is the newest of the mass media. Although commercial television officially began in 1941, the medium was operating on a limited basis by 1927. In the 1950's the medium started to emerge. Some 60,-000,000 homes currently have one or more TV sets, over half of them color. This accounts for 97 percent of all the homes in the nation. Sets are tuned in for an average of six hours daily. During the past five years viewing time has decreased a half hour.

There are some 700 commercial stations and 182 educational and noncommercial stations. Over 500 of the commercial studios broadcast on very high frequency (VHF), utilizing Channels 2 to 13. Fewer than 200 broadcast on ultrahigh frequency (UHF), which uses Channels 14 to 83.

Under present viewing habits, the average person will spend a full nine years of his life before a TV set. From age 3 until they are 18, children spend between 15,000 and 20,000 hours before sets. Television is the most controversial of the news media. The myth of objectivity is argued. Most people reveal their opinions and attitudes to a degree by how they appear—their facial expressions—and how they talk—their tone of voice and inflections. Being able to see the person who is talking puts much responsibility on the viewer. Human nature is more intimately involved. How magazine writers and newspaper reporters look and talk doesn't matter; one sees only their work, not them.

Radios outnumber people nearly three to one in America. Almost 100,000,000 people listen to radio on an average of two and one-half hours daily. Almost 99 percent of American homes have one or more receivers. There are some 4,300 radio stations, almost 2,500 of which broadcast on frequency modulation (FM). Music is the primary ingredient of radio programming. Most small-town stations operate only on a daylight-to-dusk time schedule. The Federal Communications Commission limits transmission power to 50,000 watts. Use of more power literally wipes out the airwaves of the smaller transmitters.

Motion picture houses reached their peak in 1949, with some 90,-000,000 people going to see a film each week. By 1956 this attendance was reduced by half. In 1968 ticket sales were down to 21,000,000 per week. Television continues to affect the film industry, but the filmmakers are producing their fare for TV now. Prime-time TV shows—from 6 P.M. to midnight—often have between 30,000,000 and 50,000,000 viewers.

Although some 6,000 have closed since 1950, there are still over 10,000 movie houses and almost 4,000 drive-in theaters. It is extremely rare for a theater to be built in the downtown area of a major city. The few theaters being built are found in suburban shopping centers. Half the adult population see a movie a month. One out of four people sees one movie or more weekly.

Movie cassettes make it possible for people to see the movies they want on their own TV sets. Most critics forecast that the cassette will be a vast contribution to home entertainment.

Thus, the scope of the mass media is astronomical and complex. Global communications are coming. One is in contact with one or more mediums at all times. One can hear a radio next door while he is reading a magazine, book, or newspaper and his own TV set is operating. If a movie is being shown on the set, then he is all but shrouded in the mass media.

Except for local news, newspapers and radio and television stations obtain virtually all their regional, state, national, and international news from the two major wire services, the Associated Press and United Press International. Only a few dozen newspapers keep a correspondent in the nation's capital or send reporters to cover wars and other major news events in the world.

The AP and UPI have men and women in all the major news centers of the world and quickly dispatch reporters to cover important news stories. The AP serves some 8,500 newspapers and radio and television stations in the United States and abroad. The UPI has some 6,000 subscribers. The two services lease over 400,000 miles of telephone wire in the nation. Each has a budget of $1,000,000 a week. Small newspapers pay $100 to $400 weekly for one of the services. A few of the largest dailies pay $6,000 weekly in wire service fees. More than 500 dailies subscribe to both services.

Media Ownership

Who owns the media? Newspaper chains have developed. Some chains own 30 or 40 newspapers. A few own more than 50. Scripps-Howard,

Gannett, Newhouse, Hearst, and Thomson are among the larger chains. The government has established controls concerning mass media monopolies. No newspaper chain may own more than a specified number of radio and television stations. Having too much of the media vested in one ownership would be contrary to the best interests of democracy.

Few cities have more than one newspaper. In the cities with two, they are generally owned by the same party, group, or chain. However, they are often quite competitive. Some papers have merged mechanical operations in order to save on printing and other expenses, but they remain competitive editorially. Only 100 or so cities have two or more papers under separate ownership. In such a situation, usually one is a morning paper and the other an afternoon. Fewer than 50 cities have total competition, a morning against a morning or an evening against an evening.

Three networks—ABC, CBS, and NBC—control all but 50 of the 700 television stations. This trio plus the Mutual Broadcasting Corporation owns the majority of radio stations. The motion picture industry is dominated by fewer than half a dozen companies. Some magazine corporations own a dozen or more publications. Some media corporations own one or more of each of the mass mediums. The *Los Angeles Times* was obliged to sell the *San Bernardino* (California) *Sun-Telegram* a few years ago because the company was becoming too large in California holdings.

The High-School Press

Approximately 18,000 of the nation's 27,924 high schools have newspapers. Only a few thousand of them publish a magazine. Some of the more modern schools have an internal radio or public-address broadcast operation for airing announcements, news, and occasional features.

"What is the function of the school newspaper?" Dr. Laurence Campbell asks in one of his Quill and Scroll Studies. "Is it a house organ, public relations medium, adversary medium, or truth shop?" This question was asked of 275 high-school newspapers among 157 other items in a questionnaire.

Of the 275 schools participating in the survey, 55 percent were public, 84 percent were coeducational, 69 percent had traditional schedules, and 95 percent were three-year, four-year, or five- to six-year high schools. Enrollments were as follows: under 500, 23 percent; 500 to 999, 24 percent; 1,000 to 1,999, 31 percent; 2,000 to 2,999, 17 percent; and more than 3,000, 5 percent.

The following tables assess their beliefs in answer to some of the questions concerning the roles of the high-school press. The replies are analyzed in three ways. "All" means the response of all schools to the question. The other two categories record the responses from "All-American" newspapers and those that have scored "Second-Class" ratings in Quill competition. "All-American" is the highest rating possible.

"Second-Class" refers to those newspapers which won the rating below "All-American" and below "First-Class." Generally, rating services stop with "Third-Class."

Concerning Table I, it is alarming that anyone would believe that the school newspaper should be dictated by the Student Council or an "In-Group." It is equally disturbing that there are persons who are undecided about sacrificing their press freedom, which is really the only freedom. At the minimum, it is the essence of all that constitutes a democracy.

The following questions were asked Quill and Scroll members about the purposes of school newspapers.

TABLE 1.—Is it the House Organ of the Student Council or an "In-Group" of Students Who Hold Key Positions of Influence, Power?

	All	All-American	Second-Class
Strongly agree	1	1	..
Agree	5	4	6
Undecided	4	1	3
Disagree	22	14	35
Strongly disagree	68	80	55

The next question evidently confused many student newspapers. An analysis of its wording must be made carefully. Perhaps the term "newsletter" was too widely or too narrowly interpreted by most. The accurate definition removes all content except news. Features and editorials are necessary to the life of a newspaper also. All three types of copy are needed. Any publication lacking one of them is not a newspaper.

TABLE 2.—Is the Newsletter of the School for Parents and Alumni As Well As Students and Faculty?

	All	All-American	Second Class
Strongly agree	12	17	6
Agree	33	39	39
Undecided	14	6	13
Disagree	23	19	29
Strongly disagree	18	19	13

According to 14 percent of the student staffs in this survey, the main function of the newspaper should be opposition to the School Establishment. This narrow concept hardly fulfills the responsibilities of press freedom. Focusing only on one topic seems rather limited coverage of the world. Again, an unusual percentage could not decide whether witch-hunting is good or bad.

TABLE 3.—Is it the Adversary of the School Establishment Which Exposes the Faults and Failures of the School?

	All	All-American	Second Class
Strongly agree	1	3	..
Agree	13	4	16
Undecided	9	17	13
Disagree	38	38	39
Strongly disagree	39	41	32

Although there are a few who apparently do not believe in truth and objectivity, the following table notes that most newspaper staffs do. Concerning the few, one may wonder what their concepts of freedom and fairness are. One may also ponder what the alternatives were for those who could not make a decision.

TABLE 4.—Is it the Truth Shop Which Presents the School "Like It Is" in Accurate, Balanced, Objective, Truthful News?

	All	All-American	Second Class
Strongly agree	48	56	39
Agree	37	35	48
Undecided	7	5	6
Disagree	6	4	6
Strongly disagree	1	1	..

Some excellent essays and articles have been written praising, supporting, and endorsing freedom of the press. One of the best declarations of the functions and responsibilities of the press to the public—every individual—is the code of the American Society of Newspaper Editors. It adopted these principles in April, 1923:

> The primary function of newspapers is to communicate to the human race what its members do, feel and think. Journalism, therefore, demands of its practitioners the widest range of intelligence, of knowledge, and of experience, as well as natural and trained powers of observation and reasoning. To its opportunities as a chronicle are indissolubly linked its obligations as teacher and interpreter.
>
> To the end of finding some means of codifying sound practice and just aspirations of American journalism, these canons are set forth:
>
> I
>
> RESPONSIBILITY. The right of a newspaper to attract and hold readers is restricted by nothing but consideration of public welfare. The use a newspaper makes of the share of public attention it gains serves to determine its sense of responsibility, which it shares with every member of its staff. A journalist who uses his power for any selfish or otherwise unworthy purpose is faithless to a high trust.

II

FREEDOM OF THE PRESS. Freedom of the press is to be guarded as a vital right of mankind. It is the unquestionable right to discuss whatever is not explicitly forbidden by law, including the wisdom of any restrictive statute.

III

INDEPENDENCE. Freedom from all obligations except that of fidelity to the public interest is vital.

1. Promotion of any private interest contrary to the general welfare, for whatever reason, is not compatible with honest journalism. So-called news communications from private sources should not be published without public notice of their source or else substantiation of their claims to value as news, both in form and substance.

2. Partisanship in editorial comment which knowingly departs from the truth does violence to the best spirit of American journalism; in the news columns it is subversive of a fundamental principle of the profession.

IV

SINCERITY, TRUTHFULNESS, ACCURACY. Good faith with the reader is the foundation of all journalism worthy of the name.

1. By every consideration of good faith a newspaper is constrained to be truthful. It is not to be excused for lack of thoroughness or accuracy within its control or failure to obtain command of these essential qualities.

2. Headlines should be fully warranted by the contents of the articles which they surmount.

V

IMPARTIALITY. Sound practice makes clear distinction between news reports and expressions of opinion. News reports should be free from opinion or bias of any kind.

1. This rule does not apply to so-called special articles unmistakably devoted to advocacy or characterized by a signature authorizing the writer's own conclusions and interpretations.

VI

FAIR PLAY. A newspaper should not publish unofficial charges affecting reputation or moral character without opportunity given to the accused to be heard; right practice demands the giving of such opportunity in all cases of serious accusation outside judicial proceedings.

1. A newspaper should not invade private rights or feelings without sure warrant of public right as distinguished from public curiosity.

2. It is the privilege, as it is the duty, of a newspaper to make prompt and complete correction of its own serious mistakes of fact or opinion, whatever their origin.

VII

DECENCY. A newspaper cannot escape conviction of insincerity if while professing high moral purposes it supplies incentives to base conduct, such as are to be found in details of crime and vice, publication of which is not demonstrably for the general good. Lacking authority to enforce its canons, the journalism here represented can but express the hope that deliberate pandering to vicious instincts will encounter effective public disapproval or yield to the influence of a preponderant professional condemnation.

The Journalist

What are the attributes of the men and women who work in the news media? They must be alert, articulate, educated, ambitious, and have the desire to help gather and distribute the products called news, features, and editorials. No other items made by man come in as many shapes and sizes. No two stories are identical. No journalist is confronted with consistent sameness.

Reporting is covering what is happening now and tomorrow. It is finding out in detail what happened. It is the ability to cope with every event of which mankind is capable. Journalism is literature in a hurry, Matthew Arnold once said.

There is drama in the profession. Old movies created the myth that many reporters are a composite of cartoon hero Clark Kent–Superman— and the best of all possible detectives. Some reporters have exhibited facets of superior beings at times. Reporters have by work and circumstance solved many crimes and produced great stories involving intrigue. But most reporters are spared or denied such situations, reality being what it is.

Not much action and atmosphere are involved in interviewing a man at the chamber of commerce concerning a new brochure designed to lure industry to the area. Listening to the last gasps of a dying man—whether he is in a hospital or pinned under a truck—while covering a story demands something of the soul of the reporter. Whether a reporter is interviewing an axe murderer, a monk in a monastery, a guerrilla leader, Miss America, or Mister America, he must adapt to each individual and his environment when and where it is.

Covering all the news and human interest events and activities of man is challenging. A desire to be involved in the dissemination of news— whether as an advertising copywriter, a television weather man, or any other position in any medium—is a prerequisite. But preparation for the profession is needed.

The education of the journalist is all-encompassing. He must have more than technical skills. Vast knowledge is important. Journalism is the written and pictorial account of all life. Journalists become repositories of information, as each story they cover or research adds to their background. In essence, a writer never wastes time. Literally everything he does, even daydreaming, is deposited in his experience bank. Academically, the journalist needs all the formal education he can get.

The Shapes of Newspapers

Newspapers have an anatomy. The title of the newspaper is just that; it is also called a nameplate or flag. On either side of the title are ears. The ears may be empty in some newspapers, but most newspapers carry some message. For instance, *The Nashville Tennessean* has a heart-shaped map in its left ear, accompanied by the motto "In the Heart of TVA." In the right ear is the slogan "Served by America's Greatest News Services."

Below its nameplate, the newspaper of the Tennessee capital carries another slogan, "At the crossroads of Natural Gas and TVA Power— Telephone 255–1221." Just below that is the volume and number of each day's issue. This line also gives the city and state of the newspaper, the date, the price, and the number of pages in the issue.

The traditional commercial newspaper is 15″ wide and usually a fraction less than 24″ long. Most newspapers have eight columns, each usually measuring 1¾″ in width. Several newspapers have converted to five-, six-, or seven-column formats, because the eight-column paper tends to be congested with type and pictures. Conversion to fewer and wider columns provides more white space. The page is open and airy, and the separation of the copy and art increases its attractiveness and its readability. The former may be debated, but reading tests confirm the latter.

Nothing but space separates the columns in newspapers with fewer than eight columns. These white alleys are also used by some eight-column newspapers, but many use thin, black lines, called column rules. Photographs are usually called such, although some veteran journalists call them cuts—going back to the days of the woodcut—or art.

The dateline is the prelude to the lead of nonlocal stories. It gives the location of the event and the source of the report, such as a wire service. A few newspapers still put the date of the event in the dateline, but most indicate the time element in the lead of the story. Local stories do not carry a dateline.

A by-lined story is one that gives the name of the journalist who wrote it. The table of contents is on page one. In the editorial section is the masthead, which may be placed in a corner at the top or bottom of the page. The information in the masthead usually includes the names of the publisher and the highest-ranking editors, the street address of the newspaper, and often some statements concerning its history. The editorial aims of the newspaper may be stated or a slogan used. High-school, college, and institutional newspapers often have much more detailed mastheads. Their length is almost invariably a liability.

Display advertising is scattered throughout a newspaper. Classified advertising is restricted to its section. Metropolitan dailies have several sections. Smaller papers usually have no more than two sections, news-editorial and sports.

Tabloid newspapers differ primarily in size. Most measure 12" by 15". By tradition they generally use more photographs than the bigger versions. More progressive full-sized newspapers that have fewer than eight columns are using more and more photographs and artwork. The eight-column format makes this less feasible.

CHAPTER II

Journalism: The Vehicle History Rides

Words and pictures are the raw materials of the mass media. Man must have them to communicate. His survival and progress depend on his ability to send and receive messages.

In the beginning—and man may be 2,000,000 years old, some anthropologists say—man communicated with his primitive neighbor with grunts, groans, and sign language. After eons, alphabets and languages developed, making him more fluent. Stone Age man recorded picture stories on many cave walls.

Handwritten news sheets were posted in public places in Rome half a century or more before Christ. The *Diamond Sutra,* published in 868 A.D. by Wang Chieh in China, is the oldest known printed book. Passages or pages were painstakingly carved into wood blocks. Movable type was probably first used by the Chinese around 1045. But it was not until the 1440's that Johann Gutenberg, a German craftsman, popularized movable type, with the individual letters on separate pieces of metal.

Newspapers began to appear in various European cities in 1609. The printing press liberated knowledge. Previously, newsletters, books, and other publications were handwritten, and their high cost restricted them to the wealthier classes. Printing made public education possible. It also altered political structures.

William Caxton, an author and scholar, established the first press in England in 1476. With the backing of King Edward IV, Caxton began publishing books and informative sheets in an effort to increase the culture and education of his countrymen.

By 1534 printers had to have permission from the crown to open a shop. By the middle of the century the crown was arresting the printers and distributors of folk-song sheets critical of the government. In 1620 newspapers published with the consent of the crown began to appear in London. Called "corantos" and restricted mostly to foreign news, they were rarely larger than 8″ by 10″ and usually consisted of only one sheet, sometimes printed on both sides. The corantos had to carry the legend "Published with Authority," and they were read by the crown before being released for distribution.

This censorship was still in effect when the first newspaper was printed

27

in the New World. Benjamin Harriss established a newspaper in London in 1679. Convicted by the crown of having seditious literature in his possession, Harriss was confined for several days in a pillory set in front of his shop. Later, he was jailed because he could not pay a heavy fine.

In 1686, Harriss, learning that he was to be arrested again, fled with his family to the New World. He opened a coffeehouse and bookshop at State and Washington Streets in Boston. There were already seven bookstores in the city, but the exiled printer was a good businessman. He prospered. His establishment attracted some of the most influential people of Boston. His finances and his fame increased further when he wrote a spelling primer that became a best seller for many years.

On September 25, 1690, Harriss published a four-page newspaper, *Publick Occurrences, Both Forreign and Domestick.* Measuring 6″ by 10¼″, it was printed on only three pages. The fourth was left blank for the reader to add his own news items before passing the paper on to someone else. But *Publick Occurrences* was banned by the crown after only one issue.

Fourteen years later, John Campbell, the postmaster of Boston, began publishing the *Boston News-Letter* with the consent of the crown. This is considered the first permanent newspaper in the New World.

Why did it take ninety-seven years for a newspaper to become established in the colonies? The first permanent settlement at Jamestown, in 1607, was hardly in a position to publish anything. John Smith and the others had enough problems trying to survive—building shelter, securing food, exploring the area, and warily watching the Indians.

Plymouth was a much better environment than the Virginia settlement. But it was eighty-four years after the *Mayflower* docked in New England before Campbell published his first issue. Two printers were among the colonists on the ship. Thus, lack of technical skill could not have been the primary handicap. Harvard College was two years old when the first press in New England was installed in 1638.

English newspapers arrived periodically on ships from Europe, but they were often two months old. The Boston coffeehouses invariably had the most recent papers from Europe. By 1700, New England had a population of 100,000.

There were plenty of printers, but no newspapers. Each colony had an official printer, who produced all the pamphlets and documents issued by the Colonial governments. Almanacs, sermons, books, and broadsides were among the materials coming off the hand presses. On at least two occasions, issues of the *London Gazette* were reprinted by the Colonial printers; demand for the papers was much greater than the number of copies the ships had brought.

England had enough problems with printers at home. It certainly did not desire any from those in its colonies. The attitude of the crown towards free speech and free printing was strict censorship and licensing. Every printer was a potential libeler, the crown believed. Sir William Berkeley, governor of the Virginia colony for thirty-eight years, reported to the crown in 1671:

"But, I thank God, we have not free schools nor printing; and I hope we shall not have these hundred years. For learning has brought disobedience and heresy and sects into the world; and printing has divulged them and libels against the government. God keep us from both."

The New England governors were not so narrow-minded. They encouraged education and its leader and ally, printing. The Southern colonies were not so populous. Farms and plantations were widely separated, villages were smaller, and agriculture was the basis of the Southern economy. New England was industrializing, developing paper mills, shipbuilding, fishing, shipping, and a host of other enterprises.

Colonial life and culture in New England was focused on Puritanism, the major expression of the early Colonial mind. Church and state were much more synonymous in the North than in the South. Religious and political leadership often overlapped in New England. The church bound the people together. Residents of Boston and other major population centers did not have to be self-sufficient like the residents of the South. Southerners could not step down the street to retail stores for goods and services. Most farms and almost all plantations were self-sustaining, making almost everything they used and growing almost everything they ate.

Early postmasters were in an ideal position to become the first newspaper publishers. As it is today in smaller towns, the post office was a meeting place of sorts. People strolled in together to get or leave mail, and a townsman would often leave a message with the postmaster to give a friend when he came to pick up his mail.

John Campbell became the Boston postmaster in 1700. His newspaper evolved naturally. He began preparing handwritten newsletters to correspondents and postmasters in other colonies, telling them of meetings, proclamations, legal notices, shipping schedules, and other news of interest from the largest city then in the colonies. After four years, Campbell saw that reporting everything in longhand was going to be impossible. He went to a printer, and the first newspaper was begun.

The *Boston News-Letter* was the sole newspaper in the colonies for fifteen years. Campbell's news did not have the impact of Harriss' newspaper attempt. *Publick Occurrences* carried stories on an Indian massacre and on some vices of the French king. Much of the first issue of the *Boston News-Letter* had been clipped from the most recently available

London newspapers, which were weeks old. The first issues were approximately the same size as *Publick Occurrences* but consisted of a single sheet printed on both sides.

Most of the content of the *News-Letter* continued to be taken from the stale English newspapers. About one-third of its stories were local and timely. Campbell tried to publish all the English news he considered significant, but by 1718 he was more than a year behind. In an effort to catch up on this time lag, he expanded the paper to four pages. But there were times when no ships arrived from England for six months.

On two occasions, once for two months and once for eight months, he suspended publication because of financial difficulties. His circulation rarely exceeded 250 or 300 copies per issue.

"Published by Authority" was the inscription under the *News-Letter* nameplate. Each issue was read by the governor or his secretary prior to publication, so that Campbell avoided any conflicts with the crown. Occasionally he was even given financial assistance from the public treasury. Campbell kept his newspaper going for five years after he retired as postmaster.

William Brooker, the new postmaster, wanted the newspaper, but Campbell refused to give it away. Brooker established his own paper, the *Boston Gazette,* and when he left office after only one year, he let his successor have the *Gazette.* It was published by four succeeding postmasters over the years.

James Franklin had been printing the *Gazette* for Brooker. When Brooker's successor started having the paper printed at another shop, Franklin missed the business. He also had some journalistic ambitions. Although he had been educated in England and learned his trade there, he disliked the rigid rule of the church and the state.

Franklin had friends who were also critical of the crown and the Colonial religious structure. With their backing, he published the first edition of the *New England Courant* on August 7, 1721. It was one of the boldest and most brilliant newspapers of the century. It was not "published by authority" like its predecessors, but more "in spite" of it. Modeled somewhat on the best English newspapers, which stressed literary excellence and satire, the *Courant* was the first newspaper in the colonies to use features and literary reviews. It was the first to introduce entertainment in a newspaper.

Smallpox was prevalent when the *Courant* was established. The powerful Puritan-leading Mather family favored inoculation against the disease. Franklin, most historians agree, capitalized on the opportunity to attack the Mathers, and the *Courant* campaigned against inoculation. Franklin no doubt knew the value of vaccination. He merely used the issue to attack what he and his friends considered the worst of the religious mores of the time.

In one issue, Franklin solicited "some short Pieces, Serious, Sarcastic, Ludicrous, or other ways amusing." Most of the *Courant* writing was done by Franklin's friends, but he himself did some of the work. He had to drop some writers because their editorial attacks were too vicious. James's half-brother Benjamin was apprenticed to him at the age of 13. Benjamin set type, swept the shop, delivered the newspapers, and did other jobs for his brother, who was some ten years older. Benjamin was an avid reader and had studied the leading English essayists of the era. He wanted to write for the *Courant* also, but knew James would not consider it.

One night in 1722 Benjamin wrote a piece of satire, signed it "Silence Dogood," and left it in the shop as if it had been stuck under the door during the night. He was elated the next day as his brother and friends praised the unknown satirist. Thirteen more of the mysterious essays appeared under the door between March and October. Focusing on the issues and controversial people of the day, they attracted much attention. Finally, Benjamin confessed to his brother that he had written the articles. James was not happy and made him stop.

In the summer of 1722 the *Courant* editor was arrested for sarcastic writing. Pirates had been operating off the Massachusetts coast, and James charged the Colonial government with being slow in pursuit of some of the privateers.

"We are advised from Boston, that the government of the Massachusetts are fitting out a Ship, to go after the Pirates, to be commanded by Captain Peter Papillon, and 'tis thought he will sail some time this Month, wind and weather permitting," the *Courant* reported.

The comment evidently spurred the governor because the ship sailed the next day. Franklin, however, was summoned to testify before the Governor's Council. He was sentenced to one month in jail. The *Courant* continued to publish while Franklin was in jail, and on his release he resumed his editorial attacks on religious and political issues.

In an effort to control the *Courant,* the Colonial administration declared that "James Franklin be strictly forbidden to print or publish the *New England Courant* or any Pamphlet or paper of the like Nature. Except it be first Supervised, by the secretary of this Province." This was merely a reaffirmation of the licensing power. Technically, James got around the order by making Ben the official publisher of the newspaper. But, also technically, Ben was relieved of his apprenticeship. He couldn't hold both posts.

In 1723 Ben ran away to Philadelphia. His brother continued the *Courant* for three more years before abandoning it, and then became the official printer for the New Jersey Colony for a few years. In 1732 James founded another newspaper, but it failed. Never did it achieve the impact and popularity that he had enjoyed with the *Courant.* His most important contribution to American history and journalism was his courage in publishing freely in defiance of English "authority."

Although Ben arrived in Philadelphia virtually penniless, in five years he was a prosperous printer and well-known young citizen. His editorial enterprises—newspapers, almanacs, magazines—developed soon afterward. He was wealthy before he was 30. Ben invested money in several newspapers. He chose ambitious young journalists and financed them in buying or establishing newspapers. He created the first editorial chain of newspapers. His most significant contribution to journalism was in making it a highly respectable profession.

The friction that had existed between the Franklin brothers for most of their lives was ameliorated somewhat. When James was dying, he asked Ben to take his son and raise him as he would his own. Ben did so.

Colonel William Cosby was the royal governor of New York in 1733. His administration clashed with the popular party, a group composed of some of the colony's most articulate and ambitious men. Among the anti-administration figures was James Alexander, a prosperous young attorney who was the surveyor general of New Jersey and a member of the governor's council.

Alexander and his faction wanted a newspaper to support their charges against the governor and his administration. They persuaded a young immigrant who had served his apprenticeship at the typecase to found a newspaper. John Peter Zenger had a small shop and some editorial ambitions. With financial backing and promises of editorial assistance, Zenger published the first issue of the New York *Weekly Journal* on November 5, 1733. With Alexander as a silent editorial partner, Zenger condemned the administration. He himself was not a very good writer, but some of his reporters and correspondents were. The small, four-page newspaper was vivid and exciting compared to its competition in the colonies.

Alexander had ample targets. He charged in the *Weekly Journal* that Governor Cosby had destroyed a deed in which the Mohawk Indians had given 1,000 acres to the city of Albany. The paper asserted that the governor was trying to get control of the property for personal gain and also accused him of trying to gain possession of 112,000 more acres. Most historians agree that Cosby was corrupt while in office. He tried to explain that one deed was counterfeit, which cast even more suspicion on him.

The *Weekly Journal* also condemned the governor for interfering with elections, attempting to influence the courts, and other actions. Although Cosby knew Alexander was responsible for the exposure and harassment by the newspaper, he could not prove it. Cosby therefore focused his power and anger on Zenger. When he could not persuade the grand jury or city council to indict Zenger for libel, he finally induced his own council to have Zenger arrested on a charge of seditious libel, in November, 1734. For nine months Zenger helped edit the newspaper from his cell and offered editorial advice through the few visitors he was allowed. Alexander and his colleagues continued to publish exposés and accusations concerning the governor.

In August, 1735, Zenger was tried. His friends and supporters secured him the most famous of the "Philadelphia lawyers." Although in his late 70's, Andrew Hamilton—not to be confused with Alexander Hamilton, the secretary of the treasury under Washington—was persuaded to come out of retirement to defend the young editor.

The prosecuting attorney of the New York colony was shocked when Hamilton admitted that Zenger had indeed printed the stories on which the charge was based.

"Then the jury must find a verdict for the King," the attorney general said, "for supposing the libels were true, they are not the less libelous for that. Nay, indeed, the [English] law says their being true is an aggravation of the crime."

"But the words themselves must be libelous, that is, false, scandalous, and seditious, or else we are not guilty," argued Hamilton.

"You cannot be admitted, Mr. Hamilton, to give the truth of a libel in evidence," Chief Justice Delancey said. "You are not permitted to argue against the opinion of the Court."

But argue well Hamilton did. He ignored the judge and the Royal Court and concentrated on the jury. With brilliant oratory, the elderly lawyer denounced tyranny and corrupt rulers. He heralded liberty as the only defense against such oppression. The common people who filled every seat in the building and stood outside on the street knew the defense included their own souls. The jury returned a verdict of "Not guilty." The cheers were so wild that the justice threatened to send the spectators to jail.

The Zenger case was the first major legal move toward freedom in the colonies. After that verdict, truth became admissible as a defense against libel.

The Stamp Act, which was passed in March, 1765, and went into effect in November the following year, ended up by branding England instead of the colonies. It demanded that all newspapers, books, official papers, and documents be printed only on stamped paper, which carried a special tax. The cost was prohibitive for newspapers, amounting to a halfpenny for each copy of a two-page newspaper. Four-pagers cost a penny. The English accepted a similar tax at home, but the Colonials defied it.

The Stamp Act alienated journalists and lawyers, two of the professions most involved in politics. Not many newspapers bought the stamps.

A few suspended publication for a short time. Some bordered their front pages to form an outline of a tombstone, symbolizing the death of free expression. The time lapse between the announcement of the Act and its effective date gave the Colonials some seven months to protest the tax. Public resentment was so intense that when the Act went into effect no one would take the job of selling the stamps. Tax collectors had been hanged in effigy in several newspapers. They feared a realistic reenactment of the same, rope included. The Act was removed in March, 1766. Almost all newspapers had evaded it in their own way.

Benjamin Edes and John Gill were the editor-publishers of the *Boston Gazette*. This was the same newspaper that had been started in competition with the *Boston News-Letter;* it had passed through a succession of postmasters until it reached this dynamic editorial team. Edes was a member of the radical Sons of Liberty. Both editors were friends of Samuel Adams, "the father of the Revolution." The *Gazette* published some of the most vehement attacks on the Stamp Act. The Massachusetts governor tried to press libel charges against the paper but was unsuccessful. Its defiance and daring increased its circulation to over 2,000, the largest in the colonies.

The *Gazette's* staff was composed primarily of political activists who also constituted an unofficial radical press corps. Officially, this clique called itself the Caucus Club. It was a judicious mixture of merchants, shipyard laborers, and some uptown intellectuals. In addition to the *Gazette* editors, Sam Adams, his cousin, John Adams, John Hancock, James Otis, Thomas Cushing, and Paul Revere were among the members.

Isaiah Thomas was one of the youngest of the group. He was 21 years old in 1770 when he established *The Massachusetts Spy*. Tall, muscular, and handsome, he was brilliant but lacked the formal education of some members of the club. Sam Adams had a master's degree, and a few others had college educations. Thomas tried to be very objective in his newspaper. Under its nameplate he carried the slogan "A Weekly Political and Commercial Paper—Open to All Parties, but influenced by None." As the temper of the colonies moved toward war, the *Spy* openly endorsed the case for freedom.

Thomas did not become resentful spontaneously, however. He was very much agitated by the Stamp Act, and he was just 17 at the time. He had started working as a printer's apprentice when he was 6. Boston became the center for Colonial dissent, and Thomas became a leader in the underground movement. He was the man who signaled with the lantern in the Old North Church for Paul Revere to begin his historic ride.

The *Spy* and the *Gazette* had to leave town during the British occupation. Their presses were smuggled out of the city in wagons to Worcester and Charles Town respectively. Thomas continued to prosper as an editor and publisher during the war. His plant expanded to seven presses and 150 employees. Over 400 books were published by his presses. He was the first American to publish John Bunyan's *Pilgrim's Progress, Mother Goose Tales,* and *Little Goody Two-Shoes.* Daniel Defoe's *Robinson Crusoe* was published as a serial by several Colonial newspapers, but Thomas was the first to publish it in book form.

Sam Adams never was prosperous financially as was Thomas. He failed as a businessman. His friends often had to lend him money to keep him sheltered. Freedom and rebellion were his major concerns from 1765 to 1783.

Called "the grand incendiary" by the New England Tories, Adams used his forceful speech and pen to condemn and harass the British. He was in the House of Representatives from 1765 to 1774, part of the time serving as a clerk. Between 1770 and 1772 he wrote over forty inflammatory articles for the *Gazette.* He led the band of radicals to the Boston Tea Party on the night of December 16, 1773. Dressed as Mohawk Indians, they dumped 342 chests of the commodity from British ships anchored in the harbor. The raiders had donned their disguises that evening in the *Gazette* office.

"Where there is a spark of patriotic fire," Adams said, "we will kindle it."

But England feared one man even more than Adams. James Otis was even more magnetic and explosive in inciting the Revolution. A Harvard graduate like Adams, he became a lawyer in 1748. By 1761, he was renowned for his stature in the profession and considered the most eloquent and unyielding defender of Colonial rights. Adams wrote of his friend many years later, "Otis was a flame of fire." Otis forecast the Declaration of Independence by demanding that people have the rights of life, liberty, and the pursuit of happiness.

Despite his brilliance, Otis was not a stable man. He was highstrung and often could not check his temper. In 1771 he was declared insane. His death was as dramatic as his life. He was killed by lightning in May, 1783—the year the Revolution ended—while standing in the doorway of a farmhouse near Andover, Massachusetts. One of his adversaries said, "He set the province in a flame and perished in the attempt." Even after his mental illness removed him from public life, Otis' oratory still echoed in the consciousness of the colonies.

Thomas and his *Spy* continued to advocate freedom and Colonial unity. His newspaper's trademark was a snake sliced in segments with the caption "Join or Die." Ben Franklin had used a similar cartoon in his *Pennsylvania Gazette* of May 9, 1754, calling for Colonial unity against the French and their Indian allies. The royal governor warned Thomas to tone down his attacks, but the young editor ignored him, and the Crown was afraid to arrest him for fear of precipitating war. Thomas was one of the twelve men already on the hanging list who had been excluded from the amnesty offered by Britain in an effort to avoid war. Edes, Gill, and Adams were also on the list. The other eight were not journalists but were frequent contributors to the crusading Colonial newspapers.

Thomas covered the first shots of the Revolution, and he was at the Battle of Lexington. His account was one of the most notable examples of reporting during the war.

The pamphleteers had started campaigning by 1767. John Dickinson, more than any other man except Otis and Adams, did much to prepare the public for the conflict. He was for peaceful separation from England if it could be achieved. His series of articles titled "Letters From a Farmer in Pennsylvania" was printed in newspapers and pamphlets. A Quaker, he was conservative, but his political commitments were strong and notable. Dickinson belonged to the elite propertied class, and he convinced many of his class that they must defy British rule.

A 37-year-old former corset-maker from England did more with his editorial inspiration than any other person to keep morale from ebbing during the Revolution. Thomas Paine was a drifter who had worked at several manual and minor jobs. From a poor family, he had little education, but he was not content with his fate. Fortunately for America, Paine met Ben Franklin when he was visiting London. The journalist-statesman-inventor gave him a letter of introduction and a promise of a job if he went to the colonies. In 1774 Paine did so. He got a job as an editor for the *Pennsylvania Magazine* in Philadelphia.

A natural crusader, Paine was a fanatic looking for a cause. And he found it. His first criticism was an editorial attacking the institution of slavery. He was probably the first man in the colonies to denounce it with such force.

On January 10, 1776, Paine published a 47-page pamphlet titled "Common Sense," blasting King George III and his government. In three months it sold 120,000 copies at two shillings each. Nothing published during the Colonial period ever achieved such scope and impact. Undoubtedly, it gave great impetus to the Declaration of Independence signed on July 4 of that year.

Paine enlisted in George Washington's army. At night by the light of a campfire, he continued to write. And the "Crisis" papers began to appear.

A copy of the first "Crisis" article reached General Washington the day before he attacked Trenton. He had it read to each squad before the fight. He lost, but he later said, "The 'American Crisis' did not win the battle, but it was as good as another regiment." Each time the Colonial cause seemed doomed to crumble because of bloody defeats, Paine came up with another piece of writing that renewed the souls fighting for freedom.

Paine never got rich from his writings. He gave all his earnings to the war effort. Congress deemed him too valuable to leave in the ranks. In 1777 he was appointed Secretary to the Committee on Foreign Affairs, but he angered France and was forced to resign. He became a clerk of the Pennsylvania Assembly. When Washington was pleading for money to feed and clothe his cold and hungry troops in 1780, Paine undertook a campaign to raise it. He went to France, which he had offended, and was nevertheless able to collect cash and supplies.

After the war, Paine was again restless and broke. He had thought it morally wrong to earn royalties from suffering. The public, as it invariably tends to do, almost forgot his significant contributions. Washington had the State of New York grant him a 300-acre farm, and Congress and the State of Pennsylvania gave him $5,500. But Paine soon left for Europe and became involved in other revolutions. However, he was never to gain another such climax as his achievement in America. During World War II, one of Paine's "Crisis" papers was used often to support the morale of the Allied nations when times were particularly bad. During the Nazi invasion of England the crackling radios often came through with these immortal lines:

> These are the times that try men's souls. The summer soldier and the sunshine patriot will, in this crisis, shrink from the service of their country; but he that stands it NOW deserves the love and thanks of man and woman. Tyranny, like hell, is not easily conquered; yet we have this consolation with us that the harder the conflict the more glorious the triumph. What we obtain too cheap, we esteem too lightly; it is dearness only that gives every thing its value. Heaven known how to put a proper price upon its goods; and it would be strange indeed if so celestial an article as FREEDOM should not be highly rated.

The most famous Tory paper before and during the Revolution was James Rivington's *New York Gazette,* which he began in 1773. Rivington came to the colonies in 1762 after losing over $50,000 at racetracks. His family had been the official publishers of religious books for the Church of England. Rivington remained loyal to the mother country because he was still a member of its established church, and to rebel against England would be to reject the church.

Rivington regained his fortune through a profitable chain of bookstores in New York, Philadelphia, and Boston. As a newspaperman, he was competent, successful, and highly respected by the Tories. He had been commendably objective prior to the first shots of the Revolution. Then he became a propaganda agent for the Tories. When his presses were destroyed during the war, he returned to England and came back with new ones. He continued to publish against the rebels until the end of the Revolution silenced the skilled Tory voice. As Adams lied concerning some charges against the British, Rivington lied concerning American leaders.

Of the 35 papers in the colonies when the Revolution started, only 20 survived. During the war, some 35 others were founded, not all of which survived. There were about as many papers after the war as before it.

In 1787, a Constitutional Convention was held in Philadelphia to revise the Articles of Confederation or to draft another Constitution. Nine of the thirteen states had already incorporated freedom of the press in their constitutions. Most delegates to the convention were prosperous landholders, who naturally favored the propertied class. They were conservative and wanted to retain as much power as possible in the hands of a few. But the general public was wary. It wanted some concessions and got them. Otherwise ratification of the document would never have been possible

One of the primary additions to the Constitution was the Bill of Rights, comprising the first ten amendments to the Constitution. The first draft of the document stated that ". . . no state shall violate the equal rights of conscience or of freedom of speech . . ." When the amendment went to the House and Senate, it was modified to include that all-important prepositional phrase, "or of the press." The omission was not exactly intentional by the framers of the document. Some delegates assumed that the protection of the press would be handled by the states, since all but four had already offered that guarantee. The First Amendment was ratified in 1791.

Those who favored adoption of the Constitution crystalized into a party called the Federalists. They were of the landed gentry, but many were members of the clergy, the medical profession, and the merchant class. Alexander Hamilton, the secretary of the treasury under President Washington, was the party leader. Thomas Jefferson, the secretary of state under Washington, led the opposition.

Jefferson's followers were for strong states' rights and a weaker central government. They were primarily small farmers and those owning no property, the poorer working classes. They clamored for the Constitution to express the freedoms for which they had fought the Revolution. And they felt that the moneyed property holders would not permit them an equal voice in government.

Those for adoption of the Constitution were spearheaded by Hamilton, James Madison, and John Jay. The trio wrote eighty-five essays during 1787 and 1788. The collection, called the Federalist Papers, first appeared in the *New York Independent Journal.* Other newspapers also printed them.

The party press started developing in 1789 when the Federalists launched the *Gazette of the United States,* a political organ based in New York City, with John Fenno as editor. Jefferson's party picked a brilliant soldier of fortune, Philip Freneau, to edit its newspaper, the *National Gazette,* which was launched October 31, 1791. Dubbed "the Poet of the Revolution," Freneau wrote some of the most highly acclaimed verse during the war. His poetry was as fiery as Paine's prose, and in its own medium also helped morale. The American-born French Huguenot was a close friend of Jefferson. At Princeton University—then the College of New Jersey—he roomed with James Madison. Aaron Burr, Harry Lee, and Hugh Brackenridge were among his classmates, all to become important then and to history for their exploits.

Freneau had captained a privateer for a short time during the war. He was captured and spent miserable months in the hold of a prison ship anchored in New York Harbor. The ordeal had taxed his health considerably, but not his spirit. As the *National Gazette* editor he proved he had no peer in political prose either. Hamilton was disturbed by Freneau's brilliant writing. Under pen names, the secretary of the treasury wrote articles attacking him in the Federalist newspaper. It is not known whether Jefferson did any writing for his party's organ, the *National Gazette.* The paper died in 1793 when Jefferson left his cabinet office. Freneau closed its doors during an epidemic of yellow fever, and it never reopened. It could not have reopened anyway because there was no money to support it; Jefferson had not been able to secure enough financing to keep it going. Freneau is best remembered today for having designed the street system for Washington, D.C.

In the summer of 1798 the Federalist administration of John Adams tried to muzzle the opposing party press with two pieces of legislation. In June, the Alien Act was passed, providing in essence that foreign-born editors critical of the administration would be deported. Another provision of the Act allowed the President to deport foreigners he considered subversive. Two shiploads of men were deported.

The Sedition Act was passed the following month. It stated: "That if any person shall write, print, utter, or publish . . . any false, scandalous and malicious writing . . . against the government of the United States, or either house of the Congress . . . or the said President . . . or to excite against them the hatred of the good people of the United States . . . or to resist or oppose, or defeat any such law . . . shall be punished by a fine not exceeding two thousand dollars, and by imprisonment not exceeding two years."

Both acts were in effect for two years. Even Hamilton deemed them too severe. Former President Washington left his sick-bed to protest them.

Jefferson decided that the best course was to try to nullify the acts through states' rights. The results were the Virginia and Kentucky Resolutions, which declared that freedom of the press should remain. Madison wrote the one for Virginia. John Breckenridge was thought to be the author of the other, but twenty-five years later it was disclosed that Jefferson had written it. He could not admit authorship because at that time he was vice-president and the action would have violated his oath of office to uphold the federal government.

Matthew Lyon, a congressman from Vermont, was the most famous of the ten men fined or jailed under the Sedition Act. Fifteen more were arrested and released. Lyon was sentenced to four months for writing a letter critical of President Adams to a newspaper editor. Although he was imprisoned in October, 1798, he was nevertheless reelected to Congress. When he was released the following February, his supporters were waiting, and the newspapers reported that the procession behind his carriage as he left jail was twelve miles long at times.

When Jefferson became President in 1800, the United States had several daily newspapers. New York had five; Philadelphia, six; Baltimore, three; and Charleston, three. The first daily in the nation was established in 1783 in Philadelphia, Benjamin Towne's *Pennsylvania Packet and Daily Advertiser.* Newspapers began to grow with the new nation. By 1820 there were more than 500 newspapers, 24 of them dailies, 66 semiweeklies, and the rest weeklies. Circulations rarely exceeded more than 1,500 copies per issue.

In 1823 the Penny Press era began in New York City. The population then was over 200,000. Industrial expansion effected an urban boom, and by 1860 the city's population was over 1,000,000. Aliens poured from the poverty areas of Europe to the New York City docks. The working man began to exercise his influence through political parties and unions. The transition from an agricultural to an industrialized society brought social and political changes along with it.

The penny newspaper made it economically possible for many more people to read the daily paper than ever before. Mass readership dictated some content changes. More feature and human interest stories were used, with enormous impact. Realistically, they mirrored the news from all levels of society for the first time. This new emphasis was not all good. There were some editorial abuses. Sensationalism and indecency were by-products of the profiteers. Some were papers disreputable by design, but the majority adhered to high ethics and ideals.

Benjamin H. Day published the first issue of the New York *Sun* on September 3, 1833. Others had tried a penny paper and failed, and Day studied the faults of their experiments. Born in New England, he moved to New York in 1831, when he was 20-years-old. He opened a small printshop with the money he had saved working on a newspaper, but he wanted to found a successful penny paper. In two months he had built up a circulation of 2,000, and two years later it had reached 15,000. Day made police reporting popular. Crime news, he discovered, had extremely high human interest. He employed the first full-time police reporter in America, and the police news beat was born on the *Sun.* The paper was also the first to put newsboys on the streets.

The second successful penny newspaper was the *New York Herald.* James Gordon Bennett started it with not much more than the price of one of his papers. The 40-year-old Scotsman emigrated to America in 1819. After teaching school for a short time, he started working as a newspaperman. He tried to get a job on Day's *Sun,* but could not.

With $500 in savings—made mostly by writing short stories free-lance for newspapers—Bennett opened an office in the basement of the building at 20 Wall Street. His furnishings were few. He put a plank across two drygoods boxes for his desk. He had a box for his files and a second-hand chair. The first *Herald* appeared May 6, 1835, but the second issue did not follow until a month later. Because of his financial plight, Bennett had to operate on a day-to-day basis.

A year later Bennett was doing well. He raised his price to two cents because, he said, his paper was twice as good as most penny papers. He concentrated on sensationalism and made it sell. His emphasis on scandals and crimes upset his competitors and some segments of the city, but their moral war against him was defeated. The *Herald* continued to become larger and more profitable.

"This success," Bennett said in 1837, "has undoubtedly arisen from the entire novelty which I have infused into the daily press. Until this epoch of the World, the daily newspaper press has been a mere organ of dry detail—uninteresting facts—political nonsense—personal squabbles—obsolete rows—tedious ship news—or have infused life, glowing eloquence, philosophy, taste, sentiment, with wit and humor into the daily newspaper. . . . Shakespeare is the great genius of drama—Scott of the novel—Milton and Byron of the poem—and I mean to be the genius of the daily newspaper press."

Bennett was usually first with the news. He sent boats out to meet ships coming from Europe. Reporters would go aboard and get the latest news from across the Atlantic, then get back to shore hours ahead of the ships. Bennett started using carrier pigeons to carry dispatches from point to point. When the telegraph was invented by Samuel Morse in 1844, Bennett became a major user. The *Herald* introduced a financial page, sports news, society news, and critical review columns. Bennett established pension and annuity plans for his workers. He contributed much to charity and crusaded for improvement of the slums.

As the Civil War loomed, the *Herald* was the only Northern newspaper that upheld the constitutional rights of the South, and it was generally against the abolition of slavery. After the war began, the paper gave editorial support to President Abraham Lincoln. After the war, Bennett's son, James Gordon Bennett, Jr., joined the staff. The elder Bennett moved to Paris in 1877 with some of the $30,000,000 he had made. He continued to guide the newspaper to some extent by telegrams. And he lived, as always, lavishly.

Bennett, Jr. made his most notable achievement when in 1871 he sent a reporter named Henry Morton Stanley to Africa. Stanley's assignment was to find the missing missionary, Dr. David Livingstone, who had disappeared in 1869 while searching for the source of the Nile River. After an adventurous two-year expedition, Stanley found him. His greeting is one of the classics of understatement: "Dr. Livingstone, I presume." Stanley was so impressed with his jungle beat that he couldn't bring himself to leave it. He became an explorer himself.

Horace Greeley was one of the most forceful and important editors of his century. Born on February 3, 1811, in Amherst, New Hampshire, to poor, hard-working parents, he evinced his genius early. He began his formal education before he was 3-years-old. Already an avid reader, the infant prodigy had read the Bible in its entirety by the time he was 5. School was easy and entertaining for him.

"When brother Horace was 13-years-old," his sister, Esther, said, "he was taken out of school, as the teacher could instruct him no longer."

"Having loved and devoured newspapers—indeed, every form of periodical—from childhood, I early resolved to be a printer if I could," Greeley wrote. He tried to become an apprentice when he was 11, but he had to wait four more years while working on the family farm. He deplored the use of tobacco and alcohol. At 5 he sampled a cigar and later reflected, "From that hour to this, the chewing, smoking, or snuffing of tobacco has seemed to me, if not the most pernicious, certainly the vilest, most detestable abuse of his corrupted sensual appetites whereof depraved man is capable." While a teen-ager, Greeley organized one of the first temperance societies in the northeast, so strong was his attitude toward drink.

When he was 20, Greeley moved to New York City. At first he had trouble finding a job because of his poor appearance, but in three years he had a prosperous printing plant. He founded a weekly, *The New Yorker,* which died in financial difficulties in 1841. On April 10, 1841, he founded the *New York Tribune.*

"The *Tribune,*" Greeley said in an ad concerning it in another paper, "as its name imports, will labor to advance the interests of the People, and to promote their Moral, Social, and Political well-being. The immoral and degrading Police reports [this was in reference primarily to Bennett's *Herald*], Advertisements and other matter which have been allowed to disgrace the columns of many of our leading Penny Papers will be carefully excluded from this, and no exertion spared to render it worthy of the hearty approval of the virtuous and refined, and a welcome visitant at the family fireside."

Some historians maintain that Greeley's main motivation in establishing the paper was to promote social reforms and welfare. He battled for the common man. He hired some of the most noted scholars and thinkers of the time as editors and reporters.

Greeley was against war. He wanted the South to dissolve the Union legally through a formal secession at a national convention. The rotund, high-voiced editor almost ended the Civil War a year early. He got involved in a spy drama at Niagara Falls, Canada, where secret negotiations almost ended the conflict in 1864. Greeley tried to arrange for some representatives of the Confederacy to negotiate with some agents from the United States, but he was unable to get the two parties together in a situation where officials could negotiate. Greeley gave much money to help the poor. His personal wealth was never large; he did not desire it. Although the *Tribune* made millions, he gave some 90 percent of its control to members of his staff and others who had helped him. He ran for President unsuccessfully against Ulysses S. Grant in 1868 and died four years later.

Many historians contend that the Civil War was motivated more by sectionalism than slavery. The land-based economy of the South was different from the urbanization and industrialization of the North. Plantations were self-sufficient. Neighbors were not close. In the North, the city was the core of society. People were dependent on one another. In the North, one could go down the street and buy many items not available in Southern stores.

Abolition of slavery was a contributing factor to the splitting of the Union. The treatment of the issue by the press, more than the institution of slavery, caused much of the alienation of the two segments of the country. The first antislavery newspaper, *The Emancipator,* began publication on April 30, 1820, in Jonesboro, Tennessee. A Pennsylvania Quaker, Elihu Embree, published it until he died eight months later.

In January, 1821, Benjamin Lundy founded *The Genius of Universal Emancipation.* The abolitionist editor, who wanted to dissolve slavery by persuasion, started in Mt. Pleasant, Ohio, just across the river from Wheeling, West Virginia, which was a slaveholding area. Ironically, he also went to Tennessee and set up up in Greenville. Most abolitionist papers were founded in the North, which was more receptive to condemning slavery.

The Liberator, founded January 1, 1831, was the most notable abolitionist organ. William Lloyd Garrison was fearless and fiery in his crusade against slavery. Some historians assert that he caused more public reaction than any man since Thomas Paine.

One abolitionist editor was killed because of his convictions. Elijah

P. Lovejoy, editor of the *St. Louis Observer,* was forced by public disapproval of his editorial views to move his press to Alton, Illinois, across the Missouri River. Many citizens of Alton objected to his upsetting the tranquillity—or apathy—of the community. Mobs destroyed his press twice in 1834, and on a third occasion killed Lovejoy. He had been publishing for one year.

The South was not impressed with the abolitionist press. Some Southern states made it a prison offense to be caught with an issue in one's possession; in Georgia a violation warranted the death penalty.

The Union and the Confederacy censored some news. More control was put on the Northern press. The war was one of the most extensively covered in history. Correspondents were present at almost every battle and skirmish. Summary news leads came into being during the war. Reporters learned the precaution of sending a summary lead on stories, since the telegraph wires might be cut by the enemy at any minute. Also there was naturally competition among correspondents to be first with the news. A young reporter once sent his story and kept control of the telegraph line by having the operator transmit a few dozen pages of the Bible. His story was printed and delivered almost before other reporters could send their releases.

The Southern press was so desperate for materials that at times it printed issues on wallpaper taken from plantation houses. Some newspapers had to become mobile during the war, sometimes loading presses on wagons and fleeing the Union army. During Reconstruction, from 1865 to 1872, the Southern press suffered indignities from carpetbag administrations.

Mark Twain fought in the war for a few months before going to Nevada to prospect for gold. The only money he found he earned by working as a reporter during the war for the *Territorial Enterprise* in Virginia City. The newspaper, which is still publishing, was a flashy vehicle during the gunslinging era of the West. Twain did not start writing about Tom Sawyer and Huck Finn until a few years later.

Henry W. Grady was one of the great editors of the 1880's. At the age of 19 he was associate editor of the Rome (Georgia) *Courier.* The editors did not like his attacks on local corruption, and he resigned. In 1880 he bought an interest in the Atlanta *Constitution.* He stressed quality reporting. His primary ambition was to better the South in all aspects. The term "The New South" came from one of his speeches. He preached an industrialized South. King Cotton was dead, he said, and the South had to rebuild from the debris of the war. Grady died in 1889 at the age of 39. Today, Atlanta has a statue to Grady and a hospital, school, street, and other features bearing his name.

Joseph Pulitzer, born in 1847 in Hungary to wealthy parents, left home at 17. He wanted action. Successively, he tried to join the Austrian army, the French Foreign Legion, and the British army. All rejected him because of his poor eyesight and frail physique. In Europe, through an American agent there, he signed up for the Union Army in the United States.

Arriving in Boston Harbor in 1864, he and a companion jumped ship and swam ashore, having decided that they would rather collect their own enlistment bounties. Pulitzer's service in the cavalry was uneventful, and six months after the South surrendered he left the army without having seen combat. He made his way from New York City to St. Louis on freight trains. After holding some odd jobs there, including tending army mules and firing a boiler, he got a job as a reporter on a German-language newspaper. After achieving some journalistic renown and becoming active in local and state politics, he bought the *St. Louis Dispatch* for $2,500. Three days later he combined it with the *Post,* which was owned by a friend. After a year, Pulitzer bought out his partner.

The *Post-Dispatch* crusaded against graft and corruption. It promoted and aided in many reforms. In 1883 the prosperous editor and publisher purchased the *New York World* and made it a crusading paper also. It provided many public services: it bought coal for the poor in winter, furnished them with ice in the summer, provided summer recreation for poor children, and kept doctors on call night and day for the sick who could not afford to pay for medical attention.

William Randolph Hearst was born in 1863. His multimillionaire father mined much of the Comstock Silver Lode. The elder Hearst was somewhat rough and coarse, compared to his refined and cultured wife. When young Hearst was 19, he entered Harvard University, but he did not take his studies very seriously. Owing to his practical jokes and violation of school conduct codes, Hearst was expelled after two years. His service as business manager of the campus magazine was one of the few assets he derived from his time there.

Hearst inherited the San Francisco *Examiner* from his father, who died in 1891. His share of the estate also included $7,000,000. Four years later he bought the New York *Journal.* Then the Pulitzer-Hearst competition began. In the hectic 1890's they competed to be the most sensational with their New York newspapers. At times, they intentionally printed untrue statements, they exploited crimes and scandals as never before on such a monumental scale, and they fought bitter and gaudy circulation wars.

Despite this period of "Yellow Journalism," Pulitzer performed some outstanding public service. In 1885, France gave America the Statue of Liberty, but neither the U.S. government nor the public had provided a pedestal for the huge work by the renowned sculptor Frédéric Bartholdi. As an immigrant, Pulitzer felt deeply about the project, and the *World* began a campaign to raise the money. The newspaper asked its readers for nickels and dimes, anything they could contribute. And it raised the $100,000 needed to build a foundation for the symbol of freedom.

The great journalist was far ahead of his time in his concepts of government and labor. He called for a luxury tax and urged the government to tax most heavily those who could best afford it. He argued that the so-called privileged corporations should be taxed and that monopoly businesses should bear heavier taxes. He urged legislation to punish crooked politicians, stressed the urgency of reforming civil service, and demanded that employers stop coercing employees as to how to vote. Pulitzer paralleled Greeley in his desire to improve the life of the poor working classes.

One of Pulitzer's most heralded publicity stunts was sending a reporter, Nellie Bly, around the world. Her real name was Elizabeth Cochran and she ranks as one of the best reporters. Feigning insanity, she had gained admission to the asylum on Blackwell's Island and written an exposé of the inhuman treatment of the inmates. She had exposed crooked lobbyists and bad prison conditions. Her mission to circle the earth was inspired by Jules Verne's novel *Around the World in Eighty Days.* The *World* offered a prize to the reader who came closest to predicting how long it would take Miss Bly to go around the world, and almost a million people submitted entries in the contest. Traveling by ship, trains, horse, burro, and on foot, she made the trip in 72 days, 6 hours, 11 minutes, 14 seconds. This was considered an amazing adventure for a girl traveling alone in that day.

Hearst's *Journal* also contributed some outstanding exploits. The paper secured the rights to interview James J. Corbett and Bob Fitzsimmons before their bout for the world heavyweight championship. The *Journal* paid Mark Twain—then famous—handsomely to go to England and cover the 60th anniversary of Queen Victoria's coronation. Fact and fiction merged in "Yellow Journalism."

The Cuban insurrection began in March, 1895. Spain and the United States went to war in April, 1898. Cuban datelines appeared in the New York City newspapers almost daily during that period. When the battleship *Maine* was blown up in the Havana harbor, newspapers and much of the public were more than ready for battle. Historians still debate who sank the ship. Some say it was done by an outside agent, others blame sabotage, and still others say it was the work of a Cuban sympathizer. Regardless of who blasted the *Maine,* 266 American sailors died on it. The *Journal* offered a $50,000 reward for information leading to the arrest and conviction of those responsible.

Hearst became deeply involved in the war of 1898, sometimes suspiciously so. He was linked to some spy dramas concerning forged letters.

He went to Cuba and covered some battles himself. Both the *Journal* and the *World* assigned famous reporters to cover the war, including Frank Norris, James Creelman, and Stephen Crane among others.

Richard Harding Davis, still considered by some the most glorious epitome of the war correspondent, reported for the New York *Herald*. He led one battle charge and was praised by Teddy Roosevelt.

More war was waged in editorial ink and sensationalism than took place between troops. The times were perhaps in part responsible for the war and the way it was handled. Many years later, after he had served as President, Roosevelt reflected on the war.

"It wasn't much of a war, but it was the best war we had," the former Rough Rider said.

S. S. McClure is usually credited with launching the exposé era of 1900–1910. When he founded *McClure's Magazine* in 1893, he was already a successful businessman. One of his staff writers was Ida Tarbell. He assigned her to do a series of articles on the operations of the Standard Oil Company. For five years, she researched and wrote fifteen articles. She showed that the company was indeed a model of efficiency and organization, but she also reported that the methods involved to acquire this perfection included bribery, violence, fraud, corruption, and a host of illegal and unethical practices. The project cost the magazine some $60,000 to publish.

Lincoln Steffens was McClure's second exposé writer. His first assignment resulted ultimately in several books, the most notable of which was *The Shame of the Cities.* His articles exposed corrupt governments in Minneapolis, Pittsburgh, Philadelphia, Chicago, New York, and other cities. With evidence, he proved that the cities were run by political gangsters.

Upton Sinclair's stories on the filth and appalling conditions in some food and meat packing plants resulted in the passage of several laws for the benefit of the public health. After reading Sinclair's *The Jungle,* on the meat industry, many persons became vegetarians. Under crusading editor Edward Bok, the *Ladies Home Journal* exposed the evils of the patent medicine industry. Its war against dangerous and false medicines had much influence on the passage of the Pure Food and Drug Act of 1906.

When President Theodore Roosevelt applied the term "muckraking" to those magazines that championed progress and justice, he was branding them gratuitously. Magazines and reform writers made the world aware of the range of evils seething in almost all phases of life. Some chroniclers have criticized them. They exposed things that needed exposing. They did not always have solutions for the terrible situations they discovered. But they did their duty in reporting and clamoring for legislative corrections. The magazines of the times retorted that they were publications, not politicians. Moreover, the exposé era ushered in much of the cleanliness and honesty found in life today.

The 1920's were christened the age of Jazz Journalism. Again, it was a time between wars. The decade was wild and zany, and so was the press. It has been called the only decade that really roared. More news broke during it than possibly in any other.

Probably 1927 was the climax year of news coverage in this century to date, despite the exploits and events of recent years. Why so much happened then is still baffling. Man ushered in modern technology and amalgamated it with merriment and madness. It was Prohibition's wildest and wettest year. The marines landed in Nicaragua, posing an international situation with a high war potential. Crime's most notorious cast was coining nicknames and killing people. Al Capone, Ma Barker and her murdering brood, Legs Diamond, Baby Face Nelson, and hordes of other hoodlums were attending and making funerals. John Dillinger, Public Enemy Number One, was in jail that year.

Charles A. Lindbergh flew the Atlantic, and two Army pilots flew from California to Hawaii. Al Jolson starred in the first talking picture, *The Jazz Singer.* The first television demonstrations were made. Henry Ford made the Model "A." Vaudeville, Will Rogers, barnstorming aviators, and electrifying persons and events were everywhere all the time, it seemed. The greatest Mississippi River flood in history inundated half a dozen states, with much loss of life and property. Sacco and Vanzetti were electrocuted in one of the most celebrated cases in history; people still debate whether they were anarchists or martyrs.

The monumental scoops of that wondrous year covered all of life. It is the most talked-about year in sports history. Babe Ruth hit 60 homers. Jack Dempsey and Gene Tunney fought with such savagery that at least two men died while listening to the fight on the radio. Ty Cobb was spiking around the bases. Willie Hoppe was the billiards king. Johnny Blood generated so much backfield drama that he is still more immersed in fiction than fact.

Tabloid newspapers appeared in the 1920's. The small format was—and still is—primarily pictorial. The New York *Evening Graphic,* which existed from 1924 to 1932, was the most famous. It not only faked some news, but often faked photographs, superimposing heads on other people's bodies. The resulting composographs contributed to an astronomical number of highly scandalous and flashy stories. Bernarr Macfadden, founder of the *Graphic,* was one of the most colorful journalists. The physical culture fanatic founded a newspaper and magazine empire that still exists; some major magazines today are owned by the communications group he established. A flamboyant showman, Macfadden was making $10,000 a day from his magazines during the decade. *True Story* was one of them.

No other man in America, however, has ever lived as lavishly as Hearst. He spent over $40,000,000 on one of his half dozen houses, San Simeon. Built on a California mountain, the fabled residence is now open to the public for tours. It is one of the most ornate palaces in the world. Hearst's personal living expenses averaged $1,000,000 a month. He once built a 90-room beach house in California for a girl friend. Hearst owned the Metro-Goldwyn-Mayer film studio and other holdings just as hobbies. He once had a river frozen during the summer so that an ice-skating scene could be filmed. At his peak, he owned at least 25 newspapers, 8 magazines, 2 press syndicates, and property worth tens of millions of dollars. For many years, he was the most powerful private citizen in the nation. Few men have ever approached living on such a palatial scale. When he died in 1951, his art collection was sold at the largest private auction in American history. Millions of dollars worth of famous paintings and other art works were still packed in crates at his beloved San Simeon.

The Depression of the 1930's also affected the press. Some newspapers had to cut their staffs of reporters. Some journalists were employed by the Works Progress Administration to write articles, brochures, and books. They wrote histories of a few cities, New Orleans among them.

E. W. Scripps was a contemporary of Hearst and Pulitzer. The freckled, red-haired farm boy was born in 1854 in Illinois. In his youth he worked for the Detroit *News,* owned by his half-brother.

The thirteenth child of a thrice-married Englishman, Scripps was dynamic of mind, but not of body. In the 1880's he bought the Cleveland *Press* and the Cincinnati *Post.* He founded the first big modern newspaper chain. Between 1892 and 1914 he acquired outright or the controlling interest in 34 newspapers in fifteen states. He amassed a personal fortune of over $50,000,000.

"Bluffing" was responsible for his success, Scripps said. But this was only one facet of his character. He did not like to work. His vices were so legion that he was half-blind, physically wasted, semiparalyzed and had palsied hands by the time he was 46. Realizing that he had to change his habits or die, he concentrated on rebuilding himself. For eighteen months, he rigidly avoided anything detrimental to his health, and he restored himself enough to live another twenty-six years. Scripps was a man of little patience. Although he rarely visited any of his newspapers, he wrote voluminous memos to his editors.

The Scripps papers became champions of the common man. Most of the papers he purchased were in industrial cities. He selected newspapers that were not financially strong, bought them with a down payment of some $50,000 each, then appointed an editor from his empire to run each paper he acquired. If the paper did not soon make a profit, he sold it. When a paper became very successful, Scripps rewarded the editor by giving him 50 percent of the stock. His autobiography, *Damned Old Crank,* reveals much about the man.

The Scripps chain was left to his son Robert and young Roy Howard. Howard was born in 1883 in Ohio to very poor parents. For a time he worked on Pulitzer's *St. Louis Post-Dispatch.* After being denied a pay raise, he went to Scripps's Cincinnati *Post.* By 1920 he had become business manager and chairman of the board of the Scripps empire. He died in 1964.

H. L. Mencken was born in Baltimore, Maryland, on September 12, 1880. His German immigrant father owned a tobacco factory. A prodigy, young Mencken was doing serious creative writing by the age of 12. When he was 23, he became city editor of the Baltimore *Sun.* He covered the Scopes Monkey Trial—he coined the name—at Dayton, Tennessee. Another of his neologisms was "the Bible Belt" for the conservative South. He founded the political magazine *The American Mercury.* A great lover of hoaxes, he made literary history with several stories. He satirized almost everything and everyone.

"The world is a vast field of greased poles flying gaudy and seductive flags," Mencken once wrote. "Up each a human soul goes shinnying, painfully and with many a slip. Some climb eventually to high levels; a few scale the dizziest heights. But the great majority never get very far from the ground. The effort is too much for them."

The irrepressible iconoclast wrote one of the most famous scholarly works in America, *The American Language.* Of all his statements, this is one of the most quoted, "The truth to the overwhelming majority of mankind is indistinguishable from a headache." Despite his biting sarcasm, he had a warmer, if somewhat bittersweet, personality than he liked to project. The "Bad Boy of Baltimore" died in 1956.

One of the most fabulous journalists of the 1930's was Mark Hellinger, a jet-haired, pale-blue-eyed writer who scaled the heights of success, starting as a cub reporter. During the Depression, he made $1,000 a week as a Broadway columnist and another $3,500 a week as a movie producer. He lived luxuriously but, like many other wealthy journalists in history, he had compassion for the poor. He was never without a pocketful of $2 bills folded to stamp size. When down-and-outers greeted him on the street, he would grasp their hand and palm them two dollars. Hellinger's fashion trademark was a blue suit and white tie. The suave writer died in 1947 at the age of 44, having written more than 5,000 short stories for magazines that almost no one remembers. The only extant monument to his memory is a New York City theater bearing his name.

Guys and Dolls author Damon Runyon (1884–1946) is another of the immortal journalists. Among the characters he created in his hundreds of short stories, books, and plays are the "Lemon Drop Kid" and "Harry the Horse." One of his first jobs was as a reporter for the Denver *Post.* In his late teens or early twenties, he reportedly went to a newspaper and applied for a job. The secretary told him the editor wanted to see his credentials. Runyon had none, nor had he any experience. Spying a deck of cards in the office, he picked them up, extracted an ace, and told the girl, "Give him this." Legend says that thus the "ace reporter" cliché was born. He got the job.

An ace journalist he was, and he made much money from all his writing and reporting. One of his major areas of reporting was sports. Runyon was a slightly built man, but his clothes reflected the color spectrum. He wore expensive attire, particularly shoes. To break in a new pair, he would hire a man to wear them for a week or so. Broadway was his street, and he wrote about his beloved thoroughfare and its people with an unapproachable depth.

He liked the concerto of bright lights, show business, a repertoire of unusual but always interesting characters, and the exciting journalism of the period. Toward the end of his life, he lost his voice and was obliged to rely on a note pad and pen. Even though he could not talk, he communicated as few men ever have with his fellow man. When he died, his will requested that he be cremated and his ashes scattered over Manhattan. And it was done, his friend and World War I and II aviation hero Captain Eddie Rickenbacker flying the plane. Another friend, columnist Walter Winchell, established the Damon Runyon Cancer Fund, which has raised many millions of dollars for the fight against the disease.

Journalism history—American history—is studded with hundreds of other men and women who contributed much to mass communications, the nation, and the world. Henry Luce founded *Time, Life, Fortune,* and *Sports Illustrated.* DeWitt Wallace founded *Reader's Digest,* the U.S. magazine with the largest circulation. Radio and television have their histories of award-winning staffs in electronic journalism.

The history of American journalism is more than the evolution and revolution of mass communications. It is the emergence of a democracy, a New World, and modern times. It is the New England coffeehouse, the Colonial newspaper, the American Revolution. Journalism is the vehicle history rides. History is yesterday, the yesterday of a year ago and of eons past.

Journalism history encompasses the communication of ideas as well as technological advances. Each contributed to the march of the mass media on its way to the unbelievable scope it covers today. Journalism history is happening this second. Something new is being contributed to the flood of occurrences called news, now and a minute from now.

CHAPTER III

The Journalist's Word Workshop

Writers of all kinds, including journalists, are word workers. They design and build stories with them. Everyone has a given number of words in his vocabulary, and the rest are in the dictionary. They are construction blocks. Masons use mortar to bond bricks together. Writers have adhesive techniques and devices to arrange words in informative and entertaining shapes.

All words can be classified in one of the eight parts of speech. Nouns are the most numerous. They identify people, places, objects, ideas, and qualities. Pronouns are relatively few in number. They are substitutes for nouns. They function like nouns, but they do not give the precise name. They help tighten up the language and keep down repetition. Rather than cite the same word again, they refer to it.

Nouns:
> River-front *parks* often lack *scenery* and *sanitation.*
> Heavy wood *tables* course its rolling *terrain.*

Pronouns:
> *Sheldon* dismantled the typewriter. *He* used a wrench.
> *Cactus* stands in grotesque geometrical shapes, and *it* is not all prickly.

Verbs express action or a state of being. They give life to nouns. The verb is the only part of speech that has voice. Verbs in the active voice act. They have direct objects, but passive verbs do not. Passive verbs are forms of the verb *to be* combined with a past participle. The most effective verb choice is invariably in the active voice. Sentences using the passive voice are generally longer and always weaker in impact.

Active:	*Passive:*
Jean *chose* a red sports car.	A red sports car *was chosen* by Jean.
Carl *climbed* the ladder.	The ladder *was climbed* by Carl.

Adjectives and adverbs are modifiers. They influence the meaning of the words they modify. Adjectives modify nouns and pronouns. Adverbs modify verbs, adjectives, or other adverbs. Modifiers should be used with extreme caution. Many beginning writers feel they must use them in abundance to achieve vivid writing. This is not true. Modifiers are spices that should season the natural flavor of sentences only when absolutely necessary. Note the effect of careful choices in the following examples.

Adjectives:
>   Her *blonde* tresses billowed as the convertible accelerated.
>   *Blue* and *white* streaks of electricity penciled across the sky.

Adverbs:
>   He shuffled *listlessly* as he eyed the ball.
>   The wire felt *extremely* heavy.

Prepositions, conjunctions, and interjections are relatively few. The preposition establishes relationships between events or things. It relates or links a noun or pronoun to the whole of the sentence. Conjunctions are simply connectors, joining together two words, phrases, clauses, or sentences. Interjections are the fewest in number. They inject sudden or strong feeling or emotion. They are somewhat isolated from the rest of the sentence, but they give it a dash of living.

Preposition:
>   *Of* all the items *on* the table, she bought the art book.

Conjunction:
>   Shelby *and* Carl Howard are going, *but* they will drive the old car.

Interjection:
>   *Oh,* that was a valuable vase!

Too many beginning writers feel they can communicate emotion and intensity with an interjection and an exclamation mark. Unfortunately, this is asking far too much of one word and a punctuation mark. The interjection can be used with subtle events, too. An exclamation point is rarely needed. Punctuation merely defines the starts, stops, and pauses of communications; words must convey the messages.

Words are arranged into phrases and clauses. A phrase is a group of words that works as a single part of speech. There are verb phrases and prepositional phrases. A clause is a unit of words containing a verb and its subject. There are two types of clauses.

An independent clause is actually a sentence by itself, although it is often used in conjunction or coordination with one or more dependent clauses. The dependent clause is not a complete thought; it must rely on the rest of the sentence for full expression.

Words have various values depending upon their use. Each word has its worth. Some are weak, some strong. Each word in a story—regardless of the type—must contribute to the overall effect. Words are money to the selling writer, and he chooses what he puts in the till with the utmost precision. Good writing is tight writing. It is thoroughbred lean and has speed. Pedestrian prose is boring. One of Ernest Hemingway's greatest contributions to the modern literary scene was that he helped to remove the tradition of wordiness from the novel. Most people talk too much and write the same way.

Never select a word to do a job simply because it is different. A thesaurus can be of help to the beginning writer, but one should not become addicted to it. Looking up a synonym just for novelty is bad. There should be a reason to do so. The seasoned writer rarely uses a thesaurus because his repository of words is generally large enough that he has the selection already in his mind.

Words can be arranged into four types of sentence construction. Every sentence must have a subject and a verb and express a full thought. The simple sentence contains one subject-verb unit, and so does the clause. The complex sentence contains one independent clause and one or more dependent clauses. The compound sentence has two or more independent clauses and no dependent ones. Compound-complex sentences have at least two independent clauses and one or more dependent clauses. Following is an example of each type. Note the subjects and verbs.

Simple:
> *Rain turned* the asphalt into a black mirror of shimmering neon.

Complex:
> When the *ice cream melted* on her dress, *it got* sticky.

Compound:
> Black *cars* with low mileage on them *were* in the second row, and green *cars* with air conditioning units in them *were* in the last section of the lot.

Compound-Complex:
> Even though *he was* hungry, *he waited* two more hours, and *she servèd* him a huge steak.

Effective writing mixes the four types of sentences. There must be a variety of constructions. One cannot write a quality story—fact or fiction —using only one type of sentence. Simple and complex sentences are used much more often than the other two types. The compound-complex tends to get a little long.

Some grammarians contend that there are no restrictions on sentence length. In theory, this may be true. There is a limit, however, to how much readers will tolerate and can comprehend. Although the writer works for himself, he is also a reader. He is an extension of his audience, and he must know what it will and can endure. Generally, no sentence should exceed thirty words. If one cannot read a sentence aloud in one breath, it is too long, providing one has average lung power.

There must be a variety of sentence lengths. They cannot be all of relatively the same length in a story. There must be some short ones, some longer ones, and some at various points within that range. Good writing has movement. Too many short sentences jerk the reader along. Too many long ones bore him. Pace is very important. The reader wants to go on an entertaining and informative literary safari. To transport him in the way he prefers takes a literal literary license.

Sentence length and construction must be allied with the use of varied sentence openings. The same type of opening on every sentence becomes boring. Each of the eight parts of speech can be employed to launch a sentence. The three verbals—infinitives, participles, and gerunds—are also in the arsenal of openings.

An infinitive, consisting of the preposition *to* and a verb, can serve as a noun, adjective, or adverb in a sentence. A participle is a verb form ending in *-ing* or *-ed* that can be used only as an adjective. A gerund is a verb form that ends in *-ing* or *-ed* used as a noun. Verbals can be used in any part of a sentence. Gerunds and infinitives are often used as subjects or objects. When a participle is used to open a sentence, the phrase must always be followed by a comma and must modify the subject of the clause it introduces.

Infinitives:

> *To impress the candidates,* he wore a $300 suit.
> *To scale the cliff,* he drove in spikes with a special hammer.

Participles:

> *Smiling,* he soared over the dunes on the kite.
> *Considering the scope with the end caps,* he hefted it from its case.

Gerunds:

> *Taking the car to be waxed* was a good idea.
> *Walking on his hands* made several men stare at him.

Misplacing a participle distorts a sentence. The participle should be next to the word it modifies. Editors know that stories containing misplaced modifiers are not from competent writers. Note the distortion in the following example. The sand is not climbing the dunes, but the words in this order say that.

Incorrect:

> *Climbing up the dunes,* the sand seemed more solid than it looked.

Correct:
>   *Climbing up the dunes,* he found the sand more solid than it looked.

Although students are introduced to all the literary equipment in English courses, they rarely employ all the tools of language. One may recall them in detail, but they need to be lubricated with use. The figures of speech are important in any drafting of words. Laymen are most familiar with similes and metaphors. The former is a comparison of two unlike things by using *like* or *as.* The latter is an implied comparison. Good figures of speech help make writing vivid, colorful, and forceful. They intensify sentences.

Similes:
>   Blisters of *crystal* sprayed the wall *like* little *ice* explosions.
>   The *bulldozer* crawled across the strip *like* an armored *insect.*
>   Her *dress* was *as* yellow *as* a *lemon.*

Metaphors:
>   The *volcano* was a *furnace* stoked in hell.
>   *Stands* of oaks were *fences* on the perimeter.
>   Her *hair* was just another *center* of a sunflower in the garden.

Hyperbole, intentional exaggeration for effect, is often used in daily conversation. It can add emphasis to statements. Someone says, "The window broke in a million pieces when he homered through the living room." The glass did not really break in a million pieces. It may tally out to a few hundred perhaps. A million? No.

Hyperbole:
>   You have a *thousand* things to do today.
>   A *million* firecrackers exploded when the powder caught fire.

Personification is giving life to an inanimate object. Human qualities are attributed to a nonliving thing.

Personification:
>   Fog *digested* the tops of the building.
>   The moon *stared* through a slit in the tent and reflected on the radio.

One of the most flexible shapers of words is alliteration, or the repetition of initial letters or sounds. Man likes its rhythmic sound, but care must be exercised not to abuse it. If word choices are forced, the effect is always detrimental. One must be careful not to lace words together, striving so much for a musical quality that they result in a singsong effect. Then it becomes juvenile. Alliteration is a sensitive device and must be used with delicacy. A beginning writer must be careful not to turn it into a word game. Some acceptable alliteration examples are:

Alliteration:
> Women have used sensual smells since the beginning of *civilized sniffing.*
> *Perfume* and *passion* are synonymous with romance.
> Graphologists say that *people's penmanship* reveals some of their character traits.

Sometimes it is appropriate to use alliteration because the word choices pertaining to the topic make it natural. Word patterns that cannot be read aloud without difficulty are generally ineffective. Some clichés are alliterative. Note those on the cliché list.

Clichés are worn-out words. They have been used and abused so much that they are worthless and deadly. Such words taint work. They are errors so monumental that they can destroy all the good. They are subtle thieves that steal into the work of even some of the most noted professionals when they relax their vigilance. Clichés are dead words, but on occasion they can be converted to assets if circumstances are such that one may use them as a play on words. Unfortunately, clichés rarely disappear, and new ones are added yearly. The following is only a partial listing of expressions to avoid:

Trite Expressions

sweet as honey	strike a bargain
black as night	laud to the skies
tall, dark, and handsome	short and fat
deader than a doornail	sadder and wiser
smooth as silk	like a bird
slow as Christmas	gone but not forgotten
the grim reaper	

Good writing is visual. To show the reader the story, one must let him see all of it. Don't just tell him that people and things are there. He wants to view them. Description is an essential part of almost every story.

In essence readers must be taken on an excursion of a story. They become concerned and involved if the subject and its treatment impress them. One must develop a pictorial exhibit in prose, but an exhibit consists of details. Writing must be in specifics, not generalities. Don't say that the tree is tall. The reader wants to know more. He demands it. Show him the tree. Let him see that it would cover half a football field if felled. Let him feel the wind fluttering its canopy of yellow and brown leaves in autumn.

Past tense is the most common approach to fact and fiction. The writer says that something was there. He states that someone *was* walking up the street. If he says that someone *is* walking up the street, it is happening then, and the logical time element is upset. Generally the writer must say the stream *was*—not *is*—a muddy scar zippered into the red clay mountain.

Description

Description must be vivid, authentic, and concrete. Good description uses intricate detail to build graphic word pictures. A good story is a language tapestry produced by the writer's ability to exercise his penetrating vision and translate it into the right words. The professional writer can write an amazing amount of wordage about the smallest and simplest objects when necessary. But he does not overdescribe either. He must realize when the scene is developed enough. One most likely will never have to consider the chemical composition of the paint on the chair, but he must be aware of every possibility, even the most minor technicalities, on occasion. The writer has to see every possible atom relating to the content of his stories.

Effective writing focuses on all the senses, not just the eyes. Readers cannot grasp a story by peering at it from a distance. They must be able to see, smell, feel, taste, and touch, through words, the total story. All their senses must be involved. Their perception should be allowed contact with every sensation. Their eyes tell them the world is visible; other sense organs tell them it is tangible, audible, odorous, and savory. Words have to signify what is there that can be experienced.

Atmosphere, tone, and other elements influence description. An ancient, decaying mansion on a hill with its shuttered windows and heritage of superstitions may be just a commonplace item of the landscape on a hot July day at noon. But that same structure twelve hours later during a rainstorm adopts another role. Wind, lightning, and night are the accessories then, and their effect on the emotions is generally rather eerie. Some mystery writers can irradiate such scenes with terrifying realism. They are well aware of how weather and darkness can establish or affect moods. These, also, are dimensions of description.

A spooky house can be viewed with humor, too. How scenes are portrayed depends on the intended effect. Slant dictates how the story, and the people and things described in it, will be handled. The attitude of the story has to convert the attitude of the reader. If it doesn't, it isn't successful.

The following passage is designed to show the reader a street scene. It could be a view of almost any city in the world at night with electricity. Weather is not involved, and neither are people. It is a simple picture in an unadorned frame.

Gnarled neon tubing scrawled its way down the block. Some signs winked and blinked in a multicolored code that screamed the commerce of the city. Mannequins hawked their attire in some of the lighted shop windows.

There is light alliteration in the first two words of the opening sentence. *Scrawled* is a fair verb choice. In the second sentence the first four words make subtle alliteration, and the *multicolored code* makes stronger rhythm. *Screamed* is a workable verb, but *telegraphed* might be more appropriate. *Hawked* and *attire* are the best word choices in the third sentence. No words are wasted in the three-sentence painting, and the image is sufficiently detailed.

Landscape descriptions are geographical word surveys. They must be real, not a glossy postcard reproduction with an artificial sheen. If there is dust, the reader must sense it on his own shoes. Words are tour guides taking him around the scenery.

Cliffs blemished the sides. Bands of limestone slashed into its canopy of green. Rocks lacerated the sculptured fullness of the crest. A stream was there, a pipeline of trout and clean water, etched into the folds of the mountain.

Notice the variation in sentence lengths. The first sentence counts four words, the second, nine, the third, eight, and the fourth, eighteen. There are cliffs defacing the mountain, and *blemished* is a strong verb choice here. In the second sentence, *band* does its job, and *slashed* follows through with a play on band, reflecting that these factors of the mountain are injuries of sorts to it. *Lacerated* adds to the emphasis. The fourth sentence is understatement because the stream is not described with as much force as are the other things. The elaboration on the stream, calling it *a pipeline of trout and clean water,* gives two additional facts about it. *Etched* and *folds* are the words that give the sentence some power. Note that *mountain* is used at the end of the bit of description. *Sides* and *crest* and the other information attest that it is a mountain.

Sound is the motive of the next example. To make the reader hear the scene, as well as see it, is the purpose of the piece. The example is as close as the nearest hairdresser's parlor.

Dryers hooded their heads with hot sounds. The humming cycled the room. Syllables of gossip rode the air currents from the vents, and combs and curlers hitting the stands punctuated the ritual of permanents.

The first sentence has the three *h*'s for alliteration. *Dryers* and *sounds* say it for the ears. In the second, the muted *syllables of gossip* is stronger than *words* would be. The *combs and curlers hitting the strands* contribute another source of noise. Generally, the stronger the scene, the easier it is to show the reader. The louder and harsher the din of sound, the simpler it is to let the reader hear.

Scenes with odors in them are as difficult as the odors are to identify. If one knows what something smells like, then he has to let the reader sniff it in terms of what he has used his nose on before. The reader must get a good breath of whatever is there.

> Jeweled cosmetic containers and elegant decanters were arrayed on the dresser. Sensual odors wafted from the fragrances, caressing the femininity of the room. Perfumes combined into an overpowering chemistry that titillated the nostrils rather than irritated them.

These odors are sophisticated and pleasant. A skunk would be on the opposite end of the sniffing scale. The opening sentence shows the source of the smells. *Sensual, wafted, fragrances,* and *caressing* are the major words in the second. *Perfumes* is another word choice to help convey the sense, while *chemistry* adds a little naturalism to the scene of reality.

Touch is the most intimate sensation. Words really have to rub the reader's nerve endings to let him feel things. He must be allowed to grasp an object. He has to get the heft and texture.

> It was more than a piece of luggage. The leather bag was a status symbol in the most posh resorts. She glided her palms across the perfect skin. The steers had always been stalled for fear they would mark their hides in some way. Her fingers moved over the gold hardware, and she relished the gleam.

The feel comes through as part of the excellence of the product. She magnifies its richness with the praise of her hands. Explaining that the bag was made from unmarred hide commands more respect for it. Readers know what fine leathers feel like. They can identify with touch.

The sense of taste is aimed at people's enjoyment of good things to eat. Advertising copywriters call their food description "hunger copy." And they are superb craftsmen at making people crave their tasty wares. Studying some of their advertisements helps some students comprehend how to handle edibles.

> Chocolate pastries filled several trays. Little white cones of cream perched on some cookies. Brownies and doughnuts cooled on the counter racks. Pies and cakes dominated the fantasy of desserts.

Most of the word selections react on the taste buds. *Perched* is a fair verb in the second sentence, and there is some alliteration in all but the first sentence. *Fantasy* is the best word choice in this example. It calls on the magnificence of a bakery to move the appetite.

Describing people is one of the most provocative and challenging tasks in writing. People are puppets of their emotions and logic, and this causes them to adopt many roles. This flexibility of the living makes portraying them a constant creation. More than the surface of people must show. The inner person must be probed and revealed. His character must be diagnosed. Some people who see in total but not in detail tend to say that everyone looks alike. They are not looking. No two people or things are alike. "Identical" twins really are not. There are always distinguishable differences.

Character Labels

Character labels define each individual. The most basic items are height and weight. Human beings vary by only a few feet and a few hundred pounds. So a lot of people are in the same superb or miserable shape, with the mass of humanity falling between the extremes. Some people are synonymous with one or more character labels.

People in the entertainment world capitalize on their labels more than those in any other profession. Everyone should be able to think of one or more show-business personalities for each of the types of character labels. If one can do so easily, he will find employing labels to be somewhat easier than perhaps anticipated. Some names are known for their tallness, their shortness, their thinness, their obesity.

Starting at the top of the anatomy, one can list celebrities who are recognized for their unusual hair or lack of it. Now the eyes. Some are renowned for their big eyes with which they can do comical things in expressions. The western gunslinger's "cold, blue eyes" have become a cliché. Noses. Several entertainers, especially comedians, talk about having a prominent proboscis. Mouths. Some actors and actresses have cavernous mouths. Some have been known for their teeth. A few noted thespians have had unusually large ears, which became their trademark. Beauty and build are labels. Some people are synonymous with these. Handsome physical specimens are models of humanity. In addition to these physical labels, there are others of equal importance.

Object labels help establish individuality. Some people are associated with things they carry with them or are frequently near. A scholar who always wears an honorary key on a chain is an example. The special wallet of the route truck driver in which he carries money and receipts is an object label. Each trade or profession has its tools. A teacher with a piece of chalk in his hands or in his pocket is allied with the object.

Movies and television series have long employed character labels, as has every medium. The hero invariably has strong character labels. In the low-grade western, he always has the best horse, the best saddle, or the best something else. In modern drama the sleuth always has an unusual weapon or carries it in an odd place. Main characters, and supporting ones, have toted every odd weapon the writers can conceive. They carry funny looking rifles, half rifles, whips, knives, and assorted other things. Daniel Boone and Davy Crockett were famed for their long rifles. Jim Bowie became immortal for the fighting knife he designed. Sometimes a person is nicknamed for his label. Buffalo Bill killed a lot of bison. The nickname is particularly associated with the underworld. Almost every celebrated criminal has had a nickname as his label, such as Scarface Al Capone and Machine Gun Kelly.

Some people walk in an unusual way. They have a unique shuffle, stride, or gait that characterizes them. Speech labels focus on some offbeat way of talking. Very high or very deep voices become symbols. A Southern drawl or a clipped Yankee manner of speech are regional speech labels. People can identify familiar voices from perhaps all others. There are even odor labels. A carpenter smells of wood and sawdust. A teacher gets a chalk scent on his clothes. A baker smells like his bread.

People who dress out of the ordinary have a clothing label. A person whose wardrobe consists primarily of one color or design has a label. A. Conan Doyle did not have to give Sherlock Holmes a funny pipe and a hat, but he did, and these labels help make him one of the most memorable characters in literature. Ben Franklin without his spectacles would be an unbelievable portrait.

The way a person stands, sits, and moves is important in portraying him. If he whistles or jingles the coins in his pocket, these mannerisms are of potential use in parading him before the reader. Everything that can help demonstrate that characters are living must be considered. Literary allusion can be effective in rare instances. Saying that a man has a scowl like Captain Hook's communicates with the masses.

Gestures label some people. A person who habitually tugs at an ear lobe or brushes his hair with his hand in a peculiar manner helps pronounce his identification. The way a woman dangles her foot or carries her purse might be unique enough to call to the reader's attention.

In face-to-face interviewing the reporter must watch what the person is doing while he is talking. These movements help to tell the story. How a person tells something is part of it. Does he pace, fiddle with an object, gaze into space, or talk in a monotone? The source and his surroundings often are part of the story. Consider the following examples:

His face was half pate and glasses. The baldness would have coursed right to his chin, but the horn rims sliced the nudeness.

The nose was Grecian when he was on-stage. Off, it was bent. But it blended well with his features. He was handsome despite it. And it added that unknown appeal with masculinity to make the face worth millions in movie tickets.

She had a sensuous mouth. Her lips were full and could pout or smile with her alternating moods in an instant. The eyes and the mouth were in absolute unison with each expression. She was that good an actress.

Baxter's hair was oily. It looked lubed, but it was just glossy with globules of sweat. Still, when he rubbed the heavy, white towel over his head, it absorbed a gray wetness.

She didn't wiggle into the raincoat exactly. Her roundness just bunched up the coat, and it wouldn't drop down over the flare of her big hips. She methodically buttoned it to the bottom though, then tugged it down.

He rolled the pencil across the desk with one finger. He was careful to flick it in the middle so it would roll straight.

Dialogue is a necessity in almost all news and features. There must be some direct quotes when possible. When the reader glances down a column and sees quotation marks, he knows the story has someone making a statement. Conversation helps "humanize" a story.

Direct quotes can be paragraph beginnings also. Quotes should not be buried. Some should open paragraphs. This is extremely important when there are only a few quotes. When there are several quotes, it is not necessary to bring them *all* to the front of paragraphs. Another factor in their use is to choose the proper verb of saying at the right time.

There are hundreds of synonyms for *said*. The repetition of one verb of saying can be very harmful to the story. Following are a few of the substitutes for *said*. Each differs and must be used properly to report its relationship to the statement.

added	demanded	pondered
announced	ended	pronounced
asked	frowned	related
blurted	grinned	remarked
bubbled	hissed	screamed
concluded	implied	shrugged
considered	indicated	smiled
consoled	injected	snapped
contended	inquired	stated
contributed	laughed	whispered
croaked	noted	winked
	pointed out	

Note how dialogue and gestures are combined in the following.

"Counterfeiting antiques is a multimillion-dollar business," he said, peering at the 18th-Century desk. "Crooked dealers make new stuff out of old wood."

"Diamonds have as wide a range of quality as anything else." The gemologist pushed the little stones across the velvet pad. He chewed on his thumb pensively for an instant and looked up from the rocks. "I can let you have these at a discount though."

"You can buy land that will triple in value in two years," the broker sighed. "But you have to show the cash," he frowned as he pulled a watch from his coat, "and there isn't much of it around here."

Peering gives the speaker a little movement. His eyes at least are doing something while he is talking. In the second example, there are no verbs of saying, but the gestures make it quite clear who is talking. *Sighed* is more accurate and graphic than *said* in the first sentence of the third piece. The passage after the quote in the second sentence shows facial expression and movement.

The sentence fragment is also a legitimate literary tool. In the section a few pages back on character labels, this writer used some fragments because it was appropriate to do so. They were also used to see if the reader was at all aware of the technique. He should not have been, because when the reader becomes conscious of how something is expressed he is not thinking about content. His concentration must stay on the story.

CHAPTER IV

News at School and Away

News is any disruption of the status quo or any deviation from normal. It is the glut of occurrences that will happen today. Millions of events are taking place now. Some have news value. Some do not.

How do reporters and editors determine whether an event is news? Five major guidelines assay the worth. The size or magnitude of an event must be considered. If Congress passes a bill this morning that affects only millionaires, the masses are not interested, except for human interest. A rule affecting only seniors does not disrupt freshmen, sophomores, or juniors. The number of people affected determines the scope of a happening.

Importance is a second aspect to consider. On a logical scale, some things are more important than others. People are supposed to be of more consequence than property. The number of persons killed or injured is supposed to be more important than the extent of property damage. A big tree falling on a street during a storm is of some slight news value. If the tree hits something expensive, the news weight increases. If the tree kills or injures someone, the news value becomes greater. If the tree strikes someone famous, the accident becomes of page one importance.

Prominence is a third factor. Local prominence, such as that of the mayor or well-known business or professional persons, is of more interest and perhaps consequence to local people than news involving a national or international celebrity who resides somewhere else. Almost anything a celebrity does has some minor news value. A sprained ankle on an alluring film actress gets media attention. A tonsillectomy on a high-ranking senator warrants a little newspaper space.

Proximity—the nearness of the news to the reader—is the fourth factor that must be measured. The closeness of an event has a direct relationship of relevance to the reader. A major fire in Hong Kong doesn't have the reader identification of a local fire. The burning of a local shopping mall may affect many local consumers who will have to trade elsewhere, maybe at much more expense and inconvenience. An explosion in Africa is of much less consequence to local citizens than a bomb dropped on their back lawn.

Timeliness, the fifth factor, is essential. Newspapers must have new news. The recency of an event may be an important aspect of its impact. The electronic media are often able to report events as they are taking place. Printing takes more time than broadcasting.

If there is a major crime today in the Northeast, it will get headline attention on page one, assuming nothing of greater news value happens. As the story is relayed around the country by the AP or UPI—or both—it receives less space and less prominent display. Chicago papers may use less than half the copy the northeastern papers devoted to the story. By the time the story reaches the West Coast, it may get only a few inches of coverage deep inside the paper, or it may not be used at all.

News has many other qualities and characteristics. News is as varied as life. As with most terms, there are almost as many definitions of news as there are journalists, the hordes of pseudo-authorities and pseudo-critics of the press notwithstanding.

Super-journalist William Randolph Hearst said very early in the century that news is anything that makes readers exclaim, "Gee whiz!" Charles A. Dana, while editor of the New York *Sun,* said, "News is anything which interests a large part of the community and has never been brought to their attention."

"The first thing which an editor must look for is news," Dana said. "By news I mean everything that occurs, everything which is of human interest. I have always felt that whatever the divine Providence permitted to occur I was not too proud to report." For those literary hypocrites who don't consider newspaper writing legitimate, there is a stock answer: Journalism is also literature in a hurry.

Glancing through a metropolitan daily reveals the variety of news subjects. Most stories reported by the press come under one or more of the following headings:

Accidents	Biggest-smallest
Accomplishments	Oldest-youngest
Animals	Fires
Celebrities	Health
Contests	Heroic Acts
Crime	Historical Finds
Disasters	Hoaxes
Discovery and Invention	Labor and Management
Economy/Business	Law Enforcement
Education	Medicine
Exploration	Natural Catastrophes
Extremes:	Nature
Shortest-tallest	Politics and Politicians
Lightest-heaviest	Promotions and Demotions

Public Health:
  Environmental Sanitation
  Epidemics
  Mental Health
Religion
Research
Revolutions
Riots
Science
Social Problems:
  Alcoholism

Moral Issues
Prison Reform
Racism
Suicide
Speeches
Sports
Technology
Vandalism
War
Weather

Hundreds of types may be outlined under some of these broad areas. Consider the types of crime. Some libraries are devoted to certain of these subjects. And many libraries have scores—often thousands—of books under each heading.

Some news is predictable. Political and governmental stories are standard. They are covered on the local, state, national, and international scenes daily. The time and place at which most of these happenings will occur are rather definite.

Accidents are happening now, but they are less predictable. An editor can't tell a reporter to go to a particular place at a precise time and get a story on a burning building, an auto accident, or a bank robbery. Some locales are much more prone to have these become realities than others, but they can't be regulated by clocks and calendars. This unpredictability is part of the drama of the profession of journalism. On occasion, reporters encounter something of greater news value while en route to cover a given story. Reporters must be as spontaneous as their product.

High-school news encompasses almost all the subjects noted above. Among the many specific news sources on the secondary education scene are:

Accidents—student or faculty, either at school or away
Accomplishments of student or faculty
Crime
Contests
Business and economy related to the school
Fire prevention
Health
Politics and politicians related to education
Promotions or demotions
Research by students or faculty
Social problems: alcoholic parents, moral issues, prison reform
Speeches
Sports
Vandalism

Teachers and students number many millions. They are often directly or indirectly included in many news stories. The scope of the high-school newspaper must be as broad as the happenings in which students and faculty are involved. Local coverage must be the primary objective. But national and international affairs also affect high schools in some situations, as all society is touched in some manner. The high-school paper must look at the total world because the view of everyone must be much more universal in order to understand and cope with change. No institution or individual can exist in a vacuum or thrive in isolation today. Communication is the brain—possibly the soul—of modern man.

Society cannot ignore news from the secondary education press and vice versa. Everyone is associated with public education in some way in addition to taxes. Few things are as controversial as education. Good and bad school systems—and good and bad colleges—are certainly affecting life with the quality of students they produce.

Effective communications depend on the quality of the writing. News stories must be tight. They must focus only on significant facts. The total story must be told in the minimum wordage compatible with the fastest readability. Most news happens with incredible speed, and it must be consumed the same way. Each word must contribute to the story. No embellishments are permitted.

Good writing in any medium is lean. Some so-called classic books are literary tranquilizers. Most were considered good during the eras when they were written. Writing must stay as contemporary as the people or be interred with them as they die. Redundancy and rambling were once legitimate in literature. Not now. Generally, people talk too much and write too much. Much "heavy" literature literally is. One can almost get a hernia hoisting some of the bulky volumes from the shelves.

Maybe it is the lucid brevity of news writing that offends aficionados of wordy literature. Books often have the option of deviating from the central theme. News must not stray a syllable. Neither should a lot of books.

A news story has a beginning, a middle, and an end, as all logical prose must have. The opening is the lead. With rare exceptions it should consist of one sentence. There are summary and salient leads.

Summary leads try to answer as many as possible of the 5 W's and the H: Who, What, When, Where, Why, and How. Journalism jargon refers to them as the 5 W's. If these six questions are answered concerning any news happening, the story will be complete. One point is usually much more important than the others. What happens is almost always foremost. If it happens to a celebrity, who he is may be of more importance than the event.

The majority of straight news stories use summary leads. It is easy to find the formula for them in any daily paper. Thousands of summary leads are being written right now. The facts summarize the story in one sentence.

Who? . . . . . . John Smith, 29, a hardware salesman, 123 Pearl Street
What? . . . . . . was killed
When? . . . . . today
Where? . . . . . Central Avenue and 12th Street
Why? . . . . . . his car collided with a truck.

Simple accident stories with similar information have leads like this:

John Smith, 29, a hardware salesman, of 123 Pearl Street was killed today when his car collided with a truck at Central Avenue and 12th Street.

"Why" and "how" commonly merge. "Why" something happens sometimes remains a mystery. Why does a hawk smash into the cockpit of an airplane, causing it to crash and kill people? The above lead has twenty-six words. No lead should exceed thirty words. The longer a sentence, the more difficult it is to comprehend quickly. There is a direct relationship between length and readability. Of course, something simple may be expressed in a complex way and vice versa.

Notice that the lead says "a hardware salesman." The article *a* is often not used by some newspapers. It has become a matter of style to drop it. However, many journalists feel that using *a* or *an* helps the readability even though it adds a short word to the sentence. This author recommends using an article when identifying persons by occupation or profession. Note also that the preposition *of* precedes the house address of the deceased. If the preposition is not used, the address must be isolated with commas. Both should not be used. Use one or the other.

Although straight news leads follow a formula, this need not hamper creativity and literary variety. Writing demands self-expression even in the simplest and shortest news story. No two persons are going to select the same words when writing a story from the same facts.

Straight news presents a story in order of the importance of facts, not chronologically. When President Abraham Lincoln was assassinated, millions of people had to read hundreds of words in some newspapers before the stories revealed that he was dead. And some progress in journalistic writing had been made years prior to the Civil War. The summary lead was given impetus by the war. Correspondents telegraphing stories to their papers learned to give all the important information first; the possibility always existed that one of the armies would cut the wires.

Who? . . . . . . The Blank club
What? . . . . . . sold 350 boxes of chocolate

When? . . . . . last week
Where? . . . . . locally
Why? . . . . . . to raise $175 for a new kiln for the art instruction room.

The Blank Club sold 350 boxes of chocolate locally last week to raise $175 for a new kiln for the art instruction room.

Several variations of the above lead are possible. Reader appeal can be enhanced by writing it with more impact and interest. Such as:

Calories mean heat in other ways, too. The Blank Club sold enough chocolate last week to local sweet tooths to raise $175 to purchase a new kiln for the art instruction room.

This could be a two-sentence lead. Purists can make such leads into two paragraphs. They believe the opening sentence should always be the lead. It is permissible to do so as long as the lead does not get too long. Over forty words make a rather long paragraph in a standard newspaper column less than two inches wide. A long paragraph—especially the lead—tends to repel rather than entice readers. People are leery of long lists of words, oral or written.

Complex sentence leads offer some variation in construction and expression.

Substantive Clause

Although Principal Jones Key had 30 pounds of plaster under his robe, he passed out diplomas to the graduating class yesterday.

Despite the cast, he refused any assistance during the ceremonies. He broke his left leg in a skiing accident at Sun Valley, Idaho, last week.

Conditional Clause

If the extent of the poster campaign is any gauge, senior class officers will be among the most active politicians in the nation.

More promotion is posted around the grounds than ever before, according to the school janitors.

Participials are the most appropriate for some leads. They move the most dramatic or important elements of the news to the front. Reader interest is stimulated, and the information is quickly presented.

Past Participial

His facial wounds stitched, Howie Smith is present at school this week after being attacked by a kennel of dogs.

Smith, a sophomore, was working with eight Doberman Pinschers Saturday when one of them became vicious.

Present Participial
Casting more than 100 votes in a half hour, the junior class had the most active voting record during the election yesterday.

The anti-apathy campaign by the class recently showed other results, according to one class officer.

Infinitives
Infinitives can often open a lead with the motivation behind the news story.

To increase the potential of class participation, a variety of events is scheduled for Home-Coming.

Picnics, bicycle races, and a concert are slated for the annual affair.

Prepositional Phrase
Prepositional phrases can relate some aspects of news that should appear in the lead.

With one pitch, his side-arm fast ball, Howard Smith held the Parker High Cardinals hitless during last week's game here.

Salient or one-fact leads are generally restricted to more important stories. Despite the definition, they usually present more than one fact. Some information is usually necessary to support the primary news fact.

1. The Gymnasium roof caved in yesterday.
2. A truck backed through a wall of the cafeteria last week.
3. The president will have major surgery next week.
4. Leon Strobe was elected to the Genius Club last week.
5. War was declared today.

There are other types of news leads. They employ literary devices and techniques for reasons of readability, human interest appeal, and effective writing in general. Many are used on news features.

News features have more feature than news value or vice versa. Either way, the interest qualities are double. Whether the news element is weak or strong, it is accompanied by feature qualities. The news peg is the fact that gives the story its reason for being. It is dubbed a "peg" because it is the element on which the feature aspect must hang.

If a warehouse fire drains most of the water pressure in the city, there are likely to be degrees of feature interest. Some kids might have been planning a pool party, but the lack of pressure will not supply the needed water. A student learning to drive an auto strikes a transformer and blacks out half the city. These are called sidebars. These sideline stories are often placed near the major stories that inspire them. "Playing up the feature" is the way journalists refer to them.

1. It was a dry pool party in Briarwood yesterday.
2. The Acme warehouse fire drained water pressure throughout the city. In some sections, it was reduced to a trickle.
3. A young lady learning to drive yesterday doused the lights in half the city when she rammed a transformer.

or

A young lady learning to drive at dusk yesterday reached for her light switch and turned off half the electricity in the city. She rammed a transformer as her eyes left the road.

Descriptive leads focus on atmosphere and environment. Graphic detail reconstructs the drama. This visual impact allows the reader more penetration into the story. It may be as creative as the writer's skill. However, rhetoric must not distort for the sake of good wording. Remaining meticulously accurate and still portraying color and retaining concreteness is demanded.

1. Rain crawled down the window like clear melted wax, distorting the street of neon signs into a multicolored maze.
2. The asphalt was a black ribbon mirroring the traffic, which was thinning because of the storm.
3. Maybe the moon didn't capture the waxed glow of the car, but here and there a chrome strip tossed a slash of light on the street where the corpse was lying.

Contrast leads may add irony to some stories. Two seemingly unrelated things are meshed, emphasizing the central point. They may contrast the past and the present or some inequality.

1. After buying the bank whose floors he used to sweep, William Carl said yesterday he had seen every kind of dust except gold.
   The 64-year-old bank president recalled some of his most interesting experiences during his climb from custodian to executive.
2. Trimming the hedges around the perimeter of park, Abe Shelby said the ornamental grounds certainly no longer were reminiscent of the trash dump that was once there.

Staccato leads are rarely needed. They feature pace and action and rely heavily on description. Grammatically, they consist of a series of sentence fragments or one incomplete sentence. Sometimes they are a string of phrases separated by periods or dashes. They strive for impact.

1. Accordionlike rows . . . ramps sticking their concrete tongues out of the stadium . . . batteries of lights . . . and one man on the field.
   The lonely hero stereotype was real enough for the champ.

2. Mass hypnosis . . . maybe . . . his oratory hitting every heart or head . . .
no one . . . not in an assembly there . . . not with such attention . . .
The speaker enveloped all, shrouding the crowd in a cloak of words with
meaning. This reporter had trouble concentrating on coverage. His talk was
almost omnipotent.

Capitalizing on jokes, puns, witty sayings, or clichés may generate a
good lead on occasion. For it to be effective, the expression or epigram
must be within the realm of knowledge of the reader. Consequently, only
well-known ones may be used.

The match industry is more than a burning business.
Matchbooks are also an important advertising medium. Eight out of ten
persons with matchbooks in their pocket or purse right now can tell you the
name of the product or service being promoted.

The following refers to the song, "Catch a Falling Star."

One of the cast caught a falling star at play rehearsal last week, and she
was soft.

Parody leads get their effect from taking a popular expression—
derived from such sources as songs, books, films, or fad language—and
giving it an unusual twist.

1. A fool and his money are soon parted, particularly if he strolls through
Central Park at night.
2. A penny saved means much more to a coin collector if it has the right date
on it.

Literary or historical allusion leads focus on some widely known
passage. The current situation must make an effective comparison or
contrast to something else. One must be careful not to use trite or clichéd
references.

1. What goes up, keeps going when it has helium in it.
At the zoo last week, a balloon peddler let his stock loose. It was pretty
but not profitable, the man admitted.
2. Strip mining operators in the coal-rich Appalachians may not leave any
mountains for Mohammed.
Great machines are peeling off the slopes.

If question leads are provocative enough, they may arouse good reader
interest. They are not as forceful as those already noted. Readers want
information and entertainment rather than interrogation. But they are
sometimes effective on features and news features. The question is a good

transitional device for features. Those with the "you" approach and strong human interest are excellent for strong reader identification.

1. Can you be a better driver?
   The National Safety Council statistics on people who have had a driving course say your skill may be increased considerably with proper instruction.
2. Would you throw a rock at a burglar?
   Miss Jane Smith, 20, 319 Oreo Lane, did last night. She heard a prowler and went outside to investigate. A man was pushing her bicycle. She picked up a softball-size rock and heaved it.
   "He yelped," she told police who answered her call, "when it hit him in the back. But he dropped my bicycle." The would-be burglar got away.

Quotation or dialogue leads are the least effective type. Quote marks distract rather than add to the effectiveness. Statements have to be very explosive or interesting to grasp attention, and they almost never are. It is the weakest opening in any literary form.

Direct address leads may be used on some news features and features. As noted when writing in the second person with question leads, reader identification may be inherent. Depending on the story, these leads may establish some personal rapport with readers.

1. You may be able to charge your body like a battery if engineers can get flesh to store certain electrical charges.
2. You may soon be able to fly with just 20 pounds of gadgets strapped on your back.

Effective writing allows no deviation from perfection. Word choices must be specific. The world must have its news reported precisely as it happens. Tight copy is mandatory. Avoid superfluous phrases and unnecessary words. None should be permissible.

Wordy: All students who are interested are invited to the seminar.
Tight: Interested students may attend the seminar.
Wordy: A baby boy was born to Mrs. Leona Smith on Thursday.
Tight: Mrs. Leona Smith gave birth to a son Thursday.
Wordy: An Acme toy store was completely destroyed by fire on Saturday.
Tight: An Acme toy store burned Saturday.
Wordy: Officials from throughout the area were present on the occasion to congratulate the winners.
Tight: Winners were congratulated by area officials.
Wordy: Peggy Davis, who is a secretary, has a typing speed of 60 words per minute.
Tight: Peggy Davis, a secretary, types 60 words per minute.
Wordy: P. Sue McCormick, who used to work in Jackson for an insurance agency, attended the concert by the band.

Tight: P. Sue McCormick, once a Jackson insurance firm employee, attended the band concert.

Wordy: She lived in a swank apartment in Chicago, Illinois.

Tight: She lived in a swank Chicago apartment.

Wordy: The half-time cannon went off with a roar.

Tight: The half-time cannon roared.

Wordy: He fell off of the curb on the corner of Main Street and 16th Street.

Tight: He fell off the Main and 16th Street curb.

Wordy: The convention will be held this coming Wednesday.

Tight: The convention will meet Wednesday.

Tighter: The Wednesday convention will lure some 500 beauticians.

Wordy: Principal Jed Jones, who once worked as a lumberjack, will take part
in the archery event at the sports festival.

Tight: Principal Jed Jones, an ex-lumberjack, will enter the archery event.

Wordy: The archery contest will begin on Sunday.

Tight: The archery contest begins Sunday.

Although total objectivity is a news media myth, logical objectivity is essential in the editorial world. Objectivity in its purest meaning removes the human factor. When a reporter collects a score or more major and minor facts for a story, he must decide which ones are most necessary to the story. What he regards as trivia or almost pointless information is left out. So subjectivity is necessary even before the story is written.

Outside of this evaluation, objectivity is the epitome of importance. News must be free from opinion. It takes only one word to editorialize. The editorial section of the newspaper is reserved for enlightened opinions and attitudes. News must not be tainted by any subjective action. News consumers are interested in facts. They neither want nor need reporters or editors adulterating or abridging to distortion the information in any way. Reporters must report, not editorialize. No implications, conscious or unconscious, may enter news. Subtle or almost undetectable editorializing is more dangerous than the obvious.

Reporters must be able to see themselves before they can report for others. They must know and keep in check their opinions, political and philosophical orientations. If they don't admit having them, they may well let bias affect facts. Simple news, devoid of emotional involvement, presents no personal reporting problem. Stories oozing with strong human elements affect reporters—they are human. No reporter, even the most callous, can be totally detached or remain aloof from every story. When stories throb with pathos, sympathy, or deadly irony, facts are invariably enough to reveal the depth. The desire to be dramatic is admirable perhaps, but quality reporting always conveys it. Journalists accept the goal of objectivity.

It takes only one word to editorialize. And, unfortunately, many such

words will appear today in dozens of newspapers. But most are innocuous, and over 99 percent are unintentional.

"The bride was lovely" will appear in papers today. Who said? Reporters differ even on what constitutes ugly and pretty. "He was outstanding
in the game" will be written hundreds of times this week. State his
record. Let the facts show he was great. Reporters don't have to inject
double praise.

Some editorializing is the result of reporters leaving out attributions.
Opinions are rendered by someone, but the reporters fail to say who
made the statements. Attribution of all facts is necessary if the source
of the information is not strongly implied. As millions read auto accident
stories today, they know that reporters had to get the facts from law
enforcement officers, hospital personnel, and maybe even the wrecker
drivers who towed away the vehicles. A few years ago a famous and
highly respected reporter wrote a series of articles on a phase of a war.
He neglected to state the source of some casualty statistics. This basic
oversight by an honored newsman resulted in his not receiving the
Pulitzer Prize that year.

Most news comes from beats. Reporters have two types, subject and
geographical. The former type specifies that a reporter cover one subject
area. It may be crime, business developments, politics, or some other
standard topic. The geographical beat outlines a section of the city, and
a reporter covers a variety of general news sources. He may have a zoo,
a post office, a high school, a fire station, and other points, as well as
crime and accidents on occasion, in his own piece of reporting world.

High-school beats may be restricted to administrative offices, departments, clubs and organizations, sports, the physical plant, guest speakers, library, student transportation, city offices or agencies that
communicate with the school often, police or safety patrols, and others.
It is invaluable for reporters to establish as much friendly rapport with
the sources as possible. A reporter who is not always ethical with his
sources soon will not have any, at least not with suitable relations.
Cooperation almost invariably aids efficiency.

The following lists of some news topics from within the high school
are taken from the Quill and Scroll Foundation's *Teachers Are News-
makers* by Laurence R. Campbell. The college press covers essentially
the same beats, but the terminology differs. And campus facilities are
usually larger and more sprawling.

News in Every Classroom

Your classroom is a learning center. It is newsworthy. Some news
happens once a year; some more often. Nearly every classroom teacher
is likely to have news of:

Accreditation
Audiovisual aids
Awards, honors
Conferences
Contests
Curriculum changes
Debates, panels, forums
Demonstrations
Department meetings
Dramatizations
Enrollment figures
Equipment
Evaluation
Exhibits
Experiments
Facilities

Field Trips
History of program
Library resources
Personality sketches—faculty
Personnel—new, retiring
Professional writing
Publications
Resource materials—films
Schedules
Social events
Speakers
Supervisors
Testing
Textbooks
Visitors

Agriculture

Schools that offer instruction in agriculture will have news of such activities as these:

Contests—oratorical, experimental, cornhusking, hog-calling
Conventions and conferences—state, national
Equipment—tractors, power and hand tools
Experiments—plants, animals, soil
4-H Clubs—elections, appointments, programs, business
Fairs and shows—county, state, pet, cattle, garden
Field trips—experiment stations, farms, factories, colleges
Future Farmers—elections, appointments, programs, business, national FFA
    Week, fund-raising
Government—state, federal, regulations, projects, quotas
Honors and awards—scholarships, prizes, special recognition
Judging—contests, preparation, team, individual, tryouts
Mechanization of farms
Social events—barn dances, hillbilly shows, banquets, country music
Urban-rural relations

Business Education

Business careers appeal to many teen-agers. Often they make news in their business education courses. Typical topics:

Accounting
Advertising—slogans,
    contests
Bank operated by students
Business arithmetic

Business English
Consumer education
Contests—spelling,
    penmanship, shorthand
Courtesy in business

Distributive education
Duplicating equipment
Future Business Leaders of
    America—elections,
    meetings, programs
Honors
Insurance
Interviews
Jobs—summer, part-time
Model office

Office machines
Penmanship
Salesmanship
Secretarial training
Shorthand—for boys,
    methods
Student assistants
Typing—blindfold,
    contests, methods

English

The public expects high schools to prepare teen-agers to be effective in speaking and writing and in reading, listening, and viewing. Success in many courses depends upon the student's ability to communicate. Hence, there are many topics of interest. For example:

Academic and non-academic writing, aesthetic and utilitarian writing
Advertisements—copy writing, appeals, analysis
Boners in English classes
Books—new, rare, reviews, reports, paperback
Censorship—obscenity, pornography, heresy, sedition
Comic books, comic strips
Contests—literary, journalistic, spelling
Creativity—essays, plays, poems, fiction
Journalism study—consumer role, student journalists
Language—linguistics, semantics, slang, jargon, obscenity, rhetoric, grammar—traditional or transformational
Library
Literature—American, British, World, contemporary, regional, local, religious, political, science
Magazines
Mass media—consumer study, social role, freedom
Motion pictures
Newspapers
Professional writers and literature
Radio
Reading—speed, comprehension, readability
Surveys
Teachers—achievements, requirements
Tests—reading, university admission, vocabulary
Trends in English education

Fine Arts

Art stories rank high in reader interest, and most departments in the school constantly call upon art teachers for help and advice. Typical activities for possible stories are:

Advertising
Cartoons, comics
Ceramics
Commercial design
Fabric design, textiles
Interior decoration
Jewelry, enamels
Linoleum blocks
Mobiles
Museum of Art tour

Negro contribution to art
Painting
Plaster of paris casts
Posters
Pottery work
Sculpture
Showcase displays, exhibits
Silkscreen
Weaving

Foreign Languages

Topics suggested in the English list often may be appropriate for any language. Here are typical topics:

Audiovisual equipment and
  materials for foreign
  language teaching—tape
  recorders, records,
  language machines
Boners in translation
Exchange students
Festivals
Films
Food in foreign countries
Historic days and events

Letters from foreign writers
Plays—foreign language
Propaganda
Publications—newspapers,
  magazines, books
Special events—banquets,
  contests
Tests
Tournaments
Travel

Home Economics

Typical topics for news coverage in home economics include these:

Architecture
Boys in homemaking
Budgeting
Cafeteria assistants
Child care—baby-sitting, family life
Contests—Pancake flipping
Diet
Etiquette—in school, at games, parties, other homes
Fashion—shows, modeling, costumes, trends in fabrics, detergents
Food courses, menus, gourmet tastes, recipes
Furniture—contemporary, antique
Future Homemakers of America—elections, programs, business
General living course—home life
Home management—accounting, purchasing
Home repair—plumbing, painting, electrical
Honors—fairs, bazaars
Household appliances—use, trends, cost

Interior design
Kitchen color schemes

Sewing—textiles
Spot and stain removal

Industrial Arts

The austerity of academic life at one end of the campus is more than compensated for at the other end by the warm, colorful activity of the shops where the practical problems of living are confronted and solved. The school paper must cover all academic areas of the campus completely and assiduously, and these story possibilities should not be overlooked.

Auto mechanics
Career talks by
   plant engineers
Drafting
Drawing—mechanical,
   architectural
Electronics
Gadget making
Inventions by students
Machine shop
Metal shop
Metal work projects

Model homes
National Hobby Week
Photography
Plastics
Printing
Radio hams
Sheet metal
Showcase displays,
   exhibits
Welding
Woodwork

Mathematics

Much of the interest in mathematics—"new" or otherwise—centers in application to various fields, although there is interest also in computers, cybernetics, course changes. Stories may deal with the use of mathematics in:

Agriculture
Architecture
Astronomy
Computers
Consumer research
Engineering
Forestry

Opinion polls
Public finance
Science
Space travel
Taxes—income, sales, property
Transportation

Music

Activities and courses in music are correlated so that many students participate in newsworthy activities. These activities may include:

Band—formations, marching, dance, drum majors, uniforms
Baton twirling
Choral groups—a capella choir, madrigal singers, barber shop quartet, minstrels

Concerts—chorus, band, orchestra
Conductors—student, guest
Festivals
Fund drives
Honors
Instruments—new, rare, ancient, repair
Music appreciation
National Music Week
Operetta (or cantata)—tryouts, casts, dates
Orchestra—brass choir, woodwind concerts, contests
Original music by students and teachers
Parent auxiliaries
Radio and television appearances
Recitals
Rehearsals

Natural Science

Science teachers often are rated as poor news sources by student journalists. Hence, the science teacher may wish to expand this list, which, of course, does not include course titles. Suggested topics:

Audiovisual equipment and
  materials
Equipment—new, main-
  tenance, breakage
Experiments
Field trips
Health—diet, drugs,
  tobacco, alcoholic
  beverages
Honors
Laboratories

Museum of science
"New" sciences; phony sciences
Oceanography
Photography
Pollution
Programs
Projects
Scholarships
Science Fair
Space study

Social Studies

If the program of social studies stresses student commitment and involvement in group decisions, then it will be a source of significant news. Suggested topics:

Campus unrest
Citizenship programs,
  projects
Contemporary issues
Economics study—local
  business
Field trips—city hall "takeover"
Forums, debates, discussions

History—local, school, of
  school publications
Local issues
Maps, models
Mass media
Minority problems
Mock trials, conventions

Polls on attitudes,
   interests
Propaganda
Psychology

Stamps and history
Student council, student
   organizations
Voting machines

Speech

Students who participate in debates, plays, and other speech activities
make news regularly. For example:

Amateur shows—assembly,
   radio, television
Choric speaking
Clinics
Contests
Correction
Debates—subjects,
   schedules, teams
Discussions—panel,
   forum, radio,
   oratory
Honors

Pantomime
Plays—tryouts, casts, dates,
   rehearsals, costumes, property,
   ticket sales
Poetry—oral presentation
Puppets, marionettes
Radio, television
Recording
Stagecraft—stagehands,
   facilities
Therapy

Principal's Office

The principal's office is a major source of news—some of it almost
daily, some of it yearly. The principal interested in effective internal and
external relations should schedule a press conference for student journalists and student leaders. He should instruct his staff to cooperate with
amateur news gatherers as well as professional reporters.

In addition, members of the administration make news by speaking
in public, attending professional meetings, and performing various civic
and professional services.

Topics that may be newsworthy include:

Accounting system
Accreditation
Alumni—achievement, relations, organization
Attendance—weekly, monthly, yearly; absences, excuses, epidemics, weather
Audiovisual program, equipment, resources
Board of Education—meetings, decisions
Budget
Buildings—new, repair, age, insurance
Buses—routes, schedules, drivers, equipment, safety
Cafeteria—schedule, menu, equipment, employees, prices
Campaigns and drives—bond
Citizenship honor—civic, patriotic, educational groups
Commencement—time, place, program, regalia, number of graduates

Cost analysis of different educational services
Counseling—career, educational, health, military, personal
Curriculum—modifications, evaluation, scope, problems
Custodian—training, recognition, wage scale
Day-in-life—of principal, teacher, secretary, librarian
Education Week
Employees—new, retiring, recognition, leaves of absence, health, pensions
Enrollment—school, classes, programs, boys, girls
Equipment—new, repair, stolen, time-saving
Flag—age, procedure
Grades—system, honor roll
Grounds—care, improvements, regulations, landmarks
Halls, corridors—passes, behavior
Health—services, nursing service, special programs, health, drugs, tobacco
Holidays—exact dates, hours
Homerooms
Interns—student teachers
Library—hours, policies, acquisitions, personnel, services, exhibits, facilities
Lost and found—system, unclaimed items
Nature—birds, plants, animals on or near grounds
Office—staff, schedule, equipment, services
Open house
Parent-Teachers Association—meetings, programs, projects
Parking—regulations
Patrols—traffic
Point system
Property—protection, regulation
Purchasing—methods, bills, bids
Records—scholastic, financial, personnel
Registration—dates, procedure, regulations
Research by administration or faculty
Safety—traffic, fire drills, accident prevention, safety patrols
Schedule—fall, summer, spring
Scholarships
Special occasions—anniversaries, special weeks, conferences
Students—new, transfer, exchange, assistants, monitors, oldest, youngest, twins, redheads
Teachers—new, retiring, student, summer session, extension, professional activities and writing, faculty meetings
Vacations—exact times, dates
Vandalism
Visitors—parents, civic, professional
Youth groups in community

Guidance and Testing

Counseling activities vary from school to school, but these activities usually fall within the scope of the counseling program:

Alumni placement in business, college
Appointment schedules
Careers—Career day, information, interviews
Career Groups—Future Teachers of America, Future Nurses, Future Business Leaders of America, Future Farmers of America, Future Journalists of America
Educational Guidance—choosing programs, courses, study methods, improving grades
Health Guidance—solving problems of hearing, eyesight, physical limitations and disabilities, emotional problems
Jobs—applying and succeeding in part-time, summer jobs
Military Guidance—draft laws, opportunities in different services
Personal Guidance—problems students wish to discuss
Scholarships
Surveys
Tests—aptitude, attitude, interest, College Board
Vocational guidance—occupations, professions

Library

The library is the school's learning center. It also is the repository of school archives in which historical materials should be preserved. Typical topics include:

Audiovisual equipment, materials, resources
Books—new, donors, rare
Card system
Historical materials
Library club
Literacy
Microfilm
Magazines
National Book Week
Newspapers
Repairs
Reviews
Right to Read
Rules
Schedule—evening, week-end, vacation
Student assistants

News of Organizations

Many teachers are advisers or sponsors for an organization—big or small, formal or informal. Their importance varies from school to school; for example, public and non-public, urban and suburban, military and parochial. Major organizations often are:

Class organizations—senior, junior, sophomore
Clubs—honor, career, hobby, service, boys', girls'
Homerooms or comparable units
Living center groups (in boarding schools)
Military units (in military schools)
Student council and related activities

Typical news stories for each organization may include:

Activities—planning, short-range, long-range
Appointments to committee—members, experience
Committee activities—plans, meeting, achievements
Meetings—business, social, program, regular, special
Members—selection, qualifications, initiation, participation
Officers or delegates—election, nomination, duties
Organization projects—campaigns, methods, achievements
Recognition—at school, away from school, trophies, awards

Student Publication News

Student publications also are a vital activity, especially where there are qualified advisers with journalism preparation and basic and advanced journalism courses. Among them often are the newspaper, yearbook, and magazine. Occasionally there may be a handbook or directory or a radio-television staff. Typical stories are:

Advertising
Appointments to key staff positions
Awards to students and publications
Contests—journalistic, literary, photographic
Conventions and conferences—date, delegates, programs
Date of publications—yearbook, special editions
Editorials and editorial campaigns
Election—key editors and managers, Quill and Scroll members
Exchanges
Finance—budget, circulation
National Newspaper Week
Planning activities, budgets, summer institute attendance
Propaganda study
Ratings from Quill and Scroll Newspaper Evaluation, other services
Social event—banquet, outing
Workshops, institutes, short courses in summer
Visiting speakers

School Life

School life encompasses many activities of school-wide interest. Social events are important, yet—if overemphasized—may give the impression that students concentrate on frivolity. Standard topics include:

Assemblies—meetings, convocations, class nights, rallies
Dances, parties, picnics—school-wide, class, club
Debates—inter-school, intra-school
Dramatics and related speech events—schoolwide, class
Holidays—special days, weeks
Honors—academic, non-academic, individual, group

Minority adjustments—problems, protests
Music—concerts, operettas, recitals
Personals—individual achievements in and out of school
Residence hall activities
Social problems—early marriage, drug use, draft
Traditions—school history
Vacation—summer, spring, Christmas
Weather—floods, blizzards, hurricanes
Work opportunities—part-time, summer

School and Community Relations

Community relationships may be of increasing importance in the future. Ties with other local schools, as well as with those in foreign countries, may receive increasing attention. Students may show concern for local problems by cooperative efforts, possibly reducing the time spent on good-time activities.

Sports

The school's program of health, physical education, and recreation is important. Too often the only aspect of it that receives much attention—from the press and its personnel—is the athletic program. Indeed, in some communities the public knows little about the school aside from its sports activities.

Hence, news of sports should be kept in perspective. It is not the responsibility of the high school to provide any public with a sustained program of spectacle sports. Often this public comes only to see "a good game," not to see evidence of good sportsmanship or character building. Whatever is done, therefore, should be consistent with acceptable goals of secondary education.

Sports stories—like other news stories—should be fair and objective, accurate and truthful, concise and readable. They should *not* take sides. They should *not* alibi. They should let the team win whatever plaudits it deserves on the basis of performance.

Amateur journalists often dwell on what has happened. Actually, the public may be more concerned about the coming game than the game that has passed. There also is a tendency to play up stars, neglect team effort. Football may get the lion's share of space. Intramural programs and girls' sports often are neglected.

Advance stories may touch on these details:

Coaches' statements, announcements, forecasts
Comparative scores, related facts
Conditions of players—injuries, morale
Individual angles—development of players
Public interest—ticket sales, pre-game activities, probable attendance

Starting lineups—weights, records, experience
Systems of play
Traditions and trophies
Weather reports—significance

Coverage stories may cover such points as these:

Coaches' statements
Dressing-room story
Individual honors—don't overplay
Play-by-play—chronological account used only for key games
Side features—crowd, band, between halves, end of game, fashions, parking
Significance of outcome—on league standing, championship chances
Statistics—box score, averages
Weather—role in game
Winning play—how set up, how made

Stories on health, physical education, and recreation also may cover:

Alcoholic beverages and health	League standings
	Maintenance
Alumni—achievements in college	Managers and mascots
	Medical supplies
Awards and honors	Nicknames of players, teams
Bus driver's impressions	Physical fitness, examinations, exercise
Calling out squad	
Diet and weight control	Play days
Driver training	Posture study
Drugs and health	Rules
Equipment and apparatus	Safety campaigns
First aid	Schedules
Food, etc., consumed at games	Squad—veterans, transfers
	Summer recreation programs
Gate receipts	Tryouts—spring practice
Health and hygiene	Uniforms—cost, cleaning repair
Homecoming	

Attention should be given to activities that fit the local school. Periodic articles on sportsmanship of players and spectators are appropriate. Introduction of a new activity or game—ballet dancing or lacrosse—may deserve special emphasis.

Interviewing

Over 99 percent of all news stories come from one or more interviews. Reporters must talk to people for almost every story they write. The news media are generally not on the spot when most news happens. Spot news is unpredictable. Reporters do their reporting of accidents, fires, and most other events after they happen.

On-the-spot reporting may be done only when the spots are known in advance. The press usually covers speeches, meetings, and other news stories while they are in progress. Reporters also attend dedication ceremonies, aviation exhibitions, many governmental proceedings, and other happenings. But they have to talk to many people to get quotes, comments, and information. Merely attending an event as an eyewitness does not give them all the story. At times, what they see may confuse them even more. Getting explanations from people who know about the situation or circumstances is even more essential in such instances. What appears to be a failure to laymen and reporters may be a celebrated success to scientists. On occasion, news sources are very uncooperative with reporters. But reporters must always get their stories.

Appearance of the reporter is important. First, he must consider himself. A sloppily or poorly dressed reporter does not make a favorable impression. Neatness is always an asset. His conduct must be good. Even though he may have to be very aggressive in order to get some stories from some people, he must practice good manners as much as is possible under trying circumstances. Initial impressions are important, regardless of what may be said of them. Reporters must be able to control their tempers, despite how unpleasant a situation becomes.

Research is essential before almost every interview. A reporter should learn how to pronounce the person's name, know his title, be aware of his background—particularly as it might apply to the pursuit of the present story—know his relationship to the story being gathered, and all other necessary details. Other people may be able to furnish this information on the person. If he is an authority, he may be listed in one or more reference books or directories.

Punctuality must be observed. A reporter should keep account of the time. Some people literally work on split-second timing. Famous psychologist Alfred C. Kinsey meant it when he said he would talk to a reporter for five minutes. The renowned researcher would admit a reporter at the precise time scheduled, set an alarm clock on his desk, check it against his own wristwatch, and then tell the reporter he was ready.

There are various ways to interview people. One may talk with them face-to-face—the best and most common method—or telephone or write them. A reporter must first determine whom he needs to interview and why. He arranges an appointment at the person's convenience. Prior to the meeting, the reporter must prepare the questions he intends to ask. Since the human brain is rarely photographic, the reporter should jot down in abbreviated or detailed form the questions that must be answered to get the total story.

Basically, he should recall the 5 W's and H in outlining his questions. Who is involved in this story? What does it include? When will the situation start and end? Where will this story take place? Why is this being done? How is it organized, conducted, financed, and will it affect anything or anyone else? What are the primary challenges or obstacles concerning the story?

The following story written by Professor LaRue W. Gilleland of the University of Nevada Journalism Department appeared in the *Journalism Educator,* a quarterly published by the Association for Education in Journalism.

SIMPLE FORMULA PROVES HELPFUL TO INTERVIEWERS

by LaRUE W. GILLELAND

Teaching reporting students to conduct fruitful interviews is even more difficult sometimes than teaching them to write concise, clear news stories.

A reason may be that guidelines for gathering information—when contrasted with abundance of rules and formulas for putting information into story form—are scanty.

"I just couldn't think of the right questions to ask" is a complaint students have made to many journalism professors. It's a complaint city editors have heard also. Experienced newsmen will admit on occasion that effective questions failed to come to mind when inquiring into unfamiliar subjects, when time was short, or when they were tired or not feeling well.

A technique this writer has offered students for several years involves a simple diagram they can recall easily during interviews—a diagram suggesting questions to ask. The students are not told the technique will work in every situation, but they are encouraged to try it when they feel an interview may be going badly.

Some former students, after acquiring full-time news jobs, have written letters saying the technique worked for them, often in obtaining information with minimum expenditure of time. It also has helped, they said, on assignments which appeared on the surface to be dull. Reporters, even beginners with a minimum of formal journalism education, generally have little trouble coming up with the right questions when covering spot news with obvious widespread interest—elections, disasters, or major police cases. But interviews involving relatively routine stories can be the most difficult.

The technique is based on premises that nearly any individual or organization making news has a goal or purpose and has confronted, or will confront, some obstacle; that the newsmaker has found—or is looking for—a solution to the obstacle, or a way around it; that the goal sought originated at a point in time with somebody's idea.

The theory can be diagramed on a blackboard this way:

$$x \xleftarrow{\quad S \quad} \underset{O}{\underset{|}{}} \text{---------} x$$

$$\underset{G}{x} \quad\quad \underset{O}{} \quad\quad \underset{S}{x}$$

A student who was not impressed with the diagram dubbed it "Gilleland's GOSS formula." His remark turned out to be helpful because the acronym GOSS—Goal, Obstacle, Solution, Start—provides a memory-aiding device. It reminds the reporter, after he has jotted down preliminary information, to ask the following:

—Goal-revealing questions, such as "What are you trying to accomplish?" or "What's the real purpose of your organization?"

—Obstacle-revealing question, such as "What problems did you face?" or "What stands in your way now?"

—Solution-revealing questions, such as "How did you handle the problem?" or "What plan do you have for resolving the conflict?"

—Start-revealing questions, such as "When did the program have its beginning?" or "Whose idea was it?"

Hampton Young, newsman for KCRL-TV and AM, Reno, said, "I have found the GOSS technique is excellent when I have a story to do about a subject for which I have no background. Always before, without background information, I found myself groping for 'feeler' questions, and often there would be that one question I would forget to ask.

"With the GOSS technique, everything just falls right into place. There is no need to reach for questions. I know what I'm going to ask. When I'm through I have all the information I need for a story. No pain or mental anguish is involved."

Another student who became a sports reporter told of covering a high school track meet which was routine except that an 18-year-old pole vaulter from a visiting school broke a conference record.

Other reporters obtained the pole vaulter's name, school, parents' names, the fact that he was a senior, the height and date of the old record. They found out that he was engaged, where he planned to go to college, and they got a quote from him on how he felt about setting a record.

The sports reporter, who arrived after other newsmen had finished talking to the young man, asked him, "Did you have any obstacles to overcome in setting this record?"

"Yes," the pole vaulter said, "I had polio when I was 13."

That reporter's story contained an angle other accounts of the track meet lacked. It described how the youth had taken up running, jumping and pole vaulting to strengthen an afflicted left leg and, as a result, had become an outstanding athlete.

Let's take another story that is often treated routinely—construction projects. Reporters nearly always ask how the project will be used, its cost, location, number of floors, rooms and square footage, materials used, and they obtain a general description of how the structure will look. Too seldom do they ask if there has been any unusual architectural or engineering problem to be overcome and, if so, how it has been accomplished. That question could prod forth answers which frequently would give routine construction stories extra dimension. Other questions suggested by the GOSS technique which reporters sometimes fail to ask are: "When did the congregation become convinced it should build a church with such ultra-modern lines?" or "Whose idea was it to put a shopping center in that location?"

If the technique has worth, the writer must give credit to Schopenhauer and Nietzsche. Their philosophies of conflict suggested a long recognized news value. Their statements that human life, in seeking objectives, consists of struggle against inevitable obstacles gave this writer the idea of applying the theory to news interviewing.

Virginia Heck, a journalism student who had been interning with a newspaper, wrote: "It's so simple . . . When I first had interviews to do, I was often upset. So I started using your GOSS symbol. It brought questions to mind and I started to relax. I also began listening more intently to what the person I was interviewing was saying, because I no longer was worried about my next question."

Some people, especially those not familiar with the press, become very inhibited when a reporter takes notes. Writing down some words of the person being interviewed is the reason for the reporter's being there. Some journalism educators—but no veteran reporters—say that note-taking should be done secretly, subtly, or not at all in some cases. This has become a myth, unfortunately. Notes are necessary, and one must not be sneaky in making them.

The following article by Professor Douglas P. Starr was first published in the *Journalism Educator.* He cites why notes always must be made openly.

Permit Them to See That Notepad Used

by DOUGLAS P. STARR

Almost since the moment journalism schools opened their doors, journalism students have been cautioned often against being too obvious in taking notes during interviews. It does something to the interview, runs the admonition, making the subject either clam up or open up. Either way, the reporter loses; the interview is unnatural.

George Fox Mott, in his *New Survey of Journalism,* fourth edition, cautions that "unless the interviewee wishes to quote verbatim, avoid the use of a notebook or the too-apparent note-taking since this often makes him aware that he is going to be quoted and causes him to speak less freely. If note-taking is necessary, do it unobtrusively."

Carl Warren, in *Modern News Reporting,* third edition, takes the position that note-taking is a practical problem for reporters. "When covering a speech, perhaps notes may be made unobtrusively or during a press conference openly," he writes. "But during an interview, especially with a person unaccustomed to talking with reporters, it often must be done warily if at all."

Speaking from the vantage point of 14 years of intensive and extensive reporting as a newsman for the Associated Press in various news situations in the capital bureaus in Jackson, Miss., and Tallahassee, Fla., I must take exception to these admonitions. They are not necessarily valid. In fact, more often than not in a real news situation, such admonitions are useless.

Of course, in the case of a person unaccustomed to talking with reporters, interview note-taking must be done warily, but it must be done for the protection of the reporter as well as for the protection of the subject. As in all matters, the reporter must handle his contacts civilly. But the reporter must be in control of the news situation; he must conduct the interview; he must ask the questions, in his most professional manner; he must direct the subject to respond.

Not take notes? Take them warily? Nonsense. The working newsman merely takes out his notepad and pencil as matter-of-factly as possible and says to his subject as matter-of-factly as possible that he will take notes to make sure no mistakes are made.

If the subject balks, the reporter explains the benefits of note-taking, the importance of accuracy, the necessity of securing proper spellings of names and addresses. The working newsman takes notes as he wishes, not as his subject wishes.

Once in Mississippi, I took notes while I interviewed a man suspected in a Negro lynching. Throughout the interview, the man held a revolver in his hand and his wife held a shotgun across her lap. As might be imagined, the situation in the county was tense. Nevertheless, despite my understandable fears, I controlled the interview, asking what questions I wished and getting answers to most of them.

For the most part today, newsmen are covering activities of various governments and government officials. The men and women holding important-enough positions to warrant an interview are accustomed to talking with newsmen for quotation and publication. To them, note-taking is part of the interview, not something to be feared.

Although most newsmen take notes, they take them sparsely. Most newsmen cannot and do not want to use shorthand, primarily because that would provide more notes than they really need. Actually, during most interviews, the newsman is seeking only a few new facts upon which to build his story. In general, before a newsman begins an interview, he studies the background on his subject and the topic under discussion. This not only gives him information he needs, but it also impresses his subject, and can help overcome any barriers to communication between the newsman and the subject.

Another reason newsmen take sparse notes is that their powers of observation are usually sharper than most people's. The newsman is trained and experienced in noting mentally what people do and say, and how they appear. Note-taking is used to trigger the memory.

Although errors do occur between the interview and the writing, most complaints come after the subject has had time to reflect upon what he said and has decided that he should not have said it.

A reporter should be careful in taking notes. He should be sure where direct quotes start and stop. The marks should be clear so that the reporter will not have to wonder later whether it was a direct or indirect quote. His notes must be readable. He is allowed only one interview. It is better to get too much information rather than not enough. He can delete, but he cannot go back.

In some situations, a tape recorder is beneficial. Some persons do not like to be interviewed when they are aware that every word, including throat clearings, is being transcribed. Some will not permit a tape recorder. Poet Robert Frost vehemently objected to taped interviews. He would not talk to a reporter who used a recorder.

During an interview, a reporter must observe and listen. He should note any gestures and mannerisms of the speaker, noting whether the person sits, paces, continues to work, or gazes out the window. What the person does while he is talking may give the reader of the story some insight into it. Is the person buoyant, enthusiastic, or pessimistic?

One should note whether the person has a sense of humor. Is he serious and intent, impatient, or frustrated? When some people are upset during an interview, they may fidget, frown, squint, appear bored or irritated, or reveal other emotions and feelings. The reporter must note the person's reactions to determine how to conduct the interview as to tact and necessity. Some persons study the reporter intently. They watch for responses also.

The deliberate pause is sometimes an effective technique. The reporter asks a question. After the person replies, the reporter remains silent for a longer duration than average. This time lapse inspires some interviewees to continue talking. And possibly they will add more information, thinking that the pause implies that they have been withholding something. It makes the person uneasy enough in some instances to reveal things he perhaps might not have otherwise.

Regardless of the stature of the person interviewed, the reporter must never allow himself to be overwhelmed by authority or prominence. Reporters will interview governors, congressmen, geniuses, show-business celebrities, and a variety of other notables today. Reporters are allowed little awe. None must influence their work. Thousands of reporters are interviewing people this minute on every level of society and in almost all endeavors.

On rare occasions, reporters are told things that they do not include in the story. They understand that to reveal some things they learn about a criminal case would harm the investigation. A crime reporter does not publish the fact that a raid will be conducted in two days if such information has been revealed. Sometimes a person wants to tell something if the reporter will promise not to print it. A reporter should never commit himself until he is convinced that a fact should be withheld.

When someone is reluctant to comment on a story, the reporter must inform the person that it will be in the best interest of the public for him to speak. Sometimes a reporter can persuade a news source to talk by telling him he will seek the information elsewhere if necessary. The reporter should also point out that the second source may not be as well informed on the matter. It is always best to get the most complete story from the most informed source.

Sometimes off-the-record information puts the story being sought in better perspective for the reporter. By better understanding the story, he may better communicate it to readers. Complications arise at times. A reporter is told something by a person who does not wish it reported. Later, the reporter discovers someone who has the same information and wishes to disclose it. Ethically, the reporter must tell his first informant that the information has been obtained elsewhere. Not to tell the first person would be to betray his trust. Editors and reporters have debated off-the-record interviews since the beginning. Each interview must be evaluated on its points.

Freedom of the press enters when a person tries to withhold information illegally. Public officials must reveal public information. The press has the right and responsibility to see public records and documents.

During an interview, a reporter must not be a slave to his prepared questions. The course of the conversation should dictate the points to be covered. Sometimes a reporter goes after one story and returns with a second and more important one. The most desirable interview is one that is similar to two persons talking informally. A reporter must not monopolize the conversation. His mission is to get information. The telephone interview has both assets and liabilities. It is less personal. For some, it is the most convenient. Because of distance, the convenience of the person, or other circumstances, the telephone call may be the most sensible at times. Even when persons are very busy, they will usually devote a few minutes to a telephone conversation. A reporter must get his answers quickly so as not to waste time. Since he cannot see the person, he must be tactful. It is easy for an offended person to hang up. A tape recorder may be beneficial in some telephone interviews. The person being interviewed must be told that the conversation is being taped. State laws vary on the technicalities involved in recording telephone conversations.

Mail interviews may be appropriate when great distance is involved. The questions may be listed, leaving enough space between them for the person to reply. A carbon copy should be enclosed for the person's files, and a self-addressed, stamped envelope should be enclosed for courtesy and convenience. The letter should be as well written as any piece of effective writing. If the letter is not typed, it should at least be legible.

This prepared question interview is preferred by most Communist nations. They read the list and answer only those questions they desire.

Accidental interviews demand that a reporter be prepared. He must have a pencil and paper. And he must be versed enough in the art to ask his questions spontaneously. A reporter must be able to interview a celebrity who just happens to be in town. The governor's helicopter might set down unscheduled in the town tennis court or at a local heliport. The author once accidentally encountered the only living son of Casey Jones, the railroad engineer celebrated in American folklore. He interviewed him in a museum. Unfortunately, he had to borrow the man's pen and write on a museum brochure because he was not prepared. The author had sold two articles on the legendary engineer and was able to sell a third based on the interview with the son.

The personality interview must be employed with celebrities when there is no news peg on which to hang the story. It becomes a feature profile. The reporter tries to grasp the character of the person through proper questions.

In the random interview a roving reporter asks one or two questions of several persons. The reporter must get the reaction of a group for survey stories. He talks to them usually at some specified locale and perhaps at a specific time of day.

Symposium or panel interviews are very formal. They consist of a panel of reporters asking one or more persons questions on a particular topic. These are often open to the public and are frequently televised.

Almost every celebrity in the world claims to have been misquoted at least twice. Unfortunately, some are correct. Reporters do make mistakes. They write down what they think is correct, but often it is not. When a reporter is not sure what a person said, he should ask him bluntly to repeat it. Accuracy is the foremost objective. If a statement seems inaccurate, distorted, or ambiguous, the speaker should be requested to clarify it.

Skepticism must always be the watchword of the reporter. It must be innate. He seeks truth. And some informants are unreliable. Some people lie to the press. Some do it for sensationalism or publicity. Others have more devious motives. Reporters must check their facts. Just the fact that a person makes a statement does not insure its authenticity. Hoaxes are a disreputable part of history or tomorrow's news. Every point the reporter questions must be substantiated from a reputable person or a reference book.

For years the American Society of Newspaper Editors and other journalism groups have been urging Congress to pass a national law to protect a reporter's sources. To date, seventeen states have laws stating that a reporter need not identify his sources of information. Some other states observe an unwritten law shielding sources.

To reveal those who confidentially give information to the press might well in some cases result in their murder. Others who give important information to the press may be socially and/or financially ruined if exposed. Their friends and families also may suffer in many ways. The only time that limitations on press freedom may be imposed is during national emergencies, primarily in wartime. Newspapers may not publish information that would help the enemy. And civilian courts may impose some limitations on the news media. Judges can rule whether photographs may be taken, in or out of the courtroom, of persons involved in a case. Canon 35 of the American Bar Association maintains that dignity shall be maintained in court at all times.

A generation ago, television equipment was bulky and noisy; bright lights were necessary; flashbulbs were needed on still cameras. They did indeed hamper court proceedings. Today equipment is quiet and miniature. Cameras are almost microscopic and need only available light.

The issue is primarily one of exposure and publicity. Generally, cameras are unnecessary in court. The biggest liability they present is that the jury, the lawyers, the judges, and others may forget justice and start worrying about millions of people watching them on television or thinking that the photographs being made of them will appear in hundreds of newspapers in the nation that day. Artists' sketches are permitted. This is why such art is usually the only printed illustration of most trials.

The following feature interview—an attempt at one—is an offbeat example. Clipped dialogue helps it. The weakest point is the cliché: "guaranteed going-away present." Not being able to get the interview shows insight into the subject of it. One must interview—or try to—every celebrity who comes to town. This story appeared in the Memphis (Tenn.) *Commercial Appeal.*

'BIGGEST STAR' BREEZES IN, SHUNS SOUTHERN HOSPITALITY

by CAROLYN PAIGE

With a big cigar clenched between his teeth, Tom Jones strutted down the boarding ramp of a United Air Lines' Caravelle Jet, chartered flight No. 5379 from Nashville.

It was 12:15 P.M. yesterday and airport officials, newsmen and seven policemen had been waiting more than 45 minutes on the hot runway at Memphis International Airport.

For less than a minute, Tom Jones made the wait worthwhile.

After that, a ticket to the concert was the only way to see the gyrating singer who came to Memphis for a guaranteed going-away present of at least $75,000.

"How about a short interview, Tom?"

"No."

"How about riding with you in the car to the motel, Tom?"

"There's not room."

The big limousine was three steps away, the motor running and the door open.

Time enough for one more try.

"You make your living off female fans . . ."

"Oh, do I?"

". . . what do you think about the women's liberation movement?"

"I don't."

That was it. The show of Tom Jones—the man, not the singer—was over for Memphis.

One of the concert's producers, Rick Bowen of Miami, 27, talked about the kind of man Tom Jones "really is."

"A great guy—but face it, he's the biggest star in the world, and he knows it," said Mr. Bowen.

"You can't blame him for the security measures. In Nashville, fans broke through police barricades—they went wild, even throwing bras and panties at him."

Some seemingly simple accident stories are not. Take away the multi-million-dollar cargo from the following truck wreck, and it would not have nearly as much human interest. This story is also from the Memphis *Commercial Appeal.*

INTERSTATE IS SLIPPERY STAGE
FOR CAR-TRUCK CRASH

by JAMES KINGSLEY

A tractor-trailer loaded with 32,000 pounds of prescription drugs valued at $9,000,000 was involved in a wreck during a flash rainstorm at 5 P.M. yesterday on Interstate 40 near WMC Road.

The rig, officers said, was hit by an automobile driven by Jim Waldrup, 21, of 3723 Mallory, a carpenter, who was driving west when the car went out of control on a bridge. The car hit the bridge and bounced into the path of the westbound tractor-trailer.

James E. Allison, 48, of Dallas, owner of the $47,000 rig and a passenger in the cab, said he was en route to Dallas from a pharmaceutical manufacturer in New Jersey. He refused to list the contents beyond some "aspirin and penicillin."

Mr. Allison, who owns 10 such carriers, said a fear of "the possibilities of being hijacked" prevented him from disclosing the wrecked rig's destination for repairs. "We've had wrecks before but we've never been hijacked," he said.

Mr. Allison added it was his policy that two persons accompany drug shipments "because of the possibilities of being hijacked."

Mr. Waldrup's 1966 automobile was demolished, and the front wheels of the rig were knocked loose. A passenger in the automobile, Sterling Gammon, 37, of 1555 Echols received minor injuries. He was treated and released at John Gaston Hospital.

The rig's driver, Robert Earl Holder, 34, of Denton, Texas, said, "The automobile had passed me, hit the bridge and bounced into the front of my truck. I couldn't stop. I tried to take it up the median strip but after I saw no cars coming the other way I went across the highway."

The rig jack-knifed in the eastbound lane and blocked traffic for about 90 minutes.

Mr. Waldrup and Mr. Gammon were returning to Memphis after working on a home they are building in East Shelby County. Mr. Waldrup said the sudden downpour "made the highway slick and my car spun out of control. "All I can say is that when I saw what was happening I said, 'God help us.' It's a miracle we weren't all killed."

Officers said Mr. Waldrup was charged with improper passing.

The Tennessee maximum load limit for trucks is 73,280 pounds.

Crime reporting covers everything from crossing the street against the light to murder and larceny. Crime exists on all levels of society. The following article appeared in *Editor & Publisher,* the weekly trade magazine of the newspaper world.

POLICE BEAT: STILL THE PLACE THERE'S FAST-BREAKING NEWS

by MARK H. LITKE

Chris Holmes, the *Examiner* night police reporter, and Bob Palmer, photographer, are relaxing in the San Francisco Hall of Justice pressroom when the call comes over the radio at 1:15 A.M.:

ATTENTION ALL UNITS. A 219 AT 100 EDDY STREET. A POSSIBLE HOMICIDE.

Within minutes, Bob and Chris are standing outside the Club Mason Tavern —a tenderloin bar at Mason and Eddy. Inside the bar, a 219 has occurred within the last half hour. A 219 is a "cutting," or a "knifing." A man has just hacked his girl friend to death with a ten-inch butcher knife.

A crowd has begun to form on the corner, mindless of the chilly night air, consuming the plethora of rumors circulating freely up and down the street. Pat McCristle, a free-lance cameraman for local television stations, relates the few available details to Chris.

"It's a woman, Chris," McCristle says. "Her old man just chopped her up with a butcher knife."

"Where is he now?"

"A C.P. (a member of San Francisco's elite Crime Prevention Unit) just took him over to Central Emergency. Seems like some of the patrons grabbed him when he ran out of the bar. They beat him pretty bad."

Need picture of 'live one'

Chris and Bob confer. They could wait outside the bar and take a picture of the corpse when the ambulance attendants bring it out. But as Bob laconically phrases it, "The *Examiner* won't use photos of dead ones."

Obtaining details from the homicide inspectors is incidental at this point. That can be handled later via telephone. A photo of a "live one" is needed now to "make the story." So Bob and Chris drive quickly to Central Hospital in order to photograph "the killer."

At the hospital Chris learns from the C.P. that the suspect is an ex-con—out of San Quentin just three weeks, where he served eight years for arson. With that tidbit of "human interest" the story will almost certainly appear in print. A mental scorecard has tallied enough points to make the story newsworthy: a knifing (insufficient by itself—there are dozens of 219's each week in S.F.), a female victim (a principal element for even covering a 219), a photo of the suspect (extra points for the cigarette dangling from his lips, the glazed eyes, the blood-spattered clothes). All that is needed to break par is a photo of the knife. So, back to the scene of the crime.

Inside the tiny bar, homicide inspectors Gus Coreris and John Fotimas explain the "facts" to Chris. Bob prepares to photograph the knife being held by an assistant inspector. Dim red lights cast an unreal pallor over the eerie postmortem scene.

"Hold it at the end of the handle," Bob tells the reluctant inspector. "Yeah, that's good. I've gotta get those two glasses on the bar in the background."

The bartender is muttering to himself as he wipes up the spilled drinks on the bar. And everyone is feigning anger at the pool of blood which covers the floor and sticks stubbornly to the bottom of shoes.

The next day in the Examiner, on page 12, the public record of a crime: an eight-inch story, a photo of the blood-spattered suspect, and a photo of the knife (gleaming from the reflection of the photoflash) with the two glasses on the bar in the background.

Crime reportage has changed

The value, the fairness, and the morality of sensational crime reporting has been vigorously debated throughout the years. From the gruesome descriptions of Jack the Ripper's mutilated victims in the London *Times* of 1888, to the embroglio surrounding the much publicized Manson killings, the merits and defects of crime reportage have been argued both intellectually and emotionally.

On one side, the unabashed capitalist freely proclaims that sensationalism sells papers; or, a more rational traditionalist argues that "nothing destroys an infection like sunlight." On the other side, critics claim that sensational crime reporting both fosters and appeals to a sick preoccupation with violence; or, that it creates an unhealthy atmosphere for dealing with crime; or, that it prejudices juries.

The debate will undoubtedly continue for many years. In the meantime, crime reporting continues and the "police reporter" remains a firmly established institution in journalism.

Who are today's police reporters? What does their work entail? What are the factors which determine whether crime is reported or ignored by the news media?

The crime reporters of another era were stereotyped as a gregarious bunch of noisy, aggressive bloodhounds—that group we still see in old gangster films, sporting shabby tweed jackets or wrinkled raincoats, and crumpled fedoras with the front brim turned upward, always "hanging around," waiting for a morsel of news to be tossed by a benevolent or careless official.

More sophisticated

Today, law enforcement, and, subsequently, crime reporting is more sophisticated. The technological advancement in communications, combined with a decreasing number of competing newspapers, have rendered the police reporter's job less hectic, more routine, more detached.

Police reporters have become specialists in the art of listening to police radios and using the telephone. Communications are so rapid and thorough that a reporter need only lift up a telephone receiver, make a few calls, and a story is virtually complete. Photographs or a bit of excitement are really the only reason for leaving the office or pressroom; and knowledge usually exists beforehand as to the possibility for either one.

San Francisco's police reporters operate from the third-floor pressroom at the Hall of Justice. During the day, as many as six reporters occupy the room. There is no fierce competition between *Chronicle* and *Examiner* reporters, who share the same office space. And despite the noise and pandemonium in the room, there is rarely a sense of urgency.

News via telephone

If a reporter, for some reason, should be unable to visit the scene of a crime, he can phone the central communications room. Whoever answers the phone will tell the reporter which police officer made the "on-the-scene" report. That officer can be reached by phone also (either at the Hall or at home) and all the details will be made available. In the following day's paper, there is no way a reader can tell from an article whether the reporter "covered" the event or paraphrased an official police report.

At night, the pressroom is less hectic. But the absence of lively activity and the semblance of excitement that activity creates is more indicative of modern police reporting. Beginning at 8:30 P.M., there are only two reporters and one photographer at the Hall of Justice pressroom. And between midnight and 4:30 A.M., these three are the only active reporters working in the city.

Peter Kuell, the *Chronicle* reporter, a long-haired, bearded anomaly in the spit-shine polish of the heavily guarded Hall of Justice, does little more than watch television and play gin rummy with *Examiner* photographer Bob Palmer. Usually dressed comfortably in Levi's and a T-shirt, Kuell actually has little incentive to work. The morning *Chronicle's* first edition comes out at 8 P.M. the night before. "They're not going to bust up proof for anything less than war with China. And even that would have to begin before midnight," says Kuell.

Kuell leaves at 1 A.M. So, the duty of night police reporting really belongs to two men: 25-year-old reporter Chris Holmes and 62-year-old photographer Bob Palmer.

Stories out of the past

Palmer is a 40-year veteran of Hearst newspaper service of New York, Chicago, and San Francisco. He remembers the days when crime reporting was exciting—like Chicago during Prohibition and the gang wars. Reporters depended on their wits and on one another in those days. And Palmer has a thousand stories to prove his affection toward the past.

"We were up in this tenth-floor police room, see." Palmer begins one of his stories. "And this guy they just hauled in decides he's gonna jump. So he runs towards this open window and takes a leap. Then this bailiff we all know—George, his name was—he grabs this guy by the ankles as he goes flying by.

"Now this guy is dangling from the window. Scared to death, 'cause he don't want to jump after seeing the view. And poor old George is hangin' on—slipping a little himself—and somebody's holdin' on to him.

"So all of us photographers run down a flight of stairs and a couple of doors over. Then we all lean out this window snapping shots like crazy; yelling, 'Hold 'im George; hold 'im just a few more seconds'."

Chris (Christian) Holmes has been the *Examiner* night reporter for two years—his first job after graduating from Wesleyan University with a bachelor's degree in governmental studies. The stories he relates come from the age of electronic statistics. Subsequently, they lack that bawdy, raucous flavor imbued in the tales of the 30's and 40's.

Holmes's work has become a dreary mechanical recapitulation of official police records. He works alone. He is torn between his own empathy and the callous veneer he must affect in a nighttime world of knifings, homicides, shootings, and fires. Other than police, his only companionship during the night is Palmer, who will, at the drop of a pin, gladly bend Chris's ear with a tale of the good old days worthy of Damon Runyon.

His daily routine

Chris begins his evening in the city room of the *Examiner's* office building. He checks in with the night city editor for possible stories, which, if there are any, usually turn out to be the incomplete work of the daytime reporters.

He arrives at the Hall of Justice at 8:45. A guard sits at a table inside a glass doorway at the front of the building (the only door open to the street at night). A shotgun is propped up against the wall. The guard checks Chris's identification—even though he has seen Chris a hundred times before. The paranoia of bombings and shootings aimed at police still runs high.

Palmer is already at the pressroom. Kuell is fixing his nightly hamburger in the adjoining TV room—the noise of the television competing with the crackle of the police radio.

The first priority of the evening (and often the only major task) is "calling in the beat." This involves between 10 and 20 phone calls to precinct stations, the highway patrol, the Coast Guard, the emergency hospitals, the coroner's office, the Golden Gate Bridge ("for jumpers"), the police communications room (upstairs in the Hall), and the fire department's central communications office. If there is nothing else to do, *all the calls are made.*

Friends on 'the force'

The "trick" to successful police reporting is twofold. The first key to success is a durable remnant from the past—"making friends on the force." A tip from a friendly cop can put a reporter in the middle of a Golden Gate Park manhunt or a vice raid in the tenderloin.

Secondly, a police reporter must learn to pick out "possibles" from the maze of calls coming over the police radio; and then know the right person to call for details or whether a photograph is possible.

If a garbled or confused report sounds interesting, call central communications. If a knifing has just occurred and there is no suspect and there is no way to beat the ambulance to the scene—head for Mission Emergency Hospital. If someone needs medical attention requiring an ambulance and the police are involved, the victim is always taken to Mission Emergency.

"That type of predictability makes this job easy most of the time." Chris claims. "A rich old society matriarch could be burglarized and stabbed around the corner from Mt. Zion Hospital, and they would take her to Mission Emergency."

The usual pattern

A homicide without a suspect in custody can usually be handled with three calls: the communications room (for the investigating officer's name); the investigating officer (for the details of the crime); the coroner (for the cause of death and miscellaneous details regarding the victim's general description). The following evening, the obituary can be handled by calling the coroner again for the names of relatives, the religion of the victim, and the mortuary handling funeral arrangements (Coroner Henry Terkell is a great source of information for any news story involving a death). Finally, the mortuary is called to obtain funeral details and the "standard obit" is typed out in about five minutes.

Such is the pattern of 98 percent of police reporting.

There are nights when the tedium and boredom become so overwhelming that Chris and Bob take flight to Enrico's for a leisurely dinner and a couple of hours over coffee (always mindful to call Central Communications to ask "what's happening?"—hoping for that 2 percent chance of something big).

When the opportunity does arise to break the monotony or escape the coverage of crime, the call is rarely missed. And the energy which Chris, or any other police reporter, applies to such opportunities results in exceptional reporting or gross sensationalism, depending on how the story is written and played in the next edition.

A change of pace

Last February, when two Standard Oil tankers collided in the bay, Chris was able to escape from crime for a few days and devote all his energy to coverage of the battle against the oil slick. For three consecutive nights, he and Palmer spent long hours compiling interviews and photographs of the clean-up activities at Ocean Beach, Bolinas Lagoon, and Stinson Beach. Two weeks after the spill, Chris was still writing stories on the plight of bird rescue operations.

However, tedium is not always broken by nighttime news outside the world of crime, and altruism is not always the motivation of the reporter. The unusual also comes in the form of "spectacular crime," such as the Ohta family murders in the Santa Cruz hills last October.

The story of the *Examiner's* page-one splash of the murder began when Chris picked up a bit of sketchy news from a police communications officer. The fact that he was hearing news of a Santa Cruz murder from the San Francisco police meant that something big was happening. When the S.F. crime lab and homicide bureau were notified at 11 P.M., Chris and Bob "got a tip" on the address and headed for Santa Cruz.

When they arrived at the bottom of the dirt driveway leading to the Ohta home, they were stopped by a police barricade—no friendly cops around to break the gag rule. Stymied by intransigent (and heavily armed) police, Chris burst forth with his craziest (or most brilliant) idea since becoming a reporter.

He and Bob drove to a small airport outside Salinas. After checking with the city desk, they rented an airplane. Flying over the Ohta home at a low altitude, Palmer leaned out the open hatch and snapped aerial photos that were front page material for the next day's *Examiner,* and eventually picked up by the wire services.

Why does police reporting continue? Increasingly, there is a little more to do than listen to the police radio and transcribe an investigating officer's impressions of a crime. Even worse for the journalist, the incessant attacks on police activities have driven criminal investigation underground—the gag rule is becoming more the rule than the exception. So, why do newspapers still both bother to staff dingy pressrooms in police stations? Chris Holmes has at least one answer:

"It's the only fast-breaking news in town."

The following crime story appeared in *The Lion,* the student newspaper of Lyons Township High School of LaGrange and Western Springs, Illinois. It carries the by-lines of three reporters who did a commendable job of reporting and writing.

ASSISTANCE KEY TO MURDERERS' ARREST

by JUDY PIPER
GARY POSSELT
TERRY SCHMITT

Authorities say they know who murdered Alan Fredian, '74, but are not ready to make arrests.

Two Cook county state's attorney's investigators told Lion reporters last week they are interested mainly in four south campus students. Two of these are believed to know who killed Alan and two allegedly witnessed or committed the act.

ALAN'S BODY was discovered Oct. 17 in the "hole," a wooded area opposite south campus that since has been cleared. He had been hit with a piece of concrete and, although he would have died from the wounds, he was asphyxiated when buried alive.

The investigators, who wish to remain unidentified, are sure at least four boys know what happened.

"Of the four youths who have the necessary information, we feel that at least two committed the act," said one of the investigators. "The others had to have prior knowledge of what might happen, because they were busy calling Fredian's house that night.

"ONE WAS SO concerned that he made four or five calls because he was 'super-scared' about what might happen to Alan. He was mad at the person who was going to the 'hole' with Alan to allegedly get dynamite."

The investigators said "dynamite" could refer to explosives or a high grade of marijuana, but laboratory reports indicate that Alan was not on drugs.

THE LIVES OF students who have knowledge of the case, especially those who know who committed the murder, are in danger, according to the investigators.

"Whoever killed Alan Fredian knows that somebody knows he did it," said one. "Sooner or later the killer is going to think, 'He poses a threat to me. He can put me in a penitentiary. I've got to get rid of him'."

THE INVESTIGATORS have much physical and circumstantial evidence. They say they can prove who dug the grave. The investigators said they know where the shovel is that was used to dig it. They can link the suspect to a burned LT swim team T-shirt found in Waiola park. They can also link the victim to the same burned clothing and the suspect to the victim.

The investigators said there are students who know something of the murder but have remained silent. "We have lacked cooperation from students and parents," said one.

"THE MINUTE THE spotlight focuses on a student as a target suspect, his parents obtain an attorney for him. This cuts off communication because the attorney has advised the students to say nothing.

"Some of the kids we felt might have had knowledge of the case have been cleared through a voluntary polygraph (lie detector) test with parental permission. Others have refused.

"THE PARENTS OF the boys who have taken the polygraph test have cooperated fully. They believe in the children and believe their children are not involved in any way.

"A few parents are afraid of getting involved and feel that the police will dig up information without their kids testifying."

The investigators feel that someone had to see something related to the murder.

"AT THAT TIME of the evening with that many people around that area, with the dance going and the party at a sophomore's house, somebody must have seen something," said one.

"We've got a list of 15–20 kids who were going back and forth through the 'hole' that night. Maybe whoever they saw they know and they don't make any connection.

"THE AREA ISN'T that big and there are only a few paths through it. Alan was buried on one of the primary paths."

Although the police are sure they know who murdered Alan, they do not know the motive. They have constructed possibilities from circumstantial evidence.

Of these, it is most likely that Alan was killed by students he knew were trafficking in "dynamite."

"When Alan Fredian went into the 'hole,' he must have considered those with him friends," said one investigator. "I don't think he'd go there with a stranger or somebody he didn't like."

The case has taken to long to solve because of the lack of cooperation from the students, parents and community, said the investigators. "A case that could have been and should have been cleared up in a week is now five months old."

Important business news often is used on page one of newspapers. Business reporting is indispensable to the public. Readers must be kept informed of significant developments in all areas of business and industry. Management and labor problems and circumstances are aspects of this coverage area.

A big industrial plant moving to town affects almost all aspects of the community and its people. Economically, local citizens will be employed. Executives will move to the locale, affecting its population and in other ways. A new building in town may add much to revenue. A new hotel or motel downtown with convention facilities may add much money to local cash registers.

When a large bread bakery or dairy has a labor strike, many citizens in the area may have to do without the items for days. Or a fire or other accident could force some businesses that supply important products or services to the public to close for some time. Business news may have great bearing on people, directly and indirectly.

The following business story from *The Nashville Tennessean* is important. Construction of a big parking garage downtown may add much to retail sales, increase the convenience of shoppers and workers, and make it much easier to reach entertainment or other facilities in the city.

10-STORY PARKING GARAGE SLATED

A 10-story parking garage, costing $5,800,000 and creating 1,000 additional downtown parking spaces, will be built on an entire city block adjacent to the Public Square.

Jack Herrington, director of the Nashville Housing Authority, announced yesterday the facility will be constructed and developed by Public Square Co., consisting of Commerce Union Bank, First American National Bank and Taylor and Crabtree Architects.

THE FACILITY, featuring the latest in electronic parking aids, will be on a 50,631-square-foot block bordered by Third and Fourth Avenues, North, Charlotte Avenue and Deaderick Street, according to Warren W. Taylor, a partner in the venture.

The site faces the Metro Courthouse and is near the State Capitol and other major state and private office buildings.

"It is a pleasure to have such a vital part in planning and developing this functional and sorely needed public parking facility for the motorists of downtown Nashville," Taylor said.

"But an equally important aspect of this project is the effort made to insure that the building will be esthetically advantageous to the overall urban renewal redevelopment at the same time, including the latest in architectural techniques," he said.

THE BUILDING will cover 39,760 square feet of the site area with 10 parking levels making up 367,263 square feet of parking space. The building, standing

125 feet tall, will be centered between Third and Fourth Avenues with an attractive, landscaped plaza at each end.

"Since the block will include 27,500 square feet for commercial rental property," Taylor said, "these plazas will make the rental area facing them more attractive and more accessible."

The building's functional design and operational concept, he said, was developed by National Garages Inc. of Detroit to provide the "most acceptable facility available today."

The structure will be designed for customer self-parking but will incorporate a new structural concept that will eliminate the necessity of parking between concrete building columns.

"THE EXPRESS helical exit ramp system, unique in Nashville and the Southeast, has been designed and located to permit existing vehicles to enter the traffic ramp every half turn around the building from any parking level," Taylor said.

There will be two elevators at each end of the building for easy access to all parking levels. Entrances will be on both Charlotte and Deaderick with automatic ticketing equipment and electronic devices to inform drivers if parking space is available on a certain level without leaving the ramp to find out.

The building is designed to fill to capacity quickly and can empty as rapidly as external street traffic will permit.

Suspended interest—also called O. Henry-type—stories hold the punch line or climax until the last sentence. They may concern humorous or serious situations. Facts and circumstances must be conducive to their development. The following UPI story has a lot of emotional impact. With brief character sketches, it establishes strong human elements.

DEVOTED COUPLE DIES IN EACH OTHER'S ARMS

MENLO PARK, Calif.—(UPI)—Fred Seibezeder, 76, was once an Austrian imperial Marine officer. Tall, striking and blue-eyed, he married a fair-haired girl named Bertl in the town of Graz.

After the Hapsburg empire fell in 1918, he studied law and became a corporation attorney. When Hitler's divisions overran Europe, he came to the United States as a lawyer for a large European-based electronics company.

His wife, eight years his junior, was briefly separated from him when the couple fled Europe. But after they were reunited in New York in 1941, they were never apart again.

Ten years ago, Seibezeder retired. He and his wife moved to Menlo Park, a comfortable community near Stanford University.

The Seibezeders had no children, but they were the adopted grandparents of the neighborhood children and provided in their will for the college education of the children of a neighbor who was killed in an airplane crash.

In 1957, Bertl survived an attack of cancer. About five years ago, her husband's health began failing.

Last Friday, both the Seibezeders went to see a doctor. When they came home, they told friends the preliminary diagnosis was that they both had cancer. They were to go back again for a later appointment with a specialist. Some time after that, Seibezeder wrote a note and left it inside their house: "Garage is full of carbon monoxide."

He and his wife went out to the garage, shut the doors, and started their car. Their pet dog jumped in back. As the fumes filled the garage, they got in the front seat, put their arms around each other, and died.

The following story from *The Crusader* of Salpointe High School in Tucson, Arizona is analyzed paragraph by paragraph according to its development.

JON ALTMANN ORGANIZES UTEP, SALPOINTE'S FIRST POLITICAL PARTY

Sophomore Jon Altmann has organized Salpointe's first political party, the Unity Through Equality Party (UTEP).

In high schools everywhere, young people are searching for the reasons behind student government's lack of relevance for the student body.

UTEP thinks a political party is the partial answer.

Largely through Jon's efforts and with the help of Sophomore Co-Chairmen Joe Demer and Greg Urquhart, UTEP sponsored its first annual membership drive April 14 through last Friday.

The party backed Jim Drachman for Council USA President and Terri Negrette for recording secretary.

"These were the candidates who best represented the goals of UTEP," Jon said.

Welcomes Opposition

"As the only political party at Salpointe, we would welcome any organized opposition. In fact, a second party would make UTEP even stronger."

Jon cited a number of reasons for having a two-party system. In the first place, it would sophisticate government so that students would take a more realistic look at what government can do for them.

In addition, candidates would be forced to take a stand on school issues.

Also it would make it possible for candidates to run on a ticket. This would make it easier for class and student body officers to work together.

"Student government can function if it is made to function," Jon emphasized. "But it needs a shot in the arm to revitalize it. UTEP means a change from the traditional. I only hope the students have concern enough to seriously consider what it has to offer."

1. WHO opens this lead. WHERE is the next fact, and WHAT news the WHO has done is answered.

2. In this one-sentence paragraph, the national scope of student government's problem of pleasing student bodies is noted.

3. WHO thinks that another political party may help solve the situation at his institution.

4. The first activities of the new political party are detailed. And additional persons are mentioned.

5. The party's candidates are named.

6. A quote from the founder of the party contributes more information on the candidates.

7. Another quote expands the information on the party. Using *he said* after the first statement would be better.

8. The reporter relates the founder listed reasons for his desiring another party as opposition. He cites a reason.

9. Notes a second.

10. Notes a third.

11. A quote ends the story. The founder concludes with another reason for the establishment of his party. The "shot in the arm" cliché is the weakest wording in the story.

Preparing Copy

How do reporters write stories, literally? What kind of paper do they use? If a story runs more than one page, do they staple or paper-clip the pages?

The mechanical procedures of copy preparation are somewhat standardized, although they vary on minor points from newspaper to newspaper.

1. All stories are typed, and journalists must learn to type before they acquire their reporting skills.

2. Stories must be double-spaced, and some newspapers demand that all copy be triple-spaced. The typewriter ribbon should be black. Faint typing is difficult for the copy editors and the printers to read. The typewriter keys should be periodically cleaned so that ink blobs will not obliterate letters. Most reporters use rather wide margins, but there should be at least an inch on the sides. They learn to avoid dividing words at the end of lines, thus avoiding errors in word breaks.

3. Reporters should mark out sections and words they want deleted as they type.

Most newsrooms use newsprint for typing paper. The paper is the same as the stock on which the newspaper is printed. It is usually cut into the standard typing page size of $8\frac{1}{2}'' \times 11''$. A few newspapers use strips twice this length or longer. But this requires the reporter to tear off his copy, and short news items results in very short pieces of paper. This variety of page sizes makes the copy rather awkward for everyone who has to handle it.

4. In the upper left corner of the page, the reporter puts his name. Below it he puts a slug line or word. Slugging a story identifies it. The slug word or words may be "Safety Speech," "Fire Drill," "Warehouse Fire," "Candy Sales," "Charity Drive," or whatever sums up the germ

of the story. Slugging stories is very important. If a batch of copy gets knocked from a desk, a person may separate the pages easily if they are properly slugged.

5. The reporter starts his story about one-third down the page. This space allows the copy desk to insert any instructions to the printer. Also, some newspapers put the headline at the top of the first page of the story.

6. Paragraphs are traditionally indented at least ten spaces.

7. At the end of the story, if it runs no more than one page, some symbol should indicate that it is the end. Some reporters write "The End." Many use the traditional journalistic close of "-30-," and others use the symbol "# # #."

8. If the story runs more than one page, each successive page must have the reporter's last name in the upper left and the slug line below it.

9. At the end of page one of a story of two or more pages, the reporter writes "more" and circles it.

10. The page numbering of a story of two or more pages follows this continuity: Page one is marked "1 of 2," page two is labeled "2 of 2," and so on.

11. The reporter should edit his story, using the proper editing symbols. He should check his copy for any possible errors of any kind.

12. Some newspapers require reporters to make a carbon copy of their stories. This is good insurance against losing copy.

Chapter V

Talks in the News

Thousands of speeches are being given this minute. Tens of thousands of formal talks before groups are made daily. Every meeting has one or more speakers. Banquets, conventions, ceremonies, special occasions, and other areas of life produce an incessant flow of oratory.

Some speeches make news, some are by-products of news, and others are submitted as news. Political speeches are common news. The most important speech annually is the President's State of the Union address. Presidents have revealed things in this speech that have had major bearings on the nation and the world. They have declared they are for or against things, have made statements concerning wars that affected all citizens financially owing to tax increases, and many other items of magnitude. They have increased or decreased the states of wars.

During political campaigns on every level, from local to national, speeches proliferate. Candidates declare why they are ideal for office whereas their opponents are not. Speeches by major politicians are reported verbatim by the news media. Figures of less importance have only portions of their speeches quoted by the press.

Some speakers, including some politicians, provide copies of their prepared talk to the reporters. On rare occasions, the press receives copies of the speech prior to its delivery. Sometimes the prepared speech is distributed after it has been given. When reporters are able to obtain a copy of speeches they cover, their note-taking is reduced. Speakers often deviate from their prepared text or do not use all of it, however, and reporters must be aware of any changes in a speech.

The press reports speeches because they have some news value or because the speakers do. A politician of small stature may state in a talk that he has proof of government corruption that has been covered up until now. An internationally known Congressman may give a dull and senseless speech, but it will be reported by the news media. Sometimes the speech is more important than the speaker or vice versa.

The public must be informed that its politicians often say nothing in their speeches. Speech reporting generally bores many reporters. But dull news must be covered along with exciting stories. And not all speeches are bland. Some have inspired riots.

Modifying the 5 W's is good preparation for speech reporting. Speech stories are of two types. Advance speech stories are reported a day or more before the talks. These note:

1. WHO the speaker is, identifying him as necessary.
2. WHAT his topic will be.
3. WHEN his speech will be made.
4. WHERE he will give it.
5. WHY the speech will be given, which is usually evident: The speaker has been invited, sponsored, or paid to do so by some person, party, group, or organization.

Those responsible for securing the speaker usually are able to answer the W's. If the speaker is well known, additional information may be found in reference books. Sometimes the size of the audience expected to attend the speech is known.

Reporters often interview prominent speakers prior to the speech. The story is generally a feature or news feature. It may be of strong feature interest that such a celebrity is in town. If he has had or will have an opportunity to do any local sightseeing, his comments will contribute to his local appeal. Some speakers are pleasant, others nasty. A radical or extremist may be critical of the city in which he speaks.

Follow-up speech reporting is much more demanding than advance stories. The reporter has to learn as much as possible about the speaker and his subject prior to the speech. How often has the speaker talked on the topic? How has he been received by his audiences? What are the attitudes and beliefs of most of his listeners? Are they lower, middle, or upper class? Are they skilled, unskilled, or professional people? Are they politically conservative or liberal? Have his audiences been quiet or boisterous?

If the reporter has no knowledge of the topic, he must find books or people to enlighten him. He must study the speaker's conduct while absorbing mentally and taking notes on what he says. The audience must also be observed. Are people attentive or restless? Do they applaud out of politeness or honesty?

How is the speech delivered? Is the speaker emotional? Does he talk forcefully or in a droning monotone? Depending on the speaker, is he factually correct in all statements? Hundreds of speakers today will cite incorrect statistics and make other mistakes. If the reporter suspects something is incorrect, he must verify it. And he must be able to produce proof of the error, citing it in his story. If the speaker uses gestures and mannerisms, they should be woven into the story. If he has one or more pronounced character labels, they too should be noted. Sometimes how people say something is much more important than what they say. The way a message is delivered is part of it.

Speakers also are capable at times of making ambiguous or distorted statements. Everyone may be confused but the speaker. The reporter must check any gaps in his story. This sometimes requires the reporter to interview the speaker, if possible, after the speech. The reporter must be careful not to distort or inflate a single word out of context. If there is a question-and-answer period after the speech, it must be handled with the same fairness. And the way questions are asked may help humanize and give impact to the speech story. A person with a Southern or Western drawl may ask a question. Noting this may be important to the question or the speaker. The person may be from an area that is pro or con the ideas of the speaker or his speech.

As the audience leaves after a speech—sometimes some leave before it ends—some random comments from people concerning it may be significant. On occasion, the reporter may ask some people what they thought of the speech; he may not necessarily have to identify the persons who comment.

When a speaker verbally blasts someone, it is possible on occasion for the reporter to contact the person criticized for his comments or rebuttal. This is usually only fair play.

As the reporter organizes his notes after a speech, he decides on the most important or most interesting point to develop his lead. Too many speakers start with a joke or pun, but the beginning may be important to the story. The body of the speech must be assayed for the core of the talk, and the ending must be studied for any news value it may contribute.

Attribution is one of the most difficult aspects of speech reporting that beginners must learn. It must be very clear that every word is the speaker's, not the reporter's. If the information is not credited to the speaker, the reader must assume it comes from the reporter. And editorializing in news is despicable, deplorable, always unethical, and sometimes illegal.

How much to quote directly and how much indirectly should be dictated by common sense. Generally, only the major points are covered in speech stories.

In using direct and indirect quotes, attribution should be noted with *said* and other appropriate verbs of saying. *Revealed, announced,* or *exposed* are explosive verbs. The reporter must be sure the statement warrants the verb he chooses. Some verbs of saying are stilted and pompous. "Averred" is one of them. Unfortunately, some English instructors are under the false impression that such words add "sophistication" to writing.

Not all direct quotes should be buried in the story. Some should open paragraphs. It is not necessary to open every paragraph with a quote just because it contains one. But some must open paragraphs. This allows the reader to glance down a story and see that someone is talking.

Some description of the locale—perhaps inside and outside—of a speech may be pertinent. Atmosphere, color, human interest, and all other aspects must be considered in speech coverage. Some speeches are dull, but reporters must stay alert to so much that they have no time to get bored.

The following advance speech story from *The Nashville Tennessean* reports not only on the speaker but on the series that was sponsoring him. The stature of the speaker is noted, and the fame of previous speakers is expressed.

COLUMNIST SLATES MTSU TALK

Murfreesboro—Columnist Jack Anderson, who disclosed secret minutes of a critical White House policy session on India-Pakistan, is scheduled to speak March 13 at Middle Tennessee State University.

A university spokesman said Anderson did not announce a topic for his address in the MTSU Dramatic Arts auditorium, but the columnist attracted international attention last month when he reported on the secret government briefings.

Anderson's disclosures recorded in detail the conversations of high-level U.S. policy-makers during the brief, bloody war on the Asian subcontinent and recounted the formation of the controversial American alignment with Pakistan.

The reports subsequently were published through Anderson's syndicated column in numerous U.S. newspapers, including *The Nashville Tennessean.*

Anderson's appearance in the 1971–72 MTSU "Ideas and Issues" series will be open to the public and admission is free, said Harold Smith, series director.

In addition to his newspaper column, Anderson prepares radio and television commentary and is the Washington editor of *Parade* magazine.

In the "Ideas and Issues" series, Anderson follows columnist Art Buchwald, author Arthur Clarke, the Rev. Ralph Abernathy, chairman of the Southern Christian Leadership Conference, Harrison Salisbury, author and editorial page editor of *The New York Times,* and former Minnesota Sen. Eugene McCarthy.

Don Eisele, who piloted the command module in the 11-day mission of Apollo 7 in 1968, is scheduled to be on the MTSU campus Feb. 16, it was announced yesterday. He will appear in the DA auditorium at 8 P.M.

On the Apollo 7 flight, Eisele, Walter Cunningham and Walter Schirra performed station-keeping and rendezvous exercises and provided the first effective broadcast from outer space.

In this next advance speech story the speaker's schedule is given in detail. Excerpts from some of her previous talks add much to the story.

Feminist Heide to Meet
Women, Students, Public

Wilma Scott Heide, president of the National Organization for Women, America's largest women's rights organization, will be in Nashville Tuesday and Wednesday to address students, women's groups and a public meeting.

A trained nurse and sociologist, Mrs. Heide is concerned with the development of each person's total potential. She believes current methods of rearing children teach boys to be too aggressive and insensitive, while much of the talents and abilities of girls are wasted by limiting their ambitions and preparing them for passive, supportive roles.

"A feminist can be a woman or man who believes that women are people," she said in a recent speech. "They do not believe that we should change what we've had—male domination—to female domination.

"They believe in the legal, economic, social and political equality of the sexes. And equality is not to be equated with sameness," she added.

Tuesday morning she will appear on WLAC-TV's "Nashville A.M. Show" and WSM-TV's "Noon Show," and will meet with Church Women United at 9:30 at Trinity Presbyterian Church.

Later in the day she will appear before the "Minorities in the U.S." class at Scarritt College, attend a coffee and dialog with guests of the Scarritt Women's Club, eat dinner with students at the Presbyterian-Methodist Center, 1112 19th Ave. S., and address a public meeting at 7:30 P.M. in Underwood Auditorium at Vanderbilt University.

Wednesday she will participate in a colloquium on women's liberation at 11 A.M. in Fondren Theater, Scarritt College.

At 7:30 P.M. Wednesday she will hold a joint meeting with the Nashville chapter of NOW and the Democratic Volunteer Women's Roundtable.

NOW has actively supported the Equal Rights Amendment, continuation of the Tennessee Status of Women Committee, equal pay litigation, day care, abortion reform, and other matters especially affecting women.

Editor-in-chief Bob Redding of Elmhurst Senior High School's student newspaper, *The Elmhurst Advance,* in Fort Wayne, Indiana, won a Bronze Plaque from the American Newspaper Publishers Association and Quill and Scroll for the best news story in a high-school newspaper in 1970–71. Not every reporter has the opportunity to cover a speech by the President of the United States. It is an outstanding piece of work; such quality coverage should be applied to all speeches made by very prominent people. This story probably was better than any of those on the topic that appeared in the commercial press.

Chaos, Preparations Precede Executive

by BOB REDDING

Five minutes of near silence in the Memorial Coliseum, filled with over 12,000 people, is common only after an injury during a basketball sectional.

But for the throngs awaiting the appearance of the President of the United States, each minute represented days of preparation and hundreds of changes in plans when Richard M. Nixon came to Fort Wayne last week.

He came "for the purpose of talking about the candidates," which he did. But to many it was a visit by the President and they were honored to have him, even if he chose to read from a storybook.

From the initial tip-off that the President would be speaking, confusion commenced. Presidential aides and Secret Service men conflicted with local political figures and city police in planning the visit.

According to Allen County Republican Chairman Orvas E. Beers, "Everything changed from hour to hour." This uncertainty was felt by all those trying to arrange their schedules even down to the coverage planned by high school newspapers.

While White House aides were deciding on such things as the size and height of the platform from which the President would speak, a long distance call to the office of his press secretary in Washington was in process to secure press passes for the high schools in Fort Wayne.

One conflicting interest led to another after confirmation of the federal level that the high school press could be represented in the press corps. First the assistant city controller confirmed five passes to each school. Later the number was reduced to an uncertain two.

With a call from state representative John R. Sinks, also a guidance counselor at Elmhurst, security forms were sent out for completion. When the "Nixon News Media" passes were received, the press office reported, "You know, the Secret Service informed us this is the first time high schools have been represented in the press corps."

Once inside the Coliseum door and past security guard scrutiny, a political rally atmosphere became obvious. Posters declaring "Re-elect Congressman Adair," "Fort Wayne's Salin for Secretary of State" and "Robert D. Hanson, County Clerk, Your experienced Republican" lined the walls by flags or red, white and blue bunting.

Later, sections of the arena were almost mechanically filled. One Secret Service man and one city policeman were in assigned places at each section, while the rest of the 184 city and county police present scattered throughout the building. Volunteers then came to the areas to "trade" commercial Nixon booster signs for the homemade variety.

Public Looks Middle Class

The public part of the audience appeared to be primarily middle class, ranging in age from 25 to 60. Teenagers were concentrated in assigned groups, representing four high school bands, Concordia and Indiana-Purdue's singing groups and later grade school age Young Republicans and some teens.

Unprecedented silence followed Beers's announcement that the President had arrived at the Coliseum and would be entering momentarily.

Band Misses Cue

The band missed its cue to start "Hail to the Chief," causing many stretched necks and anxious glares. A few seconds later, President Richard Nixon made his entrance, shaking hands, smiling, patting people on the back and hurrying to greet each person on the platform.

Some seemed a little surprised at not seeing a grand, regal and somber walk to the speaker's platform. They were immediately taken in by the President's congeniality, responding with cheers during the standing ovation lasting over five minutes.

Standing room only, no boos or jeers, or attempts to drown out the speaker with protest chants, or similar incidents took place. No one made obscene gestures.

The President of the United States was in the Midwest, visiting a Republican state in an appreciative, conservative town.

CHAPTER VI

Copy Editing

Copy editing is called copyreading by some editorial personnel. The latter term is not nearly as accurate. Obviously, one has to read copy before one can edit it. In the editing process the copy is improved. Most newspapermen admit that copy editors are the anonymous heroes of the editorial world. Virtually every word must be edited in every publication.

Copy editors take the writer's work and make it as perfect as possible if it already is not. And there are probably no perfect writers. Typing errors confront all typists. Much news is gathered under hard, hectic, and harrying conditions. Reporters on occasion make errors in fact. They may make grammatical errors or use clumsy sentence construction. They sometimes misspell words, or in their haste to meet deadlines, omit words. Time often dictates that stories be written quickly and turned over to the copy desk immediately.

A copy editor must correct everything that needs it. He must be sure the facts are correct. After confirming a story's accuracy, he makes it as readable as he can. He may alter sentences, delete material, and add facts. He may rewrite most of the story. He corrects errors in grammar and punctuation. He must keep the most minute factors and the total story in perspective at all times.

The "rim" is the copy editor's domain. He is a desk man. The editors sit around a horseshoe-shaped desk with a basket beside one elbow. It is full of copy. As the editor repairs each story with the proper symbols, he initials it to show it was his work. He writes the headline for it, which has already been determined as to width and size by a makeup editor. When he finishes the story and the head, he passes them to the slot man. This is the chief copy editor, who sits in the center of the rim. As his editors finish copy, he scans each piece, checking hurriedly to see if they missed any mistakes.

Copy editors are confronted by some stories containing so many mistakes that they must be rewritten. Big-city papers have men and women who do nothing but rewrite and salvage stories that have been rejected by the rim as too poor to edit. The copy editor must be an amazing repository of information. His mind is a catalog of facts, and he is thoroughly familiar with a score or so of reference works in which he can find or check facts he does not know. In addition to a dictionary and encyclopedias, some of the most common references are the *World Almanac, Congressional Directory, World Atlas, Bartlett's Familiar Quotations, Ayer's Directory of Newspapers and Periodicals, Who's Who,* a medical dictionary, *Roget's Thesaurus* (or any good book of synonyms and antonyms), the state government reference work, and the city directory.

The copy editor is constantly enlarging his scope of knowledge, too, as he learns more with each story he edits. He has to know names, locales, social relationships, politics, and history. He does not have the time to refer to the library for everything. And he must be able to detect and remove any editorializing from news stories.

Creativity must be one of his attributes. If he sees a great story in a poor one, he must be able to write it the way it should be. Neatness is demanded. He must be able to write clearly with his thick, finely sharpened editing pencil, with which he can insert a word in a minimum of space. His writing must be legible. There is no use in correcting mistakes if the printers cannot read the corrections.

The copy editor is a mental and physical word surgeon. When some paragraphs must go and new ones be inserted, he uses scissors and glue. He cuts out the material that must be removed and with a stroke of the brush from the paste pot puts in the new material. This process avoids the necessity for retyping copy.

Despite the skills of the good copy editor, the public never sees his name in print. He gets no by-lines or publicity. He is the invisible entity between the reporter and the reader. He cannot just think something is correct. He must be positive.

Authority must not awe copy editors. They must evaluate and edit all copy, regardless of its source. Even sacred scriptures had to be edited at one time. Scholars had to put together the Bible, and they had to do some editing. One reason that some Biblical stories vary a little from version to version is that the Bible was subjected to different scholars at various times through the centuries.

Some journalists maintain that great copy editors are born. The art seems to be an instinctive gift. Some persons are simply more observant than others. They are more alert and quicker to see things that are wrong. But it is possible for a person to sharpen his editorial skills considerably. Instruction and experience can increase competency even in editing.

Copy editors are sometimes confronted with trimming or boiling down a story that already seems tightly written. This is because they must at times shorten a story to fit the space allowed it in makeup. On occasion, they must expand a story without padding it; practical information must be added. But the order is usually to shorten rather than to lengthen.

Copy editing is an intimate job. It involves changing, molding, and tampering with other people's writing, their words, their work. It is somewhat natural for reporters to be offended—particularly as beginners—by copy editors. Light editing doesn't bother most reporters. Severe editing does get to the soul of some.

Copy editors must respect as much as possible the creativity and individualism of news and feature writers, particularly the latter. Spot news follows a formula. Features are more creative and reflect a writer's personality.

Mediocre copy editors are not creative. They mark paragraphs, correct obvious errors, and jot down heads that fit but are not always the most appropriate. Not all are humdrum from choice; speed is the ogre plaguing most editors. Reams of copy are coming across their desks right now. They do not have as much time as they need to devote to each piece of copy. Some newspapermen call this type of editing "backstopping" because the copy editors do only the mechanics of editing. Creative copy editing is the supreme choice, but economics often prevent papers from hiring more editors.

Few jobs offer as much challenge as editing. Errors are constantly before the editors around the rim, and it is an incessant game to seek and correct them. Editorial writers and columnists usually read their own copy. Some newspapers have small copy desks for certain sections of the paper. The women's section staff may edit its own copy; the same is true for sports and features. Sometimes there is an international desk to edit wire copy and a state desk to take care of that copy. On such papers editors become specialists in certain types of copy.

Good copy editors command good salaries, comparable to those of good reporters and other editorial personnel. Sex presents no problem, and even persons with physical handicaps can become professional copy editors. Only mobility of mind is necessary, as with most desk positions.

Most copy editors list some seventeen faults to watch for. They are:

1. Poor lead (rewrite it if necessary)
2. Transitions needed
3. Failure to identify people
4. Paragraphs too long
5. Clumsy sentence structure
6. Style errors
7. Sentences too long
8. Spelling errors
9. Sentence started with a numeral
10. Improper or incorrect quotation
11. Ambiguous wording
12. Buried quotes (move some up front so that they open paragraphs)
13. Editorializing

14. Lack of attribution
15. Omitted facts
16. Weak continuity or flow
17. Defamatory remarks that may be libelous

Anything the copy editor does not want the printer to set on a piece of copy must be circled, including instructions to the printer as to what type sizes should be used, where boldface should be set, and any other directions needed. It is advisable to read a piece of copy through before editing it. This allows the editor to get a general understanding of the story before he begins working on it. After the editing has been done, the copy should be read again to ensure that all errors have been corrected. After the headline is written, the story may be passed to the slot man.

The following list of copy editing symbols varies little from paper to paper.

Note the following editing example:

Heads are usually written in longhand on 8½ X 11″ paper by copy editors on big city dailies, one head per sheet. The headline copy forms are printed with a place to put the slug words, the page where the head will appear, and the size of the head, and the edition in which the story will XX appear. Some papers write the head and this information on a half-sheet which is passed along with the story XXX with which it goes. But some paper feel that use using different sizes of paper does not contribute to the ease of handling or XXXXXXXXXX. Some copy desks are equipped with typewriters, editors and XX type headlines. A typewriter help head writers keep quick count by using the margins a certain way. Progressive newspapers XXXXXXXX a five, six, or seven column format in place of the traditional eight, have adopted downstyle heads to complement their streamlined appearance. Only the first word of a head is XXXXXX capitalized, and the rest are set lower case. A few papers do not capitalize the opening word if it is not a proper proper noun, and all proper np nouns must be capitalized.

Headlines—"heads" in journalistic jargon—are the pitchmen for stories. They must give the spiel on each piece of copy. Not only must they attract attention; they must also grade the news. By head size and story placement in makeup, the news is ranked according to its importance and interest.

Typographically, heads contribute to the overall appearance of a newspaper. They determine its facial image by the looks of page one first and the inside pages second. Each head heralds its story in a few words. This enables readers to scan pages and pick out the stories that interest them most. One-column heads set in small type have little lure. They hawk

Symbol	How Used	Meaning
⌐⎯⎯	today. ⌊John Smith will	New paragraph
Y	Whn the president spoke	Insert letters, words,
in Boston	today ∧ he . . .	or phrases
⌐e	left on Friday	Delete and close up
⌐I	judgement	Kill letter within word
⌐e	in the the cases of	Omit word or letter at end of word
◯	(Prof.) Sheldon Carl	Spell out
◯	(Professor) Sheldon Carl	Abbreviate
◯	(9) coeds	Spell figure
◯	(Twelve) coeds	Use figure
╱	those tribes	Separate words
⌐e	th ose autos	Close up space
≞	it was The same	Capitalize and lower case
⎓	Ft. Myers, Florida	Capitalize
∿	gathred and nuts	Transpose letters, words
⌐,	red, white, and blue	Insert comma
⌄	Hell be going	Insert apostrophe
⌄	Yes, I'll go," he said.	Insert quote marks
⊙	The speech ended ⊗	Insert or stress period
stet	The story will go	Restore deleted word or words
⌉⌉	The big man ran to the breaking timber and helped support the load.	Indent or center copy

minor happenings, not major news. Feature heads must reflect the degree of human interest of the stories.

Good head writing demands the most disciplined and creative word choices. The headline writer must conform to an allotted amount of space. A head must go on every story. It must be precise, accurate, and highly readable. The head must be in proportion to the story's length. It must be specific; the greatest pitfall of the head writer is the tendency to use generalizations instead of working for those most appropriate words, even when none seem to fit. Heads must avoid editorializing. A head can be libelous even if the story is not.

Depending on story length, professional copy editors often edit thirty to fifty pieces of copy and write a head for each story in a seven-hour shift. In extraordinary cases, four or five copy editors have worked a half hour, each trying to write an effective head for a single story. On occasion there seem to be no words that will convey the story and still fit. Head writers generally must face the same deadline pressure—sometimes greater pressure—as do any other editorial personnel.

Not all letters of the alphabet are the same width. Some are fat, others thin. A head-counting system is based on the precise width of a figure or letter. Here is a common head count:

1. All lower case letters count one unit except *f, l, i,* and *t* (and sometimes *j*), which measure one half unit, and *m* and *w,* which are one and a half units.
2. All figures are one unit, except l, which counts one half.
3. All punctuation marks count one half, except the question mark and the dash, which count one and two respectively.
4. All capital letters count one and a half, except *M* and *W,* which count two units each, and *I,* which counts one unit.

Some newspapers count the space between words as one, while others rate it one-half unit. The following head shows how to determine the count.

	1½	½	1	1	½	2	1	1	½	1½	1	1	1	13½
Plan May Ease	P		l	a	n		M	a	y		E		a	s	e

	2	1	1	1	½	1	1	1	½	2	1	1	13
Monetary Woe	M	o	n	e	t	a	r	y		W	o	e

Sometimes a "quick" count system, in which all letters are counted as one unit, can be used with fair accuracy. In the above head, there are 11 letters per line. However, this system is often identical with the precise count because of few or no *M*'s or *W*'s and the common incidence of the half-unit letters. They can be remembered more easily if one notes that they spell "flit" or "lift." The quick method is beneficial only when a head writer is composing a very challenging head. It increases his speed in determining whether a line fits.

For effectiveness and to convey immediacy, there are three important rules regarding head writing.

1. The present tense must be used, even though the story is written in the past tense. Timeliness is emphasized by the present tense, and the reader is informed of the recent nature of an event. To describe events in the future, of course, future tense is used.
2. Active rather than passive voice construction contributes to the impact of heads. The active voice is much more forceful. On occasion the prominence of a person calls for the passive voice and its constant companion of a preposition. The personality involved is of more consequence than what happens.

Name Given By
Sheldon to Dog

Sheldon Gives
Name to Dog

General Smith
Hit by Train

3. A head must have a verb either expressed or implied. Action, interest, and impact cannot be transmitted without a verb to inject life. Comparing a label head—one with no verb—with a head with a verb reveals their difference in vigor.

Astronauts on Moon

Astronauts Land in Crater

Heads with verbs are similar to sentences. They explicitly project a complete thought or enough information to warrant that implication. Expressing the central points of a story in a compact sentence is one of the best methods of working out a suitable head. Sometimes the condensed sentence can be modified enough to fit without seeking any other words. This approach also may suggest key words that can be utilized in heads. The more traditional eight-column newspapers fit tightly. They do not permit excessive white space. Many papers permit no heads to be less than two or three units from being flush left and flush right.

Newspapers follow different styles in capitalization of headlines. Some capitalize all words, regardless of their positions or part of speech. Others capitalize all words excepting three-letter or shorter articles, prepositions and conjunctions (such as *but, for, in, a*) when these appear internally within a line. Other newspapers follow a downstyle, which will be discussed later in this chapter.

Other requirements of heads include the following:

1. Do not use *a, an,* and *the* in heads.
2. Use only abbreviations known to the majority of the newspaper's readers. Abbreviations common to one locale mean nothing in another.
3. Avoid unusual, ironic, or embarrassing word splits between lines of heads. Putting "Legislature to Kill Junior" on one line and "High School Appropriation" on another is distortion.
4. *Is, are,* and other forms of the verb *to be* should be avoided.
5. Never end a line of a head with a preposition.
6. With figures, style should be followed. Generally, the numbers one to ten are spelled out, and figures are used for other numbers. Some papers spell out numbers up to 99.
7. Words may not be hyphenated at the end of a line of a head. Splitting words hampers readability and may make the meaning ambiguous.
8. Avoid general word choices. General words cannot convey specifics.
9. Avoid word repetition and redundancy.
10. Use positive rather than negative heads.
11. Only well-known names should be used in heads. If a person is not likely to be known by the majority of the audience, his name should not appear in the head.
12. The head should be attractive typographically.
13. Use only minimum punctuation, since the marks are not typographically attractive. Brevity and lucidity are also objectives. Use only those marks that aid these purposes.

A few newspapers use "banks" or "decks." These are secondary heads set in smaller type. Most are set in inverted pyramid shape. Often they are complete sentences, since their size permits more wordage than principal heads. Subheads are still used by some papers to break up the grayness of solid type. Subheads usually consist of two or three words, one of them a verb, and they are set in boldface. Most newspapers have discontinued them. To interrupt the grayness, many papers set the first two or three words of every second or third paragraph in boldface. Some cap the boldface words. This is referred to as using BFC's, or BFC run-ins.

When a story must be continued on another page, it is a jump story and has to have a jump head. Some papers use the first line of the original head, and it may be set in the same size if the jump portion of the story warrants it. Readers can find jump stories faster if the jump head repeats the first line of the original one. The number of inches jumped usually determines the head size. Some papers repeat only the first word or so of the head on the jump copy. Although some dailies have done it, it is not in the best interests of effective journalism to rewrite the head, perhaps using two or three of the major words of the main head. Some papers make it a policy not to jump a story at the end of a paragraph, on the theory that a split paragraph is more of a lure to the reader to finish a story.

A story should not be jumped too quickly or too late. Jumping a story before the reader has read enough of it to gain interest has the potential of losing him. Jumping a story near the end runs the same risk. But reader frustration is the main reason that stories should not be jumped near the end. The reader must flip through the pages seeking the one where the story continues, and he may be disappointed to find that there are only a few more words when he hoped to find much more information.

There are four types of head designs: flush left, stepped or dropped line, hanging indention, and inverted pyramid. The major head on page one that covers all columns is a banner or streamer. Some newspapers use a banner or streamer in every issue. Others feel that such a dominating and bold head should be reserved only for the most major news. Thus some papers may go for a year or more without using one. It is a matter of makeup policy on some papers to use a head that covers three, four, or five columns only for the top story of the day, at least in that paper's estimation. This type is usually called a spread head.

Flush left heads are used by some 90 percent of newspapers. They are set flush against the side of the column and should be within two or three units of being flush right, regardless of how many columns the head crosses. Two and three lines are the most common, particularly for one-column stories.

Flood Disaster
Areas Declared

NCAA Selects
District Three
Meet Entries

Bus on Wrong Side
of Road, Probers Say

Dropped or stepped line heads resemble a stairway effect. Each line drops a few units of indention from the one preceding it. The first line of the inverted pyramid head is flush left and flush right and subsequent lines are indented. In this design, there is an inconsistency in the amount of white space. Head writers must cope with the problem of fitting the lines after the first with a lesser count each time. This can be a demanding job coupled with the challenge of writing effective heads in general.

Holly Springs,
West Memphis
To Vie In Quiz

Concern For Quality Told
By AMA President-Elect

Hanging idention heads are little more than dropped or stepped line heads. Instead of the line or lines after the second being stepped down, they are flush with the second one, giving a gate hinge effect. This type of head is rarely, if ever, used today.

Inverted pyramid heads are almost extinct. The design appears primarily in the banks or second decks of newspapers that use the dropped or stepped line head pattern. It is a rigid pattern of the past and has almost no potential in the effective makeup of the modern press.

A headline schedule is one or more pages displaying the sizes and families of type styles available for the use of a publication. These often give the counts for various sizes and widths of heads. Printing plants have specimen books that give examples of the various styles and sizes of types they own. Typographically, it is not considered good to mix certain sizes and styles. Some type families are simple and easy to read. Others are elaborate and difficult to read.

Serif and sans serif types should not be mixed. Serifs are decorative designs. For instance, one leg of the *M* may be slim, the other heavy, and many letters may have decorative feet. Sans serif type is sans decoration. It is unadorned type. Strangely enough, some newspapers use only sans serif heads, but their nameplates are set in serif type. Many newspapers set their nameplates in almost ancient type. Some are extremely difficult to read, especially those in old Gothic and Roman designs. Some nameplates are a century old, carrying on the tradition of the first issue of the paper.

Note the differences between the following heads. The difference in the design of the letters is especially apparent when they are viewed together. The *A* in the two-line head contrasts with the design of the streamlined *A* in the three-line head.

Appeal Snags
Higgs' Order

Small Valley
Towns Growing
More: TVA

On big-city dailies copy editors usually write headlines in longhand on 8½″ x 11″ paper, one head per sheet. Headline copy forms have a place to put the slug, the page where the head will appear, the size of the head, and the edition in which the story will appear.

On some papers, the head and this information is written on a half-sheet, which is passed along with the story with which it goes. But other editors feel that use of different sizes of paper for stories and headlines does not contribute to ease of handling or efficiency. Some copy desks are equipped with typewriters, and editors type headlines. A typewriter helps the head writer keep a quick approximate count; he can set the left margin at zero or 10 and count each stroke or space as one unit.

Progressive newspapers with a five-, six-, or seven-column format in place of the traditional eight have adopted downstyle heads to complement their streamlined appearance. Only the first word of a head is capitalized, and the rest are set lower case. A few papers capitalize the opening word only if it is a proper noun. All proper nouns must be capitalized to be grammatically correct, but a few newspapers using downstyle heads do not cap them.

14-foot mobile homes

State's wide-load limit for highways extended

War papers bring Pulitzer to N.Y. Times

Proofreading

All copy must be proofed after it has been set in type. Excellent jobs of reporting, writing, and editing may have been done on a story, but it can be rendered unreadable in the composing room.

Typesetters make mistakes, just as typists do. Proofreaders read proofs. In letterpress printing, which is used by the majority of metropolitan newspapers, proofs are made of all copy. While the stories are still in their galley trays, the type is inked. Pieces of newsprint are placed on top of it. Pressure is applied to the paper, and inked impressions are made, proofs.

There will be literally thousands of proof errors in newspapers today. Proofreaders take the original copy and compare it to the set type by reading the proof. The symbols they use are different from those of the copy editors. The proofreader is the last person to check the story before it is printed in the newspaper. Because of the amount of copy he must read and correct, he must be fast and accurate. Even Bibles must be proofed. Every word printed should be proofed, and most of them are. On most newspapers typesetting errors rarely get past their proofreaders. The printers take the proofs marked by the proofreaders and make the corrections on their composing machines.

In offset printing there is no proof. One gets the copy that will be used in the newspaper. Corrections are marked on the copy with special pencils that will not photograph. Then the corrections are inserted by clipping and pasting.

Proof Symbols and Their Use

today. John Smith Will	use lowercase letter
Where President (b)lank spoke	use capital letter
toady he	transpose letters
le ft on Friday	close up letters
judgment ∧ was to be	close up but leave space
in the cases of ( )	use hyphen here
9 coeds who climbed down	stet means leave as is, ignore mark
Twelve cooeds	delete letter
Prof. Sheldon Carl —— / — /	use a dash
those (autos)	use lightface
In Ft. Myers —— ? /	use a question mark
Martin ∧ Tennessee	use a comma
It was ∧ red, white, blue	use a colon
however, they did so ——; /	use a semicolon
He'll be going ____ ⊙	use a period
Yes, I'll go ∧ he said	use quote marks
Yes, Ill go	use an apostrophe
Start a paragraph	begin a paragraph
those running	insert space
used wrong font	wrong font used
no paragraph here	do not paragraph

CHAPTER VII

Features

If one is not patient and persistent enough to put as much work on the opening sentence as on the rest of the story, he will never write well. The opening of anything is generally important. But with writing, it is supreme. As with news, the introduction—the first paragraph—is called the lead.

Starting something of importance requires preparation. The literary equipment must be available, and the tools must be used with skill. The lead christens the venture. If the lead—the head—of a story is not healthy, the story dies. It is in a sense the beginning and the end when it is effective because it is a bonded creation tied to the tail of the story.

The lead is so demanding for many writers that it takes them sometimes hours, even days, to compose it. Each syllable must be effective enough to attract and hold the reader's attention. If the reader doesn't like the looks of what he is starting, he will not go on. The lead is the initial salesman of the story. The lead is trying to peddle the story to the reader—and the editor.

Before one word of the lead is put down, the writer must know exactly how to develop the story. He must know the approach. Slant is the word for it. Stories are slanted toward certain types of publication. Articles on crime, war, human understandings and failings, and the gamut of life in subject areas appear in many different magazine groups. An article on crime for one of the leading women's magazines will not have the same slant as a crime story for one of the men's magazines. A women's magazine might have—and several have had—a story telling how to clean diamond rings. An article in another magazine might discuss how to shop for a diamond ring, the financial facet of buying gems. The latter would take the approach that few people can tell a high-quality stone from an inferior one. This is slant.

Newspaper and magazine features once differed only in length. This is not true today. Many newspapers use features of 1,000 or 2,000 words and sometimes double those lengths. Just as slants vary depending on magazine types, features also vary depending on the section of the newspaper for which they are written.

Slant is bringing an article idea into polished focus. This crystallizes in the writer's head. Slant must be molded in the writer's head before he puts a word on paper. The lead starts the slant, launches the story as it is going to be.

Magazines and newspapers have slants just as people do because they are published by people. Slant is editorial policy and a view toward life. Slant is more than personality. It is also character. Slant is writing flexibility. It is every word in the story—all of them—contributing to the way it is told. On controversial topics, generally, the slant should coincide with the writer's convictions. However, a writer should be able to take the other viewpoint on occasion. This is part of his innate or acquired objectivity.

Slant is handling of the reader, too. Magazines have to slant toward their audiences. A magazine with highly intellectual content and rather bland prose certainly is not read by people with a limited education. The most elite fashion magazines are not read by girls employed as store clerks who have less than a high-school education. Every market knows its readers. It knows their average incomes, the quality of houses in which they live, their preferences in food and drink, and various other facts about them.

Also, publications know what their readers will and will not tolerate in subject matter and slant. They know certain topics and slants are taboo. Those taboos must never be violated.

The lead is the beginning of a story and all or part of its slant. Since lead writing is the most difficult task, some write the lead after they have started the story. They might write the lead midway through the story or even after they have finished it. Most write it first, however, finding that the lead puts the whole story in perspective. The lead should be written as quickly as possible. As the writer advances in maturity, he will probably increase the speed of writing good leads.

A stack of articles and books on writing shows that leads vary in number and name, depending on the source. Some cite a dozen or more. The best and simplest classifications usually reduce the list to six. The following list, in its order of importance on the scale of effectiveness, is one of the most popular and the most functional: 1. narrative hook; 2. impact, action, or striking statement; 3. descriptive; 4. you, self-interest, or direct address; 5. question; and 6. quotation. Which type of lead is best for a particular article is dictated by the topic and/or slant.

The narrative hook is used more than all the others together. It is the story approach. It has drama and human interest. A narrative hook is any incident that will get the attention of the average 13-year-old boy or girl on a city street. It might be a bus backfiring, a bulldozer demolishing a building or working on a construction site, a baseball rolling under an auto, a door flopping open on a flower truck as it pulls from a curb, or any other similar attention-getting happening or circumstance. These things distract people from whatever they have been doing or thinking. Note the following examples:

> Each auto ripped up the incline screeching a tenor with its tires. They were rammed into reverse and backed into narrow slots. Some bumpers banged and gouged grilles of the cars in the back lanes. Doors were nicked and dented as they opened.

The preceding lead was used on "Beware the Parking Lot Pile-Up" by this author and was published by *Vue,* one of the men's magazines. The opening sentence of the lead has light alliteration. *Each* and *auto* have rhythm and *tenor* and *tires* complete the alliteration. It is also used in the second sentence; the third employs it more strongly.

> Maybe it was the climate. The sun was a fiery cycle of numbness that penetrated everything tangible on the island. That, coupled with the insane humidity, warped the whole sinister atmosphere. The sort of paradise where your clothes become spongy fungus overnight, and the leather molds and rots on your feet in a week.

This lead opens with a sentence of understatement. The second expresses the intense temperature. The third contributes another fact to the weather. The last sentence climaxes the impact of the story on the character and vice versa. There is some reader identification in telling how one's clothing is affected in such an environment.

The impact, action, or striking statement lead has great strength. It is a shocker that slams into the emotions of the reader. Action appeals to human nature. People crave excitement and drama. Such leads, and their stories, transport the reader to a realm of adventure. People like to be shaken from their status quo of complacency. To some degree, it is escapism. How much an impact lead arouses the reader depends on the power of its content. Note the degrees of explosiveness in the following examples:

> Sporadic rifle fire slashed the darkness. On the point, elephant guns blasted the perimeter of the paddy. The grenades pocked holes in the VC-infested underbrush.

This lead appeared on an article of the author's titled "Operation Quick Kill" in *Vue.* Gunfire certainly has impact. *Slashed* is a workable verb choice for the opening sentence. The second brings in more weapons and a dash of alliteration with the ending of the sentence. Still more violence is noted in the third sentence, with *pocked* being a fair word choice.

Suspense and mystery are reflections of the next lead. Again, *slashed* is an appropriate verb.

An alley slashed through the block, a partition of black between the buildings.

Partition and *block* are the strongest words. This sentence could be the lead, or it could be the opening of a longer one. The descriptive impact might set the scene for something ominous or innocuous.

Descriptive leads are graphic and lure the reader into the story. The scene shown must be so inviting and interesting that it baits one into the rest of the feature. Portrait descriptions are often used to open profile stories. Landscape or other physical scenes must employ all the essentials of description as noted in the last chapter. Study the following examples:

Huge drill presses burrowed into steel slabs. Batteries of stamping machines clacked in unison. An array of grinders and cutters hacked into the din. Forklifts banged around bins of parts. Mill sounds. Noise—the symphony of production—swam around the factory in a cacophony of crushing, pounding, ear-splitting sounds.

To show action and sound are the purposes of this lead. *Burrowed* is a good verb choice. It generally refers to something animals do, not machinery. The appositive after *noise* in the last sentence adds to the emphasis of the sound.

The still is up the hollow a piece. It is etched into the foothills of Tennessee's Cumberland Mountains. But the Motlow boys rarely see a revenuer. Master mash has been climbing through its coils for a century.

That lead is geographical description. It appeared in "Corn, Crocks and Copper," an article by this author on a distillery, which appeared in the April, 1966 issue of *Adam Magazine*. *Etched* in the second sentence is the best verb choice. Note that the names of the main characters are also included in this lead.

The you, self-interest, or direct address lead must have strong reader identification and communicate either a long-range or instant reward. The reader is given information that he will be able, potentially, to use in his own life either immediately or in the future. The story affects him. This is the type of lead used on the personal or intimate article. It is written in the second person. Note the reader-writer contact in the following. The amount of reader application depends upon the topic and its relationship to the reader. What is pertinent to one reader group is not necessarily of any consequence to another.

Interrogating the reader with a question lead must be handled with such tact that he wants to know the answer. The question generally is one strong point of the story or perhaps even the germ of it. Quite often the question *is* the story. People instinctively ponder over a question if it has any degree of interest to them. Questions that make the reader take a stand on something are forceful. The question must be phrased with great care so that it will in no way be ambiguous. Of course, sometimes a rhetorical question, not intended to be answered, is asked in this lead form. The question is as specific and pointed as the story it starts. Consider the following questions:

Are you in good physical condition?

Do you feel uncomfortable in elevators or closets? Do heights bother you? How many phobias do you have?

Both of the above leads are penetrating and intimate. They are universal in scope because they can be asked of all people. No literary tools are at work other than the pointed question.

Direct quotation is the weakest lead type. It is rarely effective to start any feature with a quote. In some cases, the effectiveness is diluted even more by typographical limitations. Some magazines do not use opening quote marks when they start a story. One must read the complete passage before finding out someone is actually speaking, and generally, one has to reread the lead in order to decipher its meaning. The quote must have sufficient striking force to arrest the reader. Quotes also include the old maxims, which should be avoided unless they can be adapted to effective use. Indirect statements can also be used, and they are usually more effective. Paraphrasing a quote generally makes it stronger, especially if the quote does not have the strength to do the lead job adequately. Note the following:

1. You can double your strength in two months, the physical instructors say.
2. "You can solo an airplane with two weeks' training," the flying service manager said.

The second lead would be just as effective if quoted indirectly instead of directly. Both state that the reader can do something if he desires to.

Anecdotal leads are not always true in the respect that the anecdotes happened exactly that way. But they are ethical. They did happen, will happen, or have the potential of happening. Anecdotal leads sometimes can be developed successfully by understatement. A strong situation is approached in a restricted way.

Leads can and do overlap. An impact lead can be carried on the vehicle of description. A quotation might be a striking statement. Hybrids are difficult to put in these broad classifications. When the combinations and subdivisions are totaled, there is a multiplication that gets very detailed on the analysis of leads. One should dissect every lead he reads. In reading, one must examine the various leads and the slants of various publications. He must determine why a lead is good or weak.

If it could be more effective, one must determine how it could possibly be improved. A novice should be able to evaluate how good leads are composed.

The second paragraph and all others are just extensions of the development of the story started by the lead. The transition to the next paragraph will be natural. It will flow into the mold of the story.

Some beginning writers have more trouble with the second paragraph than they do the lead. They have transition trouble. Bridging the gap between the first and second paragraph is no problem if you have your story properly outlined either on paper or in your head. All paragraphs after the lead should flow naturally. If one knows exactly what he intends to cover in his story, he knows which point should develop next. The following leads and their second paragraphs are examples of the ease with which transitions can develop if the story is fluid. The first three examples appeared in articles the author sold to King Features Syndicate which distributes its features to hundreds of newspapers in the nation.

The first one appeared on a profile of a car titled "The Rare Round Rolls." The alliteration is exceptionally strong in this lead.

Royalty has always requested, if not rated, a good ride. Some of the kings down through the ages have really been hep carriage connoisseurs. But the crown has never ridden more royally than in the Rare Round Rolls Sports Car.

King Edward VIII—the late Duke of Windsor—ordered the car built in 1930. Four years later the fabulous vehicle was completed. It cost the crown $100,000 and is as modernistic as most of today's Detroit designs.

In "Peeping on the Picket Line," the second paragraph opens with a direct quote, which is directly related to the lead, as it must be.

Management and labor are now at odds over snooping. Bugging is at the bargaining table. Labor unions are seeking to ban companies from snooping on their employees while they are at work.

"We don't like people having to work under any kind of surveillance, peep-holes, see-through mirrors, hidden cameras or microphones, lie detectors, or anything like that," AFL-CIO President George Meany said in early 1965. The announcement launched the powerful federation's campaign to stop what it labels the violation of "the basic right of American citizens to personal privacy."

"Soldiers of Fortune" is an adventure story on adventurers.

Soldiers of fortune are the most idolized adventurers. They are the most revered and most romantic fighting men. No coup or revolution can do without them.

They are independent one-man armies. Their profession has never been more lucrative and dangerous. Employment opportunities echo with every revolutionary shot. And they shoot on either side usually, depending upon the highest bid for their talents.

This last lead and transition example by the author appeared in "What Do Presidents Eat?" published by *Millionaire*.

The world's hardest job requires a lot of calories. Our presidents have always had big appetites, and White House menus have never been hampered by a grocery budget. Since the founding of our republic, the Pennsylvania Avenue address has influenced the curriculums of other households. The First Family table has likewise contributed to the mastication of the nation.

Colonial eloquence ruled the dining room in Washington during the first five administrations. George Washington preferred simple foods, but he didn't mind dinner protocol. Jefferson was an authentic gourmet. He was far more interested in food than diplomatic order. On his foreign travels he copied recipes. So enthused was Jefferson over European delicacies that Congress considered him a traitor to his domestic cuisine.

Having the ability to write effective stories is just one factor in the process of producing good work. Finding article ideas is the eternal quest. Both are creative and demanding. Many beginners finally reduce writing to one question. Which is the most important, the quality of the work or the article idea? With rare exceptions, the latter is.

The merit of a manuscript is in the topic and its slant, not in the presentation. The idea is the most important. Bad writing can be salvaged by extensive editing or rewriting, but a bad idea can not be repaired. Knowing how to find salable story ideas is part of the professionalism of the competent writer. Many beginning writers are bewildered when they first try evaluating the worth of article ideas. They must keep their interests in perspective. Just because one is intensely interested in a particular topic is not necessarily an indication that anyone else will be.

Sources of Features

What interests people? No one has ever been able to determine all the things that command their attention. People are interested in various things. This is individuality. But it is easy to make a sizable list of some topics that preoccupy them.

Self-interest ranks first on any list, human nature being what it is. People are more interested in themselves than in anyone else. Things and people that are closest to each person have the strongest appeal. Anything or anyone that affects an individual gets his interest. One must take care of himself. Self-preservation is the strongest human instinct.

Money comes next. Financial success and security are common goals.

How many more articles will be written on how to achieve success in work and life? Some publications are dedicated to these various ambitions of savings, riches, incomes, and leadership.

Sex and love have been popular since Eve ate the apple. Biology is involved, but the words are synonymous with all of life. Conflict places fourth on some lists. At this point, they do not come in order of their importance because it would be impossible to rank them. Conflict is an integral part of living. Every person is in conflict with something or someone from the time he is born until he dies.

All of life can be relegated to the four basic conflicts of man against man, man against nature, man against society, and man against himself. War is the most gruesome example of man against man. Every argument or battle is generated by the friction between two or more people. Man's inhumanity to man.

Every time a person is killed in an earthquake, hurricane, tornado, flood, or other natural disaster it is an expression of man against nature. Mother Nature can provide the deadliest of all dramas in the universe.

Man against society confronts a person when he would like to take a shortcut across a manicured plot of grass, but the sign says "Keep Off." Society imposes restrictions and limitations on people. An ordinance or law says that things will be done a certain way and/or at a certain time. It tells one when he may burn leaves in his yard and when not.

Man against himself is the most formidable conflict. If a person can get along with himself, he has made a major victory. One must appraise his thinking, ideas, beliefs, and actions. The writer knows he is, in a way, his own main character. The more he comprehends himself, the more he know about others.

Novelty has high interest. People are fascinated by unusual people, places, and things. Anything odd and unique grasps the mind. People are interested in people. Hero worship is the usual description of this aspect of attention. There are people whom others idolize or respect immensely. This aspect of human nature explains the success of many biographies, profile articles, and the fan magazines.

Mystery and suspense titillate emotions. People are thrilled and chilled by the unknown, the macabre. This facet of character supports the mystery writers quite well.

General human interest stories appear in the newspapers daily. Human interest articles are aimed at the heart rather than the head. They range from great humor to the depths of human misery and degradation. Such stories extract laughter, a grin, concern, and sometimes tears. These are the stories of life. It is the little dog trapped in a well, a child struck by a truck, the starving baby, the blind man beaten and robbed by hoodlums, the plight of those who are in great need but cannot get help. And it can be humor. Irony is an ingredient of human interest.

Events affecting large groups of people, such as political parties, religious denominations, and unions, have great attraction because of the number of persons concerned. Sports and contests rate high on any list of human wants. It is human nature to want to play instead of work. Conflict is involved. In athletic events, one invariably takes sides. People participate directly or as a spectator in events in which contestants try to out-perform one another.

Science and discovery are fields that lure thoughts. When science produces things that will change all lives in some respect, all are natu-rally interested. How will this idea or item influence living? Discovery is very stimulating. Venturing into the unknown, finding a place that has never been explored, or probing like archeologists for answers to the past make dramatic reading. Crime is another classification that fascinates man. Men make and break laws. Some of the best-selling books of all time deal with crimes.

News and the events behind it are enticing. Many news stories gener-ate feature ideas. Many magazine articles are just expanded newspaper features. This author gets many article ideas from newspapers. The germ of a good story is sometimes in a news story only an inch or two long. Big-city dailies hold more potential for ideas than smaller ones. Met-ropolitan papers are bigger, and they have feature writers. Small papers have fewer local features.

Quite often a feature on something local has national or universal interest. Every successful writer is a voluminous newspaper reader. Some free-lance writers subscribe to two, three, or more newspapers. Local features on lore of the flora and fauna in a New Mexico newspaper will be in sharp contrast to those in a Vermont newspaper. The areas differ in climate, topography, history, and numerous other ways.

Magazines and newspapers are also good sources of article ideas. Reading articles sometimes suggests others. A story on occasion brings up a point that another writer develops into another article. Browsing in a library can be quite beneficial. One sees something that dictates an idea. Radio and television news and documentaries must not be ignored. They suggest a number of articles periodically.

When one first starts looking for something to write about, he has to inventory his own experiences. If he is an authority on something, it should be assayed for any article value. This author's hobby is physical culture, and he has sold articles on training techniques to the exercise magazines. Writers are always looking for experts on strong human interest subjects who will make good profiles.

Every environment and the people in it must be analyzed. Almost every region has some characteristics that can engender features. If an area locale has already been the subject of articles, are there any new slants that have not been done? There are some 600,000 words in the big dictionaries, and most of them are nouns. Probably every one of them has been the subject of one or more articles. Libraries have been written about some of them. How many books and articles have been written about ants? Nor have the stripes on zebras at the other end of the alphabet been ignored.

After an idea is found for an article, information on it has to be assembled. Generally the writer knows what material he needs. Research is the next phase. Knowing how and where to find facts is an art. Writers who live near good libraries are very fortunate. Those who do not must employ all their detective ability to ferret out the needed raw material. The writer who resides in a small town can get the items he needs from a small library through inter-library loan. Small libraries can borrow from larger ones. Each state has a library in its capital, and the state librarian can be of great help in some research situations. He can arrange for books to be mailed to one in special instances. Becoming familiar with local library facilities and the services they can offer is an asset. Establishing friendly rapport with a library can be pleasant and rewarding.

The nucleus of research in any library is the card catalog. Every book in the library has three cards: subject, title, and author. If one knows who has written about the topic wanted, he looks at the author card. If the title of the book needed is known, that card tells where it is. The subject card refers to the section where everything the library has pertaining to the article is to be found.

Most libraries subscribe to numerous magazines, newspapers, and other periodicals. These are invaluable sources also. Some libraries have special sections where documents and other original materials are housed.

Recording research requires some organization. Regardless of what method is used to take notes, it should be orderly and efficient. Accuracy is all-important. Unfortunately, one is not always at liberty to use all the good sources he encounters. Most information is in the public domain, which means anyone can use it. A copyright now lasts for the life of the author plus fifty years. Unless there are extenuating circumstances, any written material goes into the public domain after that period.

Books on rights and the writer are available. When one is in doubt about technicalities concerning copyright, one should consult such a source. Brand names and registered trademarks—such as Coke, Kleenex, Frigidaire, and Ethyl—always must be capitalized. Companies want their names respected as they should be.

Reference books and other works will provide, most likely, the bulk of research.

Many books have a statement on the copyright page saying that excerpts may be used from them for review purposes only. Some restrict this usage to 300 words. When a reporter is not sure a source is in the public domain, he should consult the publisher. Facts cannot be copyrighted. Only the presentation of them can. One may use what is said but not exactly how it is stated. It is plagiarism to steal another writer's words. In some cases even when the information is in the public domain, it is ethical to give attribution.

Public relations pamphlets and releases are good sources for some stories. Every company of stature has PR people whose duty is to present their firms favorably to the press and the public. Some of the novel definitions of PR define its work: PR is 90 percent doing good and 10 percent talking about it; PR is the religion of business; PR is being good and getting credit for it. Journalists contend that perhaps as much as 35 percent of all news stories are filtered through public relations personnel. Since it is the function of PR to communicate goodwill, it is frequently an outstanding source of help for the press. PR workers are eager to assist writers who might be able to give their interests promotion or publicity.

Almost all organizations and associations have PR departments. Their job is to promote an entire industry or area. For instance, the American Dairy Association is composed of various dairy companies, and it promotes all dairy products. Of course, articles that might be derogatory to their interests are not going to enthuse PR people. One cannot expect individuals to aid him in criticizing something they are promoting.

One of the best research sources for the feature writer is his own clip file. He should clip everything from newspapers and magazines that might contribute to features in the future. Most writers have drawers of clippings. They can be filed according to topic. On each clip the name of the publication and its date should be noted. Knowing where they came from and when they appeared may be very important when one is ready to use them. Occasionally, this writer produces articles from his clip file alone. A good clip file is instant research if the data needed is there.

No section of a newspaper should be overlooked in the search for article ideas. Even editorials and letters-to-the-editor sometimes have story germs. A couple of well-known writers get many stories from the obituary page, doing profiles on persons—some of them not known to the current public—who have led unusual lives or accomplished notable things.

In taking notes, care must be exercised to indicate whether one is quoting verbatim or paraphrasing. It is irritating and time-consuming to be forced to return to a source to see whether quote marks should be used.

Good feature writers program themselves to recognize article ideas. Suppose one sees a very brief news story about a hunter who is rescued from quicksand. He should ponder over how many people fall into it annually. Where is the deadly stuff usually found? Can a person get out of it alone? Is there an article there? Yes. Several slants, perhaps. Boaters should be wary of stepping out on strange shorelines. Is it dramatic? Does it have wide appeal? Can it help the reader in any way? Is it entertaining? Is the interest strong enough to warrant an article on it? Will it need photographs or other art to illustrate it? Can pictures be obtained?

Journalists are always researching. They are ever alert in studying everything and everyone. The reporter is the only professional person who gets an investment out of all experience. As he learns, he increases his scope of the world.

When one is working on a story and is having difficulty getting material, his friends should be told to be alert for anything that might help him. A friend might see an article in an ancient magazine while waiting for a dental appointment.

The very first reference work to check when starting research on an article idea is *The Readers' Guide to Periodical Literature*. Published monthly and bound yearly, it is in every library. It covers the content by subject of 100 major magazines and is indexed also according to title and author's name. If one wants to know how many articles were written last year on gold, he merely looks under that heading. *The Readers' Guide* tells which magazines published them, when, and the page numbers where they can be found.

Another outstanding reference is *The New York Times Index. The Times* is one of the great newspapers of the world. *The Index* notes whether a subject has been covered. If it has, it refers to the date it was published and the page number. Almost all libraries have *The Times* in bound copies or on microfilm, usually the latter.

Information on many prominent living persons is in *Who's Who in America*. The *DAB, Dictionary of American Biography,* has biographical sketches of prominent Americans who have died. *Current Biography,* as the title states, has profiles of celebrities. Pertinent points on British and other internationally known characters may be found in *Who's Who*. Atlases, almanacs, and other reference works catalog much knowledge. To a great degree, research is limited only by the ingenuity of the researcher. A brilliant person does not know all the answers to everything, but he usually knows where to find them.

Travel Features

Wanderlust makes people read travel articles. Daydreamers are girdling the globe right now. The desire to want to go may be instinctive. Perhaps it is escapism. It could be both.

It's natural to want to go to a place better or prettier than where you are now. This writer can conjure up visions of South Sea island paradises with almost no concentration. The waves and the luxuries envisioned are Utopian. People are traveling more each year. Until the past few decades, travel was restricted to those of considerable means. Resorts that once were the domain of the wealthy now cater to the middle class of society. Today and tomorrow everyone is going, going, going.

The public is tuned in on travel articles, travelogues, and documentaries of interesting places. Virtually every type of publication uses travel articles. In addition to the travel magazines, travel sections in newspapers, and the travel stories in other publications, the transportation companies want everyone to buy tickets to go everywhere, from jungle safaris to Tibet. Advertising agencies have saturated the mass media with advertisements and commercials to promote tourism.

Travel writers contribute many stories to the media, but general freelancers probably do more. Travel article writing is fascinating work. It whets the desire to go touring. Features lure and entice millions to visit areas. The feature writer's typewriter transports them.

Travel writing is a hard, fascinating trip. Millions are on, or preparing for, vacations right now. The majority of them want to see new places and do new things. So travel writing must have aliveness, immediacy, and color, but the travel piece usually must also have long-range rewards. Accuracy and authenticity of atmosphere are absolute necessities because the competition is heavy and the standards are very high. On-the-spot reporting helps, but few travel writers are able to visit all the places they write about.

Depth is essential. This requires probing into a locale, drilling into the heart of it, not mirroring a stack of superficial chamber of commerce brochures.

Getting tourist information from cities and states is helpful as a start. The facts are generally accurate and up-to-date. One must find the facts about every conceivable facet of a place, including its people. Blending the sources into a feature is the germ of the trip. There are two approaches to the two types of travel article.

The preview piece is shorter and lighter in treatment than the depth approach. The first shows a place, reflects specifics on the assets and liabilities, surveys the cuisine, and notes the major attractions. The latter searches for anecdotes, discusses dining and accommodations in more detail, and captures the true pulse of the place. It describes the place through its people and vice versa.

Most tourist spots offer only one major attraction. Beaches, mountains, scenic spas, parks, playgrounds, and big city outings are the principal lures. Anglers and hunters are drawn to areas where fish and game are to be had for the taking. Some of the largest tourist havens have little to offer other than historical significance. Millions flock to burial grounds such as Arlington National Cemetery in Washington, D.C., and Gettysburg. Civil War battlefields do a multi-million-dollar business in tourism. The straight travel piece deals with well-known tourist areas. Scores of articles on Miami, Boston, Philadelphia, the Grand Canyon, the California redwoods, Hollywood, Niagara Falls, and others are published almost annually. Most of them will have their individual slants. Each will try to add a new bit of information or depict the area in an unusual way. Places, like people, rarely remain static. They change.

Off-the-beaten-path travel stories have high human interest. People want new places. Unfortunately, not many areas in the world have remained undeveloped or undiscovered by the public. A few beaches are left, however, where one can find beauty, tranquillity, and privacy. They have no concession stands, just unadulterated nature. And there are towns and villages that offer the visitor entertainment and have not been overly commercialized with neon signs and knick-knack junk shops with foreign-made souvenirs. As a place becomes popular owing to exposure by way of publicity, it becomes merely a resort, no longer offbeat.

People of the region must come through in the depth story. Sometimes one of the best aspects of an area is the people. Their personalities or idiosyncrasies are responsible for the uniqueness. Although the resorts do not want their liabilities publicized, the bad points must be included in the depth approach. If the insects are bothersome, say so. If there is abject poverty bordering the swank of a spa, that should be told.

It would be unethical to try to get readers to visit a place without telling them the total truth. Travel writing is also merchandising. Foreign travel is becoming more and more common. The world is the beat of the travel writer today. He must be continental in his writing, an explorer with a typewriter.

Writing a Feature

Effective writers must be able to analyze stories, syllable by syllable. They must comprehend exactly how they are composed. To see the blueprint, stories must be dissected. The following feature by this writer appeared in *Southern Living,* a half-million-circulation travel and good-living magazine. The story was inspired by the number of caverns that have been opened for public viewing during the past generation. Numerous stories on certain caves have been published by newspapers and magazines. But no article this writer could find took a survey slant on commercial caverns in general.

The feature was researched primarily from information in newspapers, magazines, reference works, and tourist brochures from several caves. Prior to writing this story, this writer had never visited a commercial cave.

The paragraphs are numbered so that after a first reading, the reader may refer to many points concerning its development.

MILLIONS ARE NOW TAKING UNDERGROUND VACATIONS:
SUBTERRANEAN SIGHT-SEEING

by CARL H. GILES

Onyx walls wind through the jeweled passageways past rock draperies and clumps of crystal. Jungles of stalactites and stalagmites jut and stab from the grottoes in an insane multicolored maze. Fluted columns sparkling with mineral formations follow no blueprint through the corridors. Veils of ivory stone fall over darker sculptured rock formations. Blisters of color spray the chambers partitioned off by nature. (1)

Underground architecture rivals the most scenic sites on the surface. Some of the most majestic grandeur is inside the earth, and commercial caves are luring millions of people annually to visit the beauty below. Subterranean sight-seeing is becoming one of the biggest tourist adventures. (2)

Probing the labyrinth bowels of the earth has always fascinated man. People have been paying for the privilege of seeing inside caves for almost two centuries. Grand Caverns, the first commercial cave, near Waynesboro, Virginia, was discovered in 1804 by Bernard Weyer and opened to the public. Early visitors had to carry latterns as they viewed the massive rooms. The Cathedral Hall is 280 feet long, 60 feet wide, and 70 feet high. Its walls are encrusted with delicate tapestries of stone spun over thousands of years by tiny trickles of water. (3)

Thomas Jefferson was one of the first to marvel at the wonderland of spectacles. A half century later Stonewall Jackson quartered his troops there briefly during his campaign in the Shenandoah Valley. Today over a quarter of a million tourists take tours through the caverns yearly. Like all major commercial caves, it has an ultramodern electrical lighting system and safe walks. (4)

Another famous cave was discovered 40 miles from Grand Caverns almost a century later. In 1878 two brothers, Andrew and William Campbell, and their friend Benton Stebbins were exploring a hill near a small cave. They suspected that there might be a bigger network in the area. They found a small fissure in the slope which was venting cold air. They dug a hole and peered into the dark pit. Andrew volunteered to go down. The other two men lowered him by rope. As he descended, the flickering illumination of his candle sprayed over the tiered columns and glittering stalactites. Andrew had never imagined such a spectacular sight. The cave was immediately opened to the public. Since then millions of visitors have been awed by its decorations. Arteries radiate from its center leading to vast rooms studded with millions of some of the most remarkable stalactites and stalagmites in the world. (5)

In Luray's huge decorative Ball Room—almost all big caves have a cathedral or ball room—is one of the most unique musical instruments, a stalacpipe organ. It's a pipe organ of sorts, but it uses stalactites instead. Each has a different pitch when cushioned electronic hammers strike them. There's no amplifier or echo chamber. The notes come right off the stalactites, a virtual rhapsody in rock. (6)

The most famous cave areas in the United States are in Kentucky, Missouri, and New Mexico. Not every state has caves, and statistics are rather scarce. Caves are scarce to nonexistent in flat country. Tennessee, which has over 700 caves, almost two dozen of them commercial, is split into three geographical divisions and is typical. The eastern section is mountainous and has about 160 caves. Middle Tennessee is rimmed by mountains and encompasses the Cumberland Plateau and some 540 caves. West Tennessee is topographically flat, and only two caves are known in this section of the state. (7)

Craighead Caverns near Sweetwater has the largest known body of water of any cave. Indians discovered the cave in the early 1800's, but the four-acre lake was not discovered until 1905. The cave, opened to tourists four years ago, has a hectic history. (8)

In 1915 an East Tennessean named George Kyle decided someone should capitalize on the monstrous cavern besides the moonshiners. Gamblers also promoted illegal cockfighting in it on weekends. (9)

He built a dance floor in one of the huge rooms, but the venture failed. A decade later Kyle decided to open the cave for its scenic beauty, but the Depression took care of his new effort to commercialize it. In 1947 its accessibility to surrounding towns inspired a new business. A guy leased it and built an underground beer dive called "The Cavern Tavern." Unfortunately, the pub's patrons couldn't determine when they had reached their capacity due to the humid air and cool temperature. (10)

Most caves remain a constant temperature the year round, usually 54–58 degrees. When they approached the mouth of the cave, they would pass out. One hapless reveler sobered up after falling into a forty-foot hole. Today Craighead Caverns doesn't need any sidelines outside of its natural beauty and the Lost Sea. Small pools and streams are common to many caves, but boating over the watery expanse deep within the earth is a very unusual cruise. (11)

One of the most publicized caves is Ruby Falls inside Lookout Mountain at Chattanooga. It is part of the Rock City complex, undoubtedly the most widely advertised tourist attraction in the world. The Twin Caves catacombing the historic mountain were discovered centuries ago. Thousands of Rebels bivouacked in the caves before the Battle of Lookout Mountain. A few years after the Civil War, a railroad tunnel was constructed which forced sealing the natural entrance to the caves. (12)

In 1923 a company was formed to drill a new entrance to the caves to make them accessible to tourists. While sinking the elevator shaft, engineers hit a new passage which coursed 1,100 feet down to a vast chamber. In it a waterfall —Ruby—plunges from a 145-foot precipice to a pool in the cave floor. Above ground it would be impressive. Below, it is an enduring sight. (13)

Mammoth Cave is the biggest network of horizontal passages. Over 150 miles of the monstrous cavern which burrows under central Kentucky have been explored. Just how much more there is to the underground wonderland is not known. Indians lived in the lair thousands of years ago. A 2,200-year-old Indian mummy was discovered three miles from one of the three entrances in 1935. The first white man to discover the cave was a hunter who pursued a wounded bear inside it in 1799. (14)

Scores of Southern caves were sources of nitre, a key ingredient of gunpowder, during the Civil War. Today, the vats and pipelines still stand in some of them. Mammoth was a major supplier of nitre during the War of 1812. One of the most unusual endeavors was the tuberculosis hospital built deep inside it in 1843 by a Louisville doctor, the last private purchaser of the cave. He hoped that the pure air and the constant 54-degree temperature would help cure the disease. Unfortunately, the experiment failed. Some of the stone cottages where the patients lived are still standing. (15)

Gigantic rooms ramble almost 400 feet below the surface. Some of the tours, which range from less than two hours to seven hours, include boat cruises on one of the three rivers or the emerald lake surrounded by 300-foot-high cliffs. Gypsum crystals and delicate travertine formations scream a silent theme to a kaleidoscope of color and grandeur that has been millions of years in the making. (16)

Although thousands came to Mammoth during the decade after its discovery, a few ventured more than ten miles inside. In 1837, an adventurous 15-year-old, Stephen Bishop, one of the cave's first guides, bridged the Bottomless Pit with a log and opened up a hundred miles that had never been explored. Bishop guided several scientists into Mammoth and showed them the sightless fish that swim the underground rivers and streams. (17)

Some of the fabulous caverns found a century ago drew so much attention that some of the most famous names in show business went underground to entertain. Edwin Booth performed in one of Mammoth's auditorium rooms. Violinist Ole Bull and singer Jenny Lind gave concerts miles inside Mammoth. The renowned Miss Lind also sang in Dunbar Cave, a commercial cavern, near Clarksville, Tennessee. (18)

Early visitors carried whale-oil lamps. The Grand Duke of Russia and the Emperor of Brazil came out of Mammoth in 1859 covered with soot and filled with awe. Today over a half-million tourists take one of the tours through Mammoth which has been a national park since 1926. Nearby Flint Ridge is honeycombed with caves, some of them commercial. One of the most impressive is the Onyx Cave, which is studded with sea coral and veined with color, primarily soft browns and purples. (19)

Six miles from Mammoth is Floyd Collins Cave, named after the most famous cave explorer of all time. The Kentuckian died in one of the most dramatic accidents of modern times. He discovered nearby Crystal Cave, which immediately became a profitable tourist attraction. (20)

On the morning of January 27, 1925, the 35-year-old Collins told his family he was going to investigate a sand hole cave on the neighboring Estes farm. He hoped it might lead to a much bigger cave. When he didn't come home the following morning, one of the Estes boys crawled into the hole and yelled for Collins. (21)

"I'm trapped," Collins yelled back. (22)

And so began one of the most tragic and emotional rescue attempts. Floyd's brother Homer was the first of several men to crawl down the small, wet, winding passage. Floyd's left foot was caught in a crevice, and a rock had fallen on his left leg. One arm was pinned against the ceiling. (23)

Grimacing with pain, Floyd told his brother that behind him was the most beautiful cave he had ever seen. For two days and nights Homer brought him food and sacks to protect him from the cold water which constantly dripped on him. Hundreds of local people came to help. But the cold dark passage was only big enough for one man to reach him at a time. (24)

The press learned of his plight, and thousands came to the site. A rock and asphalt company brought in drilling equipment and crews. The Red Cross arrived to aid the rescuers. A railroad sent 100 men. A wealthy Chicago lady sent two surgeons to amputate his foot if necessary. But the jacks, bars, strength, and prayers couldn't free Floyd. (25)

A shaft was started. Due to the danger of a cave-in, the men had to dig with picks and shovels. They struck rock and muck, slowing them down. On February 16, a tunnel was dug laterally from the 55-foot shaft. A miner crawled inside, but Floyd was dead. Thousands came from all over the country to attend his services. Floyd was buried in the cave and its entrance sealed. Years later his body was removed and buried in a silver casket in Crystal Cave. (26)

Over 20 of the hundreds of caves tunneling under the Missouri Ozarks are open to the public. The most famous is Marvel Cave at Branson, fifty miles south of Springfield. The ceiling in one of the bigger chambers is 20 stories high. Some 35 miles of Marvel's passages have been charted. (27)

Some Ozark caves were once outlaw lairs. Jesse James used Honey Branch Cave as a hideout on several occasions. According to legend Cortez buried the treasures of Montezuma in one of the Ozark caves. Treasure hunters and folklore fanatics have been exploring new and little known passages for many years in hopes of finding the gold cache. (28)

Although Arizona has only two commercial caves—Colossal Cave near Tucson and Grand Canyon Caverns near Seligman— it has some of the most romantic and most mysterious. Sloth Cave, one of the most fearsome, has yielded much scientific data. Giant sloths lived in it thousands of years ago. A few scientists suspect some still might be stalking its corridors. The National Park Service sealed the entrance, which is in the sheer face of a cliff overlooking the Colorado River Canyon, with a steel gate for further research. (29)

Most caves in America are in limestone. They were formed millions of years ago when water covered the continent. This is the reason why millions of marine fossils are found in some caves. When the water level dropped, some of it seeped inside porous rock. Over the eons it washed passages inside the earth. Cave decorations were formed by mineralized water dripping, very, very slowly in most cases, drop by drop until it built up deposits. In most cases it takes a stalactite or stalagmite 120 years to grow one inch. Some of the fantastic creations were built by nature over immeasurable millenniums. Caves that are still growing are called live caves because the water is still working. Dead caves are dry and have completed their formations. (30)

Skeleton Cave, north of the Superstition Mountains, is spooky. It was the site of a major encounter between the Apaches and the cavalry. Bones mark the battle sites inside the cavern. Not all caves have bats, even if Hollywood can't make a scary movie without them. Colossal Cave has huge squadrons of them, and some of the midwest caverns have vast numbers. Tropical caves are renowned for the large number of bats which inhabit them. Windsor Cave on the island of Jamaica has black clouds of them. (31)

Speleology is the scientific study of caves. Professional speleologists aren't too plentiful, but amateurs are. Called spelunkers, they now number over a quarter of a million. Every weekend many of them explore caves. They have formed the National Speleological Society, which has contributed to many monumental finds from dinosaurs to minute fossils. Spelunkers have also aided in important studies of cave flora and fauna. (32)

Carlsbad Caverns in New Mexico is one of the deepest caves in the world. Most of its passages are over 1,300 feet underground. Utah's Neff Cave wanders some 1,200 feet below the desert floor. (33)

One of the most famous cave areas is in the Swiss Alps. The caverns are deep and huge. The rainy weather and snow have eaten into the limestone almost a mile deep in places. Central and southern Europe stretching from France through Austria and Yugoslavia is pocked with caves. Although hundreds of old caves are yet to be fully explored, new caves are discovered annually. (34)

Spelunking is a fascinating hobby. But it also takes knowledge. Spelunkers use only the best equipment and most modern safety devices. Their most important rule is never to go caving alone. An expert should always accompany the beginning spelunker. (35)

Millions of tourists will take underground tours in the hundreds of commercial caves across the country on their vacations this year. And they will see subterranean sights in another world. A realistic, rocky fantasy land built by nature not by man. (36)

1. The lead is longer than most written by this author. It is a descriptive lead. Each word choice was selected to portray a colorful cave, a majestic view of the beauty burrowing inside the earth. The nouns and verbs are strong and show scenes of remarkable grandeur. Note the opening word of each sentence. There is light alliteration in the first three sentences, and *fall* is a good understatement verb in the fourth sentence. This lead took time. Each word was picked with great care.

2. Alliteration marks the first sentence with underground architecture and the three s's ending it. The next is a compound sentence stating that caves are popular tourist attractions and are enticing more people to see them.

3. This paragraph points out that man has always been lured to caves. What was the first commercial cave? This is answered and facts given on the cavern along with who discovered it and when.

4. Notable figures from history have been among its visitors. Statistics are given on how many people visit it, and some of the standard conveniences are listed.

5. Geographically, another cave nearby is covered. The little story of how it was discovered is told in some detail.

6. The cave in the above paragraph is not named until the opening of this one. This adds a bit of subtle mystery. The reader is finding out information about the cave. He has his curiosity aroused by this paragraph, and the cavern is named. An unusual characteristic of the cave is described. This is a strong human interest fact. The ending phrase in the last sentence adds a strong clincher.

7. Where are caves found? This paragraph relates where and gives an example for illustration.

8. The cave containing the biggest known body of water is introduced. Details are told of its discovery and opening.

9–11. The man who first commercialized the cave is named. Some activities that have taken place in the cave are listed. The tenth paragraph reveals a human interest point with the beer tavern anecdote. The eleventh notes the temperature range found in caves and follows through with an incident of humor concerning a patron of the underground pub.

12–13. Next, one of the most famous caves is located and defined. Details on it are given.

14–17. Mammoth, the biggest cave, is covered. The first paragraph tells its location, size, age, and discovery. The second points out a general factor common to many caves, the nitre. The hospital makes an interesting anecdote. Paragraph seventeen relates how a young guide found another section in Mammoth. The final sentence adds the aspect of blind fish.

18. Entertainment in caves was common a century ago. Some performers are identified.

19. Illumination in the early days of sight-seeing is described along with early celebrities who toured Mammoth. The date it became a national park is specified. In the last sentence, another cave is described. It is the only mention of it.

20–26. The saga of Floyd Collins, a famous cave explorer, is graphically told. Note that the only direct quote in the article consists of two words in paragraph 22. This just happens to be the type of story where quotes are neither essential nor available. However, this story is much better for having the one quote. Quotes should be used when appropriate.

27–28. Strong human interest points in the Ozark caves contribute to the story. Famous outlaws and treasure tales add impact.

29. The two commercial caves in Arizona are defined. Their yields of scientific data are related.

30. The composition of caves in America is analyzed. How the various formations are constructed by water is explained.

31. Some caves of interest are included in this paragraph. Events that occurred in one are told. Bats are associated with most caves. The reference to Hollywood is light for a touch of pleasant contrast. Where bats are found in abundance is added.

32. Cave hobbyists, spelunkers, are surveyed briefly but pointedly.

33. Two of the deepest caves are treated in three sentences.

34. Foreign caves are mentioned.

35. Spelunking is brought up again, and the attention to safety is emphasized. This is a sort of subtle warning to the reader that he should not start prowling in caves by himself, even though he might be inclined

to do so because of his newly acquired interest, hopefully cultivated by this story.

36. The ending paragraph ties back to the second paragraph of this story. The reader has been guided through some magnificent caverns in the article. Note that the last line is not a complete sentence, but a fragment. The reader, hopefully, has had an entertaining excursion. He may not be interested in visiting some of the underground wonders. Then, again he might.

The Crusader is a bi-weekly published by the Advanced Journalism Class at Salpointe High School in Tucson, Arizona. It is an excellent paper, a consistent award winner. The quality and quantity of its features help ensure its status. The following feature from the newspaper is a historical feature with some travel interest. The newspaper had the advantage of being in an area where ghost towns are found. But many ghost-town stories have been published by newspapers and magazines in areas where there are no ghost towns. And in the case of magazines, the stories have a national instead of a local audience.

The lead of this story is a narrative hook. It is a storytelling opening. The two feature writers who collaborated on this piece had to do some intensive research. The story and the five pictures that enhanced it consumed one page. It is a good topic, well written, well illustrated, and effectively displayed in makeup.

ROMANTIC LEGENDS SURROUND HISTORY OF ARIZONA GHOST TOWNS

by MAUREEN KING and TONY OFFRET
Crusader Staff Reporters

In the town of Total Wreck, Arizona a man named Salsig got into an argument with another man who drew his gun and fired.

Salsig would have been killed except that he had a large pack of love letters in his vest pocket. The bullet lodged in the letters, saving his life. Later Salsig married the lady who had written the letters.

Whether fact or fiction, the vast variety of stories connected with Arizona ghost towns have prompted many people to visit them.

The ghost towns of today originated as mining camps. These were a backlash of the California Gold Rush.

Most of them boasted a post office, saloon, hotel (in many cases only a tent with cots), a general store, and a schoolhouse.

In a camp, the mining company, for whom the inhabitants worked, owned everything.

Life was simple. For amusement there were baseball games between camps. In some places where women were scarce, there were stag dances and drinking contests.

Vigilante Groups

Common to most towns were vigilante groups, citizens who took the law into their own hands. This practice led to many lynchings, one of which took place in Tombstone.

In December of 1883, five armed men robbed Goldwater and Castenda General Store in Bisbee and escaped leaving four people dead.

A posse was formed with the help of John Heath, a saloon-keeper. In his desperate attempt to lead the posse away from the obvious trail he brought suspicion on himself.

Saloonkeeper Arrested

He was arrested, tried, and found guilty of being an accessory to the crime. He was sentenced to life imprisonment and taken to the jail in Tombstone.

The citizens of Bisbee and Tombstone were angered, feeling Heath deserved to die.

On February 22, 1884, a raging mob stormed the jail, dragged Heath to a telephone pole, and lynched him.

The other five members of the gang had been captured in the meantime, and their execution date set for March 8.

Invitations to the hanging were issued and some citizens built a tier of seats around the scaffold.

They intended to charge 50 cents admission. But a sympathetic group tore down the bleachers the night before the execution.

The hanging took place as scheduled, two weeks after Heath was lynched.

Such are the stories that make ghost towns places of intrigue. The towns are dead; the legends live on.

Adventure Features

Adventure is one of the most magnetic, fascinating, and appealing areas of human endeavor. Daring drama is the epitome of excitement. It is therapy—even if indulged in only in dreams—for mediocre living.

The average person never does anything dangerously thrilling, but he would like to, or thinks he wants to. He relishes witnessing and reading about daring sagas. Some say it is escape literature. If that is so, the same label could be applied to almost all prose and a lot of poetry.

Conflict is the formula, the more adventurously abrasive the better. Voltaire, the writer-philosopher, once said something to the effect, "Live dangerously, for that is the only time when we really live." Virtually every type of publication uses adventure stories to some degree. Even religion magazines use the danger theme on occasion. The Bible contains a lot of action. There are fights, battles, contests, crimes, and sundry other records of violence.

The adventure article by its nature is explosive and emotional. It must be graphic and swift. The more thrilling the topic, the more it has to be portrayed. Each adventure must be as honest and realistic as any other event. No subject should be treated in mundane terms, and adventures have to employ all the naturalism the writer possesses.

Many of the adventure stories that appear in the magazine world first make their appearance in the news. Quite often, the writer has to burrow behind the news to find the gripping stories of physical and mental encounters. Adventure is man against something or someone. Although many adventure stories are reported by the news media every day, many go unchronicled. The press cannot report everything that happens. Freelance adventure writers often come up with stories that have never been uncovered before.

Although many adventure stories are front page news, the great ones are lively, recreated tales with sweeping movement. The stories must have tremendous action, lots of it, spiced and spliced with crisp dialogue and pulsating mood. Action anecdotes are essential.

A four-inch news story noting that a mountain-climbing team has scaled Mt. Everest in record time doesn't convey much or offer any of the drama of the event. It cites statistics and identifies the people. A quote from one of the party adds another point or so. But the readers can't see the bruises, broken bones, chapped skin, and other physical hurts the members suffered. And they can't realize the pain, see the grimaces, or feel the exhaustion the climbers experienced. When were they in the most danger? When were they the most afraid? The feature writer can probe such stories in depth. Graphic writing can recreate a lot of the adventure. Using the literary toolbox with skill, the writer can take readers on the trip.

Physical dangers are inherent in many jobs and professions. Deep-sea divers are more prone to accident than bookkeepers. People with acrophobia are horrified by high-working construction men. Steel workers walk narrow girders hundreds of feet in the air. Their pay rate is invariably higher than for those men doing similar work on the ground.

In-depth profiles of dangerous occupations and professions have high reader interest. Airplane test pilots, explosives experts, spies, and show business stunt men and women are among those who risk injury or death during a day's work.

Individual heroics make good features. The person who dives into an icy river to save a dog risks his life. A girl who dashes in front of a bulldozer to grab a baby out of the way narrowly escapes death. Most of the people who perform such deeds almost daily are rather ordinary. They have that something which motivates them to do something that they never could have conceived of doing. Heroism is the broad answer, and the specifics make great stories.

Anything with an element of suspense and excitement has feature potential. The stronger the mystery and danger, the more human interest it has. Looking for buried treasure under dangerous conditions has great appeal. Wars have always generated many adventure stories. Revolutions are always in progress somewhere in the world. Soldiers of fortune who fight for money in these battles make exciting profiles.

Adventure lies, too, in exploration, whether it be in a jungle or in a research laboratory. Challenges to develop cures for ailments and diseases may be as thrilling as the muscular adventure of breaking wild horses. Scientists have died from working with certain germs. Some have been killed and injured in radiation experiments. Scientific work and investigation may have great drama for feature writers to pass on to readers.

Travel also has adventure. Truck drivers who roam the nation picking up and delivering cargoes have strong appeal to those with wanderlust. Missionaries are killed on occasion in remote places. The pilots who fly them to exotic settings are adventurers also. Alaskan bush pilots who fly fishermen and hunters to frozen wilds confront more thrills than retail store clerks.

But sometimes clerks become adventurers. A former soda fountain boy in Chicago became one of the most dramatic soldiers of fortune in the Cuban revolutions in the 1950's. Feature writers ferret out every facet of life, and they depict their stories with such vividness that readers can almost see, touch, taste, feel, and smell the interest and excitement.

The following adventure story was distributed by King Features Syndicate to scores of the nation's dailies. Although the feature was written in 1969 when there was fighting on the African continent and elsewhere, soldier-of-fortune features are among the highest in human interest. Profiles may be done on current soldiers of fortune almost any time. A survey adventure feature like this may be done periodically.

SOLDIERS OF FORTUNE— THEY FIGHT FOR PROFIT—AND ALSO FUN?

by CARL H. GILES
Written Especially for Central Press and This Newspaper

Soldiers of fortune are the most idolized adventurers. They are the most revered and most romantic fighting men. No coup or revolution can do without them.

They are independent one-man armies. Their profession has never been more lucrative and dangerous. Employment opportunities echo with every revolutionary shot. And they shoot on either side usually, depending on the highest bid for their talents.

A soldier of fortune, according to the dictionary definition, is "one who follows a military career wherever there is a promise of profit, adventure, or pleasure."

Hundreds of soldiers of fortune—many of them Americans—are fighting all over the world right now. Several French adventurers fought for the Viet

Cong in Vietnam. Many of them were veterans of Dien Bien Phu who were ousted in 1954 and returned to the conflict as mercenaries.

Scores of British and French soldiers of fortune—and one American, reportedly—are fighting with the Biafran army against Nigeria. Most of them are pilots. They fly from two former French colonies, Gabon and the Ivory Coast.

Almost every afternoon, as they have done for many months, three or four aging DC-3s or 4s will leave the palm-lined strip near Libreville, Gabon's capital. They ferry in guns, ammunition, and supplies. The 900-mile round trip to Biafra takes them about six hours.

The pilot adventurers reflect the different images of the soldier of fortune. The middle-aged RAF pilots project the neat but casual appearance. Their neatly trimmed beards and mustaches belie their coolness under combat conditions. Their slang is sprinkled with words from World War II.

The Frenchmen live in another hotel. Although it is quite plush, they don't dress for the decor of the ultra-modern building. They stay with the wrinkled shorts and sweaty shirts. But they live well. The cuisine is expensive. Meals in the evening cost $20 and up, but they can afford them easily.

One of the most renowned American soldiers of fortune was William Morgan, a former paratrooper from Toledo. While Castro was trying to conquer Batista in Cuba, Morgan became chief of staff of the revolutionaries' operation in the famed Escambray Mountains. Shortly after Castro took over, Morgan turned against him.

He fled to the hills with some of his loyal troops, but he was captured within weeks and died before a firing squad. Morgan carried his sidearm in a novel manner.

The husky, mustachioed Morgan carried an Army .45 in an open holster, butt forward, cocked with a shell in the chamber. He merely had to drop his hand to draw, letting his little finger fall on the trigger. It was not safe to be around him when a jeep backfired or someone coughed, according to his guerrilla comrades.

American adventurers are always held in esteem. Ex-GIs, especially Green Berets or other super-soldier types, have training superior to all others. Being able to read and write are big assets also.

"The peasants in these revolutionary countries are generally illiterate," a Miami-based soldier of fortune said recently. "They have no understanding or knowledge of modern warfare. They must be trained how to operate and maintain complicated weapons."

Rank in these instant armies depends on whether one is with the "ins" or "outs." His skills have a price. Most soldiers of fortune will not settle for less than an appointment as captain.

Part of their dashing drama is an act. Flashy attire, many of them say, impresses the revolutionaries. The more of a noncomformist clothing-wise, the better. Fancy boots, hats, novel firearms, and expensive gear command respect, particularly from the African and Latin American armies.

Dramatic titles help, too. The Latins take great pride in dramatic names. "Phantoms of the Mountains" or "Tigers" help build morale.

Some adventurers make contact with revolutionaries in the United States. Miami and New York invariably have several exiled Spanish types residing behind estate fences. Newspapers report regimes in danger of toppling almost daily.

Tropical heat, rum, women, and money wait for adventurers. They just have to fight for them—or sometimes die trying.

Profile Features

Profile features rank high in reader interest. People are more interested in people than in things. Profiles are of two types. Biographical features focus only on what a person has experienced or accomplished. The personality piece reveals something of the subject's character. What does the Pulitzer Prize reporter do for entertainment? What is his hobby?

There should be some overlap of the types. One cannot be totally devoid of the other. An interview helps with the former and is essential to the latter.

TV Guide publishes both types. It concentrates more on personality features because almost everyone is familiar with what the most noted entertainers have accomplished. The public sees only their show business image, so features help make them human beings to their fans. An actor who plays villains may be quiet and introverted. A petite actress who plays very feminine roles may be an avid outdoorsman who likes hiking and archery.

Survey Features

Survey features are only as interesting as what they appraise. Comparing the slums in America to those of other nations differs in appeal from a story that tells how many thousands of gallons of perfume, tons of cosmetic powder, and miles of lipstick women use annually. Or with men, how many reservoirs of after-shave lotion and cosmetics they use.

Good surveys may have impressive scope, very interesting facts, or generally just overwhelm readers with strong human interest. The challenge is to come up with great survey subjects and slants.

Almost everything may be surveyed. The size in enrollment and faculty may be compared with how an institution of learning ranks in the state and nation for towns of comparable size. Surveys require compiling facts and statistics on a subject. How many students were involved in traffic mishaps last year? How many students drown each summer? How will the tax increases benefit education now and years later? The following story is from the Memphis *Commercial Appeal*.

AREA SURVEY SHOWS TREND TOWARD EARLIER RETIREMENTS

by JEROME OBERMARK

A spot check of some major employers in the Memphis area indicates a definite trend toward earlier retirements.

More generous pension plans, supplemented by greater Social Security benefits and generally more affluence were cited as three chief factors lending to the trend.

"Prior to 1970, we never had a request for early retirement. We have had some in 1970 and 1971, and we have two requests already this year," Brandon Davis, public relations director of First National Bank, said.

More men and women at International Harvester Memphis Works also have requested earlier retirements in recent years, says J. E. Isbell, public relations director.

"Although the numbers [retiring early] are not large, there seems to be a definite trend toward this," Mr. Isbell said.

The same could be said of employees of the Dover Corporation elevator division at Horn Lake, Miss., where two office women and two plant workers have taken early retirements in recent years, Paul Boensch, public relations director, said.

While the trend was not overwhelming and for the most part limited to the past two to five years among companies contacted in the Memphis area, a national study by the Institute of Life Insurance showed the trend developing significantly in the 1960's. It is expected to increase more rapidly in this decade.

A study of major group pension plans in 1958 by the Society of Actuaries found that 21 percent of the people who retired did so early. A similar study in 1968 found that the percentage of people retiring early had increased to 33 percent of the total.

Probably the most significant factor found in the studies was what is happening with pension plans.

A survey of 641 companies published in 1971 by The Conference Board, a business research organization, found that 96 percent of the pension plans have early retirement arrangements.

Also, there is an increase in the number of pension plans which give the employee a vested right to retire at his own option. And the minimum length of time an employee is required to work before receiving a pension is lessening.

While the trend toward earlier retirements is on the increase, the great majority of workers continue to work until 65 and many work beyond.

Historical Features

Historical features may or may not have a news peg. When something from the past may be resurrected because of a current event, the story gains through timeliness. The past is almost as fertile as the future in feature ideas. Napoleon's remains have been uncovered a few times. During one of the last examinations, some scientists claimed traces of arsenic indicated that he did not die a natural death. This makes for strong human interest.

New revelations regarding any of history's mysteries provide germs for historical features. Old houses and buildings of historical significance must be torn down sometimes. Even when they have great sentimental and social impact, they must be demolished for progress. Features are essential to their burial. The present and the past often collide concerning landmarks, and news and features are often among the results.

Features have saved some landmarks from being destroyed. The press has pointed out that there were reasons for sparing the property. More than one editorial crusade has been launched by a feature.

Pure historical features with no news peg must be outstanding to grab readers. The best ones deal with little-known incidents. General history books have either ignored or distorted the subjects or covered them superficially. Historical follow-ups make good stories. Where are the guns of the legendary Western era gunslingers today? Many are in museums and collections. The stories of how they got there are often fascinating. Even one firearm owned by a famous Western lawman or outlaw has a lot of human interest attached to it. The following story is from *The Nashville Tennessean.*

JEWELS IN MUMMIES
FOUND BY X-RAYS

Ann Arbor, Mich.—(UPI)—A team of University of Michigan scientists said Wednesday X-ray photos they had taken recently in the Cairo Museum revealed priceless artifacts and jewelry hidden in the bodies of mummies of ancient Egyptian royalty.

Some of the artifacts were discovered on the mummified bodies hidden by a thick, resinous paste but others were embedded under the skin—a technique used by ancient Egyptian priests possibly to avoid the depredations of grave robbers.

Dr. James F. Harris, who headed the scientific team which conducted the experiments in December, said the X-rays showed historically priceless jewelry—possibly gold—and semiprecious stones and beads. He called it a "positively invaluable find."

It was the first discovery of royal Egyptian artifacts since the tomb of King Tutankhamen, who died at 19 in 1352 B.C., was opened in 1922, Harris said.

"These are the first personal artifacts absolutely connected to these pharaohs," he said. "Everything else had been taken by ancient and modern grave robbers."

The discovery of the artifacts was an unexpected dividend for the scientists who were conducting experiments relating to ancient diseases, body characteristics and the art of mummification.

The U-M team is the same that discovered in 1968 that what had been thought for hundreds of years to have been the mummified baby daughter of an ancient Egyptian queen actually was a mummified baboon.

Of 29 mummies studied in the museum, the researchers found jewelry or artifacts on 10 of them, Harris said.

He said the artifacts, should they be removed, would help Egyptologists ascertain the age of the queens and pharaohs at the time they died, enable them to learn more about ancient Egyptian culture and help them determine the identities of some pharaohs which were suspect.

Hidden inside the body of Queen Notmet, who died about 1080 B.C., was found a large heart-shaped scarab the size of a saucer and covered with hieroglyphics, Harris said. Four statues of ancient gods were also found inside the queen's body.

The X-rays also showed that several of the pharaohs and their queens suffered a number of bone ailments common today, such as arthritis, hip fractures and a condition that causes spinal discs to harden.

Advice Features

Advice or how-to-do-it features tell how to do things. These must be practical. The reader is seeking functional information, not entertainment. Everyone is interested in improving his life. Articles that tell how to budget one's work time more efficiently have good reader value. Tips on how to improve one's photographic or other skills are beneficial to many readers. All types of newspapers and magazines use self-help stories.

Providing readers with knowledge that they may apply for improvement is the primary function of this feature. The writer becomes a teacher or instructor once removed. Authorities are often accessible to comment on how people may profit from doing something they recommend. Local photographers may be quite cooperative in telling a reporter how people may improve their picture-taking ability. A local fireman has good tips on how to set up the safest Christmas tree or other decorations.

Mechanics may be persuaded to tell the best ways to prolong automobile tire life. The astronomical number of how-to-something books and magazines testifies to the popularity of this type of feature.

Human Interest Features

Human interest features cover the realm of human emotions. They range from belly-laugh humor to the most tragic stories of man's suffering and misery. Often no news value lies in human interest stories. A dog is trapped in a cave by a rock slide. The animal will die of starvation or lack of air. But scores of men, women, and children will spend days digging out the pet, and none of them may ever have seen the trapped canine before.

Human interest covers man's humanity and inhumanity to man. One Western pioneer was attacked by a bear. He could not walk as a result of his wounds. He crawled 300 miles on his hands and knees to get help. It was an incredible story of hardship and endurance.

Eating contests inspire some human interest features. The college or high-school student who eats a fantastic number of pies, pizzas, hard-cooked eggs, or what have you impresses readers with his capacity. Irony is another aspect of human interest. The bank robber finds the vault is empty after months of planning. A person finds a huge diamond but thinks it is a fake and throws it away. Ironic things are happening right now.

The following superb AP human interest news feature hangs on a medical science news peg. It informs, and it penetrates. The emotions and insights it presents are deep and vivid. Its forceful depth is the type that self-files in the reader's mind, permanently and with feeling each time it is recalled.

STRANGE, FRIENDLY LIGHT
PIERCES DARKEST NIGHT

by RALPH DIGHTON

Los Angeles, Jan. 5—(AP)—From a shadowy realm where eyes see dimly, mouths mumble and brains black out in the fury of mysterious electrical storms has come an almost incredible story of togetherness.

The story is that of Lennie, 28, and Ricky, 33, physically and mentally defective from birth—"human vegetables."

They live under constant observation at Pacific State Hospital in nearby Pomona with 72 others who are retarded.

Almost invariably these, the world's unfortunates, are "loners"—seemingly incapable of knowing that warm human experience called friendship.

Yet Lennie and Ricky are all but inseparably friendly.

So unique is their bond that scientists are studying them in quest of a better understanding of the elusive emotions that enable humans to enjoy togetherness.

Ricky is blind. Most of what he knows of the world comes to him through Lennie's eyes. Lennie is almost speechless, except with Ricky, but he communicates to others through Ricky's lips.

Lennie is badly crippled but he can see and he leads blind Ricky wherever the two want to go on the spacious hospital grounds.

They share everything. Lennie guards Ricky's tray at mealtime from other patients in the ward, but he is not above stealing food from other patients' trays. Lennie gets gifts from his parents and divides them meticulously with Ricky.

Ricky, who has no known relatives, does what he can in return. When Lennie is in the throes of epileptic seizures—brainstorms in which he can hurt himself severely unless restrained—Ricky cradles Lennie's head in his arms.

Each has an IQ in the 30's.

"It is characteristic of such cases to be loners," says Dr. Craig MacAndrew of the University of California at Los Angeles' Neuropsychiatric Institute, who with Dr. Robert Egerton has made a study of the strange pairing of Lennie and Ricky.

"Such cases usually are marked by callous indifference. Their relationship is that of billiard balls—they collide and bounce away unaware of the others' existence. The human relationship known as friendship has never before been observed at this level of retardation.

"But with Lennie and Ricky it does exist, therefore it is possible. This highly improbable relationship may help provide a better understanding of that peculiarly human quality we call friendship."

While psychologists puzzle over what it may be that draws them together, Lennie and Ricky live out their limited lives.

Each morning they greet one another with broad smiles. Although their conversation is largely unintelligible to others, they talk and joke together with obvious delight. When they sit beside each other on a bench in the sun, their faces and hands become expressive and Ricky's sightless eyes seem to sparkle and come alive.

They have been inseparable since Lennie entered the hospital 10 years ago. Ricky had never shown the slightest interest in other patients until Lennie arrived.

Now, Lennie frequently says to no one in particular: "I like Ricky."

And, as bedtime comes each night, Ricky regularly asks his friend: "Did you like this day?"

This next AP human interest story has a very small timeliness value noted in the next to last paragraph. Other than this it has no time element consideration. Pure features may be used today or months from now. As long as the conditions and circumstances in the stories are accurate, they may be used anytime. This is an example of features that are really depth-reporting stories.

BEGGARS PLAGUE
NIGERIA'S LAGOS

LAGOS, Nigeria (AP)—Garuba Katagum is a deformed leper whose wrinkled face and filthy tunic betray his poverty.

He supports a mother and two children by begging in downtown Lagos. His average is $3 a day.

HIS SIDEKICK, Monoh Audu, whose left leg was amputated after an accident years ago, earns half as much. Audu makes a living opening car doors at parking lots, accosting housewives at shopping centers and "just begging."

They are like thousands of others who roam the streets and beaches of Lagos. Many are from Nigeria's poverty-stricken north—a Moslem area.

They live off the generosity of urban workers, guard parked cars, for a price, grovel outside restaurants for a few pennies and make storefronts their bed.

A FEW OPERATE small protection rackets. If you don't "dash" them sixpence, you're likely to find your car tires slashed after an evening at a night club or movie theater.

Despite their condition they are generally a cheerful lot who greet regular "customers" with a smile or will wave at a passerby and shower them with Allah's blessings even if they don't get a handout.

As an eyesore in the capital of Africa's most populous nation, they provoke much discussion. A recent headline read "Lagos fast becoming a beggars' paradise." Another newspaper wrote, "Tinubu Square, the showplace of Lagos, is today inhabited by beggars and lunatics who eat, wash and even defecate right there. Railway stations are gradually being converted into leper settlements and asylums."

ONE OFFICIAL survey put the countrywide population of beggars at 20,000 with Lagos alone harboring a quarter of them. Many are deformed but the survey in Lagos also produced 40 fakes.

Two years ago the National Welfare Service herded many into camps to learn crafts such as weaving, carpentry and tailoring. Some beggars proved good mattress makers, car mechanics and masons.

Katagum, 35, sleeps in an open-air market.

"I don't like camp life." he said. "It is rigid and dull. Besides, I would get no good money being in a camp. I make more outside."

THE PROBLEM has grown with thousands of disabled victims from Nigeria's 30-month civil war with secessionist Biafra.

Image-conscious Nigerians often appeal to tourists not to take pictures of the beggars.

The following UPI filler or featurette is an example of irony. It appeared on March 20, 1969, in many newspapers.

GRAND SLAM

HOUSTON (UPI)—In a typical Texas collision, three women in mink coats driving 1969 Cadillacs collided on the southwest freeway.

Human interest focuses on the emotions more than on logic. This makes it universal. It bridges race and language barriers. It is simply the innate feeling one human being has for another.

Humor features may be satirical or pure comedy. They are extremely difficult to write. Entertainment is generally the only objective. But this vehicle may also be used to carry serious messages. Humor is used to make the point. Cutting humor may be vicious. The slant is usually a takeoff on something, a person, place, or situation.

Humor stories are easier to do if they are based on persons who by circumstance, irony, or their own sense of humor get involved in funny situations.

News features vary from a few words to thousands, depending on the subject and its slant. The news feature may have only a little news value or a great deal. The shortest featurette or filler this author has ever encountered consists of two words. The story is:

CAPISTRANO, Calif. (AP)—They did.

This Associated Press story communicated with at least half the population. Almost everyone has heard of the famous swallows that leave the California mission each year but always return on March 19. For some 200 years they have been coming back from their winter in Argentina on that same date. In 1935 they missed their schedule owing to bad weather.

The Axe of South Eugene High School in Eugene, Oregon, is one of the finest high-school newspapers in the nation. It is superior to most college newspapers and many commercial dailies. The following feature from it was well illustrated in a two-page spread on local boutiques. But it probes more than just a selection of retail establishments. It has depth. Another story on this topic was included in the layout. And the art, copy, and heads were impressively displayed.

Sundry Shops Feature Creative Handcrafts

There is a growing need to create a culture for the United States. This is the sentiment of many of the small boutiques springing up around Eugene.

In the area between Oak and Olive in the downtown district, there are a multitude of these small shops. This is almost convincing that today is the renaissance of the Middle Ages—with all the crafts and interest in doing things by hand.

Andrea's

Andrea's, located at 1036 Willamette, caters to people who want to buy handcrafts already made. Like several other of the boutiques, she also takes articles of clothing and handcrafted work on consignment. Since Andrea encourages creating personal designs, she is teaching a course in pattern design at Lane Community College Thursday nights from 7–10 P.M.

Triple treat

In the area of the old Smeed Hotel building, there are now three boutiques. The Craftsmen Center, which is coordinated by John Perry, allows amateur craftsmen to rent booths to exhibit their creations. Near by is Gold 'n Stuff, run by two metal workers, Miles Edwards and Morgan Hall. They have everything in the line of jewelry including rings and earrings, bracelets and so forth. Mendella Rugs is also in this vicinity. They sell just what they advertise—rugs. Scarborough Faire is very much like the Craftsmen Center only on a much larger scale. Craftsmen rent and work a group of stalls which include activities ranging from candle making, wood sculpturing, jewelry, a health foods department, a book stall, a restaurant and an antique shop. Right across the street from Scarborough Faire is a new boutique, Archale boutique, featuring antique furniture.

Magpie Leather

Magpie Leather shop, on 11th and Oak, is doing something a bit different from the other boutiques. They are wholesaling their designing in leather to boutiques in New York, San Francisco and Chicago.

New Moon Imports

New Moon Imports, between Andrea's and the Black Boutique on Willamette, carry lots of import items, but have a heavy interest in Indian print bedspreads and trinkets.

These boutiques, and many others not mentioned, are recreating some of the lost arts in almost every field imaginable. The handcrafted articles are made for a relatively inexpensive cost; thus they can be offered at a low competitive price—one that most people can afford.

In the following issues of the Axe, in-depth views of these boutiques will be made, in an attempt to show the creativity abounding today.

The following from *The Oak Leaf* of Oak Ridge High in Tennessee is an excellent offbeat feature. It is short, but a complete insight into an entertainment-think piece.

CAVORTING THROUGH

by KAREN OLSON

We can't live without water because we are water.

Science teachers drum into me, over and over, "The human body is 70-something percent water."

I sit in class and imagine myself oozing down a river, coursing through fresh damp ferns, sparkling inside a huge icicle.

And in the hall stands a humming gray monolith, dispensing bits of life. We can't live without the drinking fountain, because it gives us a short excused escape from class. It gives us energy when gym has sapped our sweat. It heads a long orderly line in the middle of scrambling students.

I put my ear to it once and heard low, throbbing machinery pump the water around. Almost, I thought, like my heart and blood.

How strange that a cold, ugly machine is 70-something percent of what I am.

CHAPTER VIII

Picturing Life

Photojournalism is news and features through a lens. It is the coverage of the world with a camera. Photography visually preserves pieces of reality. The pictorial record of news and events supports the written accounts.

Picture use has increased considerably during the past decade. Not only are more pictures being used than ever before, they are being run larger in newspapers and magazines. People are intensely interested in photographs. The magazines of great circulations are almost always liberally illustrated. Some are almost exclusively devoted to pictures. America is one of the most picture-conscious nations. Almost every American owns a camera. Photography is one of the major hobbies.

Cameras don't take pictures. People do. Quality photography is creative and professional. Each professional photographer sees the same scene a little differently. Their equipment might be identical, but individuals differ. Millions of hobbyists are master photo mechanics. They are experts on equipment, can load cameras, expose the film correctly with the proper settings and adjustments, and abide by all the other guidelines of good photography. Many are able to develop film and make excellent prints, technically near perfection. But it is the subject matter that separates great photographers from people who just use film.

What is the content of the picture? Photos are not in competition with the printed word, despite the Oriental cliché. A good picture is just a good picture. A photo is visual communication. It sends a message only if there is one there.

Essentially, a photograph is like any piece of art. One either likes or dislikes it. The content determines each individual's analysis. But there are guidelines for evaluating pictures to which a photo used in any publication should be subjected. Professional photos must meet professional standards. Human interest is essential to the photo. This is just another synonym for content. The more powerful the human interest, the more compelling the picture. Human interest is like a lot of iron filings. The eyes are magnets. The more interesting the metallic lure, the more attracted the eyes will be.

Action shots are the most desired by the news media. But not many

164

spot-action news pictures are made. A photographer is rarely a witness of action news. Much news is unpredictable. Editors cannot tell photographers to go photograph a car wreck. Photographers do not stand around on streets waiting for cars to collide so they can record on film the instant of impact. One doesn't know when a building is going to collapse, when a gas line is going to explode, when a bank robbery will occur, when a construction worker will be killed or injured, or when any other such event will happen.

In wars or riots, photographers are often able to record tremendous drama, inhumanity, suffering, and occasionally glory. Spot-action pictures are usually attributed to irony or circumstance. A photographer just happens to be there when something of news significance happens. Pictures of ships sinking or vessels in trouble are made only when other ships or aircraft are in the area, or when some crew member has a camera and gets photos from a lifeboat.

Photographs are usually made after action news happens. The debris and damage after an explosion, the results of an accident, the scene of the crime, the victims of crime, the weapons used, and the aftermath of catastrophes are among the types of photos that appear with news-action stories.

Photos with people in them are the most common type. People in the news often must be shown. A photo of the president of the nation giving a speech or commenting on something of great magnitude is among the standard shots of political and governmental news.

Publications use photos in various ways. A picture may be more important than the story connected with it, but usually the story is more important. And sometimes they are co-equal in importance. They are dependent on each other. And photos may stand alone—used for their own value.

Some of the strongest elements of human interest are:

1. Self-interest. Each person is first concerned with his life. Survival is the strongest instinct. One concentrates on staying alive and his welfare. Photos of people involved in danger capitalize on this range of emotions. One says of the mountain climber perched precariously on a cliff, "I'm glad I am not there." Self-interest covers everything of the greatest importance to the individual, his family, friends, and prized possessions.

2. Money. The individual's standard of living is important. He is concerned with finances whether he wants to be or not. In a cash-and-carry and credit society, one generally must save, spend, and budget, or use some method of dealing with exchange for goods and services. So wealth has human interest. Photos of treasure chests, hoards, and posh, luxurious living grasp interest as do their opposites, hunger, poverty, and pathetic living conditions of the poor. Photos of wealth itself—gold,

silver, gems—have strong appeal. Sometimes they are studies in beauty, as with some precious stones, but the desire to have is also often apparent.

3. Sex and Romance. Photos of love interest range from a portrait of a handsome man or beautiful woman to expressions of romance. Lovers holding hands may communicate much meaning when only the hands are the focal point of the picture. Sex appeal is a natural biological aspect of life. Photos of beautiful girls are standard. Sex-appeal photos are used in almost every realm of living. Advertising uses sex appeal. The entertainment industry is based on it. And the news media cover it along with everything else.

4. Conflict. People are interested in the plots of life. Actually, there are only four. Man against man is depicted every time people argue, fight, or even vote. One individual is not harmonious with another. This ranges from being most pleasant to being illegal. Man against nature. Each time people discuss the weather, tornadoes, hurricanes, earthquakes, and volcano eruptions, they are talking about man's bout with nature. The man crawling across the desert dying of thirst is an example. Man against society is represented by the individual confronted with realities. Society says one shall not walk on the grass in some places. Society says one may not park next to a fire plug. Some of society's laws upset almost all people at one time. Laws are made by the masses for the benefit of all, but this does not prevent each individual from feeling on occasion that he has been frustrated by some of them. Man against himself is the most personal conflict. The individual must cope with himself. Psychiatrists maintain that most of the mentally ill become that way because they can't cope with themselves. Photos of conflict might include two persons arguing, fighting, or expressing some other emotions, a drought area where crops are dying and causing economic hardships, a person paying a ticket for illegal parking, and the anguish, hope, help, and rehabilitation of the mentally ill.

5. Extremes. People are interested in the biggest, smallest, lightest, heaviest, youngest, oldest. Portraying these on film often makes fascinating viewing.

6. Contests. These range from sports to card games. Individuals are constantly trying to outdo others in some sort of contest. Photos may be of a fisherman trying to catch his limit, a man wrestling a bear, the intense concentration of a chess champion during a match.

7. Hero Worship. People idolize others. Everyone admires someone. Anyone who becomes the best in some endeavor has admirers. The fan-magazine business is based on hero worship.

8. Humor. Comedy is as universal as all the above human interest values. Photos showing something funny are always in demand by newspapers and magazines.

DRY SWIMSUIT, WET WINDOW SHOPPER— The woman in boots and raingear looking at the swimsuit offers contrast and tells of a miserable day with the shopper perhaps looking forward to a better one. Or maybe she is just considering dressing that way because of the weather.

PHOTO BY CARL MANNING, PADUCAH (KY.) *SUN DEMOCRAT*

9. Crime. People make laws, and some break them. The results are news. Photos involving criminal activities interest almost everyone.

10. Pure Human Interest. This is perhaps the largest category. It is the little boy trapped in a drain pipe, the children lost in the forest, the dog guarding his master's grave, the man who missed making a tremendous fortune because of his love for a person, the man who jumps into an ice-clogged river to save a person from drowning and loses his own life, the fiancé of the beauty pageant winner who will not be able to see her for months because of her responsibilities—the list goes to infinity.

Technically, print quality assays these points:

1. Sharpness. The opposite of this is fuzziness. Elements of the composition must stand out in crisp, sharp detail. The photographer determines this; he must have the correct camera settings.

2. Contrast. The contents must vary in shade. White, black, and the various hues between them must be dramatically combined for the best

COURTESY OF UNION CITY (TENN.) *DAILY MESSENGER*

FIRE, NIGHT, AND SILHOUETTES—Is the focal point the building or the officer in the foreground? Most viewers would say the building, because of the contrast, its windows filled with flames against the dark walls. The tracks make strong lines, and the traffic signal almost centers the holocaust.

visibility. Sharpness should be present in the dark and light areas of the photo. A white suit on a white background has little contrast.

3. Proportions. Certain lenses, certain angles, and other factors may cause unintentional enlargement or reduction of some part of the picture. Some portion of a subject's body may be grossly out of proportion because the camera has altered his dimensions. Almost everyone has seen photos made by amateurs showing people with huge feet or hands.

Almost all newspapers and magazines use 8″ x 10″ black-and-white photos. This is the best size with which to work. Some newspapers, particularly small dailies and most weeklies, do not use color photos because they are not equipped to print them. But color use continues to increase swiftly. Some newspapers prefer the 5″ x 7″ size for "mug shots," pictures showing only the head, or the head and shoulders. But a good photo is good, regardless of size. For professional work, the 8″ x 10″ is standard.

AGE AND DECAY—This toppling outbuilding tells us something of the place, and the junk adds a little humanity.

Evaluating Photos for Use

Content is the first factor to be considered. What is in a photo determines whether it will be used. If a photo passes the analysis of effectiveness, the second thing the editor considers is how much of the picture to use. Picture editing is called cropping. Pulitzer Prize-winning photos have been salvaged from ordinary photos by effective cropping. Sometimes just a portion of a photo is outstanding. Some superb shots have been created with the effective removal of most of what the film caught. Non-essentials to the central theme of a photo must be removed. Cropping also alters the proportions of photos for reproduction. The background, foreground, or sides of the focal point of a picture must be cut out when they contribute nothing to the message of the picture. Often, what is shown in these areas may be distracting and ruin some, or all, of a picture's effectiveness. Crop marks should be placed in the margins. Prints must never be marred.

Cropping and/or sizing may be done in two ways, using a formula or a mechanical scale. The mathematical method utilizes three known figures and one unknown. The width over the depth equals the width over the depth of the picture to be reproduced. One measures the width and the depth of the original photo. If the entire picture is to be used, it is measured from margin to margin. If the picture is to be cropped, the measurements are made on the cropped size. When an editor has decided how many columns wide he wants to use a picture, he has only to determine how deep the picture will be.

If an 8″ x 10″ photo is cropped to 7″ x 8″—this would be a vertical print, not a horizontal—the algebraic formula for running it in three columns would be:

$$\text{Cropped photo}$$
$$\frac{\text{width } 7}{\text{depth } 8} = \frac{5.5}{x}$$
$$7x = 44$$
$$x = 7.3$$

Thus 7.3″ would be the depth of the picture in the newspaper. This would be rounded off to the nearest quarter, making it 7¼″ deep. The formula also applies when a photo has been blown up, or increased in size. If the 7″ x 8″ photo were to run five columns, it would have to be enlarged. Five-column width on a five-column tabloid separated with white alleys often measures 9½″.

$$\text{Cropped photo}$$
$$\frac{\text{width } 7}{\text{depth } 8} = \frac{9.5}{x}$$
$$7x = 76$$
$$x = 10.85$$

The 10.85″ would be rounded off to 10 3/4″. This would make the picture more than three inches deeper than running it in three columns.

This formula is not used by working newspaper people. It is adequate when the editor does not have to be overly concerned with the depth of a photo.

On occasion, a photo has to fill a specific hole. The editor determines if the picture can logically be sized to fit the opening. A horizontal hole requires a horizontal photo, and logically only a vertical photo will go in a vertical slot. First, the print must be cropped in width or depth, whichever requires the least cropping. If the hole is two columns by five inches, the formula for cropping the print in depth would be:

$$\frac{\text{Photo width } 6}{\text{depth } x} = \frac{3.75}{5}$$
$$3.75x = 30$$
$$x = 8$$

The photo that was originally 8″ x 10″ would not have to be cropped again. The 8-inch depth of the original picture would fit in the 5″ hole when reproduced.

A proportion scale costs one dollar, and it is the fastest and most accurate method of figuring photos. Some newspaper editors refer to it as a "wheel." It consists of two circles, an inner and an outer. The movable inside scale is labeled "percentage of original size." The outer scale is called the "reproduction size." Most newspapers mark the outer scale in column divisions. Since newspapers vary a little in column width and in the space between columns, the scale must be marked specifically for each paper. This is done by simply measuring how much space is consumed by a given number of columns.

A proportion scale.

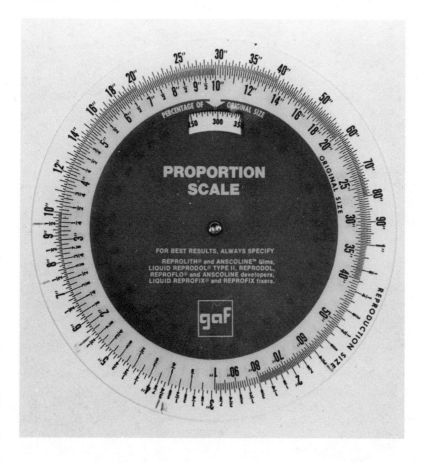

In using the scale, one knows the size of the original print and how wide he wants it to be reproduced. The width of the photo, using the inner scale, is lined up directly under the number of columns in which the picture will be reproduced. The arrow on the scale points to the percentage the photo will be run. Holding the scale firmly, one then looks at the figure directly above the depth of the print, which indicates how deep the print will be reproduced. Only one movement of the scale is needed. One merely looks at the percentage, then determines the figure above the depth of the original print. It can be done in a few seconds, and it is precise.

Information should be put in the margin of the print as to the percentage, the number of columns it will run, and the depth. Most newspapers and magazines write this information lightly on the back of a photo. Care must be taken not to write too hard and crack the emulsion. If the writing comes through on the face of the print, it will show on the reproduced photo. More than one photo has been ruined by an amateur using too much pressure when writing on the back of prints.

Cutlines

Almost all photos require a cutline. It is rare that a photo does not contain some ambiguity. It is best to assume that every photo may convey the wrong message to some people. The cutline should be written by the copy editor after he has edited the story involved. It is logical for the copy editor to do the work. He is familiar with the story and can judge how the photo should support, supplement, or play up the piece. Letting someone write a cutline for a photo when he doesn't know the content of the story it goes with is asking for a poor job. He isn't qualified to write the cutline if he knows nothing about the story. Errors and conflicting statements are much more likely to occur when story and cutline are handled separately.

Cutlines and captions should not be confused. The cutline is the information under a photo; the caption goes above it.

Cutline typography should blend with the overall makeup of the newspaper. Most traditional eight-column papers set cutlines flush left and flush right to the width of the photo. But smaller papers look much better with more white space around photos. Generally, cutlines are set a size or two larger than the body type used for stories. This helps to highlight them. Legends—capitalizing the first three or four words of the cutline—are helpful to offset the grayness of the page in general and to provide contrast. Some newspapers simply cap the first few words of the cutline. Others use legends more emphatically, capitalizing three or four words to serve as a kicker to the cutline.

Like all effective writing, cutlines must be clear, complete, concise. Many newspapers try to keep a cutline to one sentence, but this is not

PHOTO BY ADELLE STUDIO, UNION CITY, TENN.

DESERTED FARM?—This shot of a collapsed building is salvaged by the presence of the horse. It tells us that the land is not abandoned.

always necessary. Usually a photo may be explained in one sentence. But rather than overload a sentence, two or more sentences should be used. Cutlines should not editorialize. They must be objective. Superlatives are not needed. Viewers will decide if the person is handsome, ugly, skinny, fat, or a combination of other factors. The more communicative the photo, generally the shorter the cutline. Cutlines usually require the 5 W's. Who or what is in the picture? When and where was the photo made? Why it was made is evident if it is an effective picture.

Photo features are always in demand by newspapers and magazines. A series or selection of prints tells a story. A short feature may accompany them, or they may relate the story well with just the cutlines. Pictures can relate news as well as words. Sometimes they can do a better job. A news feature on an expressway may do much to explain a high accident rate. Photos of hazards on roads have strong impact. A photo news story showing how poor engineering or poor construction of a building has caused—or may cause—accidents can be significant. A photo news feature of a famous ship that is about to be retired from service may have strong human interest as well as being informative. More newpapers need to stress more photo news and feature stories.

CONCENTRATION—The teacher and her student are thinking only about their artistic task.

PHOTO BY ADELLE STUDIO, UNION CITY, TENN.

Some pure human interest photo features rank extremely high in reader lure. A written description of how a pencil is made would not hold nearly the interest inherent in photos showing steps in its manufacture. Telling how something is done is usually much less effective than pictorially revealing the steps. Photo stories add variety to news and feature coverage. More magazines than newspapers, in proportion, use good photo stories. This is largely a question of time. Magazines do not go to press daily, and few of them are weeklies. There are other reasons, including financial.

Pictures of people doing uninteresting things are the weakest type. High-school newspapers are most often guilty of using group shots. Photos of people lined up staring at a camera have almost no visual value, regardless of the characters in them. Generally, these lineups are so horrible that they should be avoided as much as possible—almost always, in fact. The person posed with a trophy or award is equally bad. These are among the worst of the picture clichés. If desperation forces

WATER SCULPTURE —The result of a small rock pitched into a river: The bottom of the splash can be seen to form the outline of a face with just a little imagination. Many experienced amateur photographers are capable of such offbeat features.

DAILY MESSENGER COURTESY OF UNION CITY (TENN.)

the use of such a photo, it should at least not be displayed very prominently.

Technically, five people should be the maximum number in a group shot. When more than this are shown, the reader-viewer must count heads trying to figure out what name goes with which person. And very few people are concerned enough to do this except for the family and friends of those pictured. The Polaroid Land camera with a standard lens cannot adequately photograph more than five people without overly crowding them.

Instead of group and trophy shots, good feature photos must be sought. Good feature photos are usually timeless. They may be made weeks, even months, before thay are to be used. It is good to have a reserve bank of feature photos always available. When a publication finds it is in dire need of a photo, it may select one in stock.

High-school, college, and other newspapers, including the commercial press in some instances, need not always have superb darkroom and developing facilities. Feature photos may be mailed to processing laboratories. This ensures technical quality.

If the photo assignment editor conceives a good photo and the photographer takes it well, the result should be impressive. Good photographers do not work solely on assignment. They are always alert for good news and feature photos wherever they find them.

Almost all newspapers and magazines use 35-millimeter cameras or those that give 2¼″ x 2¼″ negatives. Most metropolitan newspapers prefer to work with the latter size negative rather than the much smaller 35 millimeter. But the 35-millimeter camera appears to be more and more the favorite.

Seasonal feature photos should be creative. Santa Claus should be doing something of interest rather than just sitting or standing. The groundhog and the first spring flowers should be more than just mirrors of them. Inclusion of people helps shots of almost anything. Having a person picking the first blooms and a cooperative groundhog looking at the sun or the overcast sky are better than the routine prints. A pretty girl, a heap of leaves, and a tree scene are the formula for the usual fall shot. But some thought can make the contents more appealing. Piling a lot of leaves on the model conveys more than having her sit on a bench. Heaping up a huge pile of leaves and have the model feign exhaustion while leaning on a rake catches a little more attention than the standard photo. Modifying, improving, or innovating on the seasonal and other standard shots make them appealing.

Full- or half-page picture pages are commendable. Several dailies display on a single page the best selection of news and feature photos they have for the day. The pictures generally are not related but are rather an array of interesting and/or informative photos. Some newspapers use the last page for this purpose. The exhibit adds some change of pace and ends an issue pleasantly.

More photos should be used on editorial pages. Few newspapers, commercial or institutional, adequately illustrate editorial pages. This point is discussed in the chapter on editorials.

High-school staffs should have a selection of feature photos available for the first edition of the school year. During summer vacation many students make photos, and they make them in various places in the nation or world. Borrowing selections from students can prove pictorially rewarding for the paper. The faculty should also be consulted for their summer shots.

PHOTO BY ADELLE STUDIO, UNION CITY, TENN.

ANIMAL HUMAN INTEREST—The towel draped over the pup gives this shot its only reason for being. Such props help pups, as they usually do everything and everyone.

Where Do All the Photographs Come From?

Daily newspapers get photos from a variety of sources besides their staff photographers. Occasionally, free-lance photographers sell them photos. Amateurs sometimes get good news and feature shots by just being at the right place at the right time with a camera, and they give or sell them to the news media. The AP and UPI transmit pictures constantly, day and night, over wirephoto machines. The tissue-like photos are called proofs. News and feature syndicates send photos with their copy. These arrive in the form of mats—used by letterpress—or proofs—used in offset printing. Public relations sources provide free photos. These must be screened carefully because many of them are designed to promote some product, service, or cause. Some excellent prints come from PR on occasion, and PR is an excellent source for feature shots. High-school newspapers rarely take advantage of the vast photographic resources of PR. For instance, when one is looking for a photo of a certain make of car, the manufacturer will almost always be able to furnish a high-quality print of it. Tens of thousands of firms that have PR offices are happy to supply free photos. A little thought can provide some good photos from a PR source.

Every state and all major cities have a chamber of commerce, an office of tourism, or a similar organization. These are excellent sources for free photos. Areas that promote tourism and sight-seeing invariably have an agency to supply photos free to the media. Their job is to get as much favorable exposure as possible. Almost every commercial newspaper in the world uses PR photos on occasion.

Truth, Taste, and Accuracy

Many feature pictures are posed. But pictures must never be faked with the intention of misleading viewers. Pictures may lie. They can be the most vehement liars. They also can editorialize. Photographing a person while he is yawning or sneezing may be in bad taste. Some extremist publications use only "bad" pictures of people with whom they have disagreed. This is always in poor taste, and sometimes vicious. Using an uncomplimentary photo of a person famed for his or her attractiveness is usually not ethical. And things can happen to mar prints and negatives. A careless or intentional ink mark across a print or negative may come out as a scar on the face of a pretty model.

Photos that are generally taboo to the news media include obscene shots; prints of intense human misery, such as a mother crying over a dead child; and pictures of brutality or gore and the victims of certain crimes. Some newspapers never use pictures showing the horrors of war. Others use them from time to time, contending that the public must be shown some atrocities as a reminder of man's inhumanity to man. This taboo applies also to traffic accidents, which often produce photos like those of combat.

The following article appeared in *Editor & Publisher*. It adds information in other areas and underscores additional points on the necessity of stressing good photojournalism.

STRONG PICTURES IN BIG SPACE
FORMULA FOR GRABBING READERS

by LEONORA WILLIAMSON

Good news pictures, given good play, are important ingredients in the printed page's competition with the television tube, Gregory Favre, editor of the *Palm Beach Post,* said at the third annual Newsphoto Conference for Editors at Ohio State University, Athens, April 12–15.

"It is that tube we are competing with today," he declared. "We are competing for time—time spent reading the newspaper, time spent watching television. That's why we have been trying to learn for years how to reach out of a printed page and grab the reader by the lapel and say, 'Pay attention!'

"We have to sock our readers sometimes, and we can do that with pictures," the Florida editor said. He emphasizes pictures even though he is basically a word man—"a three-times-a-week column writer, an editor who reads countless stories, five or six other newspapers each day, six magazines a week and tries to keep up with the best-seller list."

Announcing his love for pictures—big pictures, impact pictures, news pictures, feature pictures, pretty pictures, all kinds of pictures from A to Z—Favre observed, "I think our readers love pictures too.

"Pictures grab them and drag them into our newspapers and that is something we all try to do. It hauls them to the words that tell them what they need to know rather than what they would like to hear."

Editorial Policy

In speaking of his own newspaper as one that is "very well illustrated," Favre said this is primarily because the *Post* has an editorial policy that emphasizes pictures.

COURTESY OF UNION CITY (TENN.) *DAILY MESSENGER*

HEADLESS?—The diver's head and shoulders are just below the water, and his good form shows. The circumstance of the graveyard in the background of the civic swimming pool adds a note of shock. Notice the crop lines, showing that the newspaper used only a portion of the picture. What was left was blown up by 145 percent.

COURTESY OF UNION CITY (TENN.) *DAILY MESSENGER*

BRIDGE SUPPORTS—Framing is the technique. Each frame seems smaller in the receding background, and the men and auto (right) emphasize the size of the structures.

"Our editors are indoctrinated toward illustrations, and our photographers love us for it . . ."

Mentioning the state, regional and national awards—including a Pulitzer—won by the photo staff during the past three years, Favre asked, "How?" The reason, he suggested, is that "as editors we want good pictures and we get them. Our afternoon newspaper shares the same photo staff and has never won a photo prize. They skimp on pictures. And the photographers probably hide the good ones from them . . ."

Favre explained that the *Post* favors the one strong picture as a matter of preference over multi-picture layout. "We go for the best picture every day for A-1. It might be a sports picture and that's all right with us . . . we'll settle for anything if we think it's the top picture of the day."

To make sure the *Post* can provide adequate space for its pictures, Favre said that two years ago "we talked the publisher" out of three open pages for

NIGHT FIRE—Silhouettes against the contrasting flames show action on the part of the firemen. The hose, too, draws some attention.

local news and local pictures five days a week. "We consider this a cornerstone of our appearance. . . . The only way you'll ever be able to play pictures as they should be played is by having a pre-set number of pages with a certain amount of space on them."

Open Front Pages

The *Post* usually has four open fronts daily, seven on Sunday. For a good series with good pictures, the paper may go for a series of days on a section front or run a special section of eight to 16 open pages without ads. As for its series on drugs ("equal doses of words and pictures") and its 12-page section on the Vietnam War, the *Post* sent a reporter-photographer team around Florida for six weeks "to find out what people were thinking about" and ran that series five successive Sundays, 15 pages in all.

The *Post's* editor added that a reporter and photographer spent four months each on the Pulitzer–Ernie Pyle–Robert F. Kennedy award-winning series on migrants; four reporters spent three months each on the drug section.

"We believe that time and talent are the two things we can spend as much of, comparatively speaking, as any other newspaper or any other news media in the country, and we do it."

The editor included the *Post's* team of four news artists in the visual orientation, adding that their work complements to a high degree what the photographers are doing.

"It isn't difficult to have a good-looking newspaper with good pictures," commented Favre, totaling the *Post* formula.

"Make good assignments. Plenty of assignments. Brief your photographers. It is my experience that photographers, taken as a whole, don't read beyond the pictures and they often don't know what is news. So brief them well."

And, said the Florida editor firmly, "Make sure you have the space to play their work. Make sure you get feedback from them—at least as much as you get from reporters who sit closer and yell louder. Have a liaison man, a coordinator from the photo department even though your desk makes final editing decisions. Praise them. Encourage them."

Part of that encouragement might be "personalizing" the photographers, Favre said in explaining the *Post* uses small signatures with the photographer's picture and name and on Sunday runs a Gallery page with sigs. "It's essentially an old-fashioned picture page, but we put the photographer there too. They love it. And apparently the reader does too."

Other factors mentioned by the editor during the illustrated talk and floor discussion included local picture priority, wild art ("We send photographers out on a regular basis to shoot wild art."), no food picture handouts. He said, "Kill a picture is not our attack . . . it's where can we move a story."

"All of us are idea men. We encourage and demand enterprise . . . our photographers work for one really great picture out of an assignment. If they get that they don't need any more."

Cult of 'Smallitis'

The cult of "smallitis" afflicts the general run of daily newspapers where top management is not committed to supporting editors bent on integration of words and pictures for the visually sophisticated tastes of today's readers.

And news and picture editors bleed just like photographers when they lose "a good one" to the dictates of a diminished news hole, poor photography, or unimaginative cropping and regimented sizing.

So run some discussions among participants in the conference sponsored by the university's School of Journalism and the National Press Photographers Association.

Chuck Scott, head of the photojournalism program at Ohio University and former picture editor of the *Milwaukee Journal* and graphic director of the *Chicago Daily News,* stressed that with a picture-conscious management, 75 percent of the job is done. The rest entails talent in the photography department—photographers who care about pictures and someone who cares in charge of the photo operations—and picture editors who will take a stand and declare that "this is the way it ought to be done," Scott said.

The conference roster of participants included managing editors; news editors; city editors in a range of word-oriented staffers, through graphics editors, picture editors, and several staff photographers. Some of the current photo and pictures editor titles were worn by former staff photographers.

They heard Steven Pyle, picture editor of the *Newark* (Ohio) *Advocate,* outline his unique operation in that he, as picture editor of the paper, gets "first crack" at all news pages and places the pictures before pages are turned over to other editors.

"Content comes first. You could have the greatest story in the world and louse it up in the presentation," Pyle commented.

Pyle likes horizontal makeup, floating pictures to get away from ads, "packaging" pictures and stories in boxes, and takes a stand against jumps—all in line with "making it as easy as possible for the reader."

Pyle, who joined the *Advocate* in 1967 as chief photographer after working as a television newsfilm cameraman in Cincinnati following graduation from Ohio University, said that his small newspaper really believes pictures are important and "uses the best photographs possible in the best way possible," incorporating all the new techniques.

He took issue with the trends of deemphasizing pictures of brides. Pyle said the *Advocate* was set to put brides on the grocery page but a readership survey proved that all age groups wanted to see the pictures. "Bride pictures are the third highest read local feature," he noted.

The art director of the *Toronto Star,* Bob De Piante, said pictures are "the most subjective things" that appear in papers. Thirty picture editors will give you 30 versions of cropping, he said. "It's a personal sort of thing."

But his general outline to the editors included:

1. Pictures look better when cropping is tight.

2. Pictures must follow the original lines of composition. The picture is the most inflexible element that the editor has to work with.

3. Eliminate the excess focal points.

4. Look for pictures of unusual size; pictures different from routine size will grab attention.

5. Make picture presentation as easy as possible to understand.

6. Learn to use picture series.

7. Learn to crop your headshots depending on what you are trying to do with that headshot.

CHAPTER IX

Editorials: Logic, Enlightenment, Leadership

Editorial freedom and freedom are synonymous. They are the basis for democracy. A place without a press has no freedom. The ability of the individual to express himself to the press is the only guaranteed security he has. Each has this freedom. Public apathy abuses it, but freedom for the public must always prevail if the soul of man is to remain unfettered from all those who would chain him.

Editorial freedom is expressed in the First Amendment of the Constitution of the United States:

> Congress shall make no law respecting an establishment of religion, or prohibiting the free exercise thereof; or abridging *the freedom of speech, or of the press;* or the right of the people peaceably to assemble, and to petition the Government for a redress of grievances.

The first ten amendments to the Constitution, called the Bill of Rights, were ratified on December 15, 1791. The power and freedom of the press have evoked classic comments from great men. Among the statements:

A news sense is really a sense of what is important, what is vital, what has color and life—what people are interested in. That's journalism.—Burton Rascoe

A journalist is a grumbler, a censurer, a giver of advice, a regent of sovereigns, a tutor of nations. Four hostile newspapers are more to be feared than a thousand bayonets.—Napoleon Bonaparte

Were it left to me to decide whether we should have a government without newspapers or newspapers without a government, I should not hesitate to prefer the latter.—Thomas Jefferson, 1787

The only security of all is in a free press.—Thomas Jefferson, 1823

The chief sources of the views people entertain, what predominantly influences those who read, is not what is said on the editorial pages but what is rubbed off, as it were, from the news columns.—Supreme Court Justice Felix Frankfurter

Give me liberty or give me death.—Patrick Henry

Of all the pages in a metropolitan daily, often 100 to 150, to the four-page weeklies, only one page is reserved for ideas and opinions. Most papers have less than a half-page of editorial opinion. Many have less than a quarter of a page. School publications—high-school and college—generally have less than two full columns devoted to editorials.

A newspaper is not worthy of its name unless it uses editorials regularly. The primary duty of editorials is to inform, influence, and entertain. Many editorials are purely informational, having no other function than to relay facts that the newspaper considers pertinent in some way. To some degree, the feature and the informative editorial overlap. Indeed, they are often identical.

Interpretative editorials demand more of the writer. Life is so progressive, complex, and challenging today that interpretation of many events is mandatory. If the reader simply absorbs a straight news diet, he will get information indigestion. Millions of news stories are happening this minute. Merely gobbling up this flood of occurrences without having some of them put in perspective may be near-fatal. It is the obligation of editorial writers to convey to their readers the importance of certain news. One cannot just report that a major bill will be passed in his state this week. The surface facts may not reveal the scope and impact that the legislation may have.

Editorials on atomic energy were necessary when it was first discovered because many people believed its only value was mass annihilation. Informative editorials outlined how such power may be converted to fuel, how it could be employed in treating some diseases, and other benefits that the discovery inspired. During World War I, E. I. duPont de Nemours & Company was dubbed one of the "merchants of death" because it made war materials. Effective editorials and the firm's public relations efforts demonstrated to the public that the company manufactured baby bottles and many general products in addition to explosives.

Editorials that intend to influence require fermentation of thought. The writer must be assured he has all the information necessary to formulate his beliefs before even thinking about writing an editorial that will try to persuade people to take his view. He may write out of emotion, but he must edit with logic. Opinions must be produced by a rational and intelligent analysis of facts. Facts cause opinions, not vice versa.

Is a school bond issue needed? Should part or more of the local sales tax be given to education? Are new school buildings needed? Is the equipment inadequate? Do the roads leading to school need repair? Are teacher salaries fairer than they were? Is there a social problem at school with alcohol or drugs? Club and organization? What is the place of one school in this nation and the world? Such questions bring affirmative and negative responses, depending on various groups and individuals. Each situation may change because variables are involved.

Some commercial dailies rarely editorialize at all, much less on any-thing of consequence. They feel they dare not offend any group larger than two, and they ignore things that they should not. They are content to wallow in apathy. Some papers are editorially strong when the targets are far away, preferring to use their editorial ammunition only on distant ills. Journalists call this type of gutlessness *Afghanistanism.* It is simply being blind to the bad when it is close and blasting the enemy when he is too far away to hear or care.

It is all right to focus editorials on remote issues and events, but it is hypocritical to do so incessantly. Some papers are outspoken on all things except locally.

The high-school press must carry editorials covering its immediate environment. The scores of schools that have underground newspapers are those that have not had sufficient editorial coverage in their official student papers. With proper advice and intelligent administrations, stu-dent papers can editorialize on topics needing analysis. Radicalism or inaccuracies will be the unfortunate results if explosive topics are deto-nated without proper precautions.

No newspaper has impact editorials in every issue. Not that many topics exist locally, despite how bad a local situation may be. Many high schools may go a year or more without encountering stories demanding the most in editorial magnitude. The same scope is true for many small-town dailies. Thanks to efficient local government and other factors, major problems that would warrant editorial attention are rare.

But there are almost always minor issues that are worthy of editorials for dailies, weeklies, or monthlies. The late Arthur Brisbane, one of William Randolph Hearst's most esteemed editors, said that editorials could teach, attack, defend, and praise. Editorials of information and interpretation fulfill the teaching function. By attack, Brisbane meant editorials intended to influence. Good causes should be defended. Praise should be recorded editorially. If something or someone deserves an accolade, it should be given editorially. It cannot be done anywhere else in the paper.

Types and Purposes

1. Information editorials
   a. outline and explain the meaning of a news story or happening;
   b. underscore and emphasize major news;
   c. stress news stories that in the opinion of the paper did not get sufficient coverage;
   d. may be documentary features with little or no editorializing.
2. Interpretative editorials
   a. put complex news stories in perspective;
   b. explain concrete applications and alternatives of a happening;
   c. define the implications and results of certain news;

    d. point out effects or significances of events, whether covered by news media or not.
3. Critical (to influence) editorials
    a. indicate the assets and liabilities of an issue;
    b. are designed to convince readers pro or con on certain topics;
    c. should examine all views equally before determining a stand and/or suggesting solutions;
    d. may defend or attack events or circumstances.
4. Entertainment editorials
    a. present humor or satire for the sake of enjoyment;
    b. point up the humor behind a news story;
    c. comment on the general comedy of life;
    d. feature humor in general.
5. Duty or dry-stuff editorials
    a. restate the policy of newspaper or institution in light of some issue or event;
    b. aid charity;
    c. stress accident prevention;
    d. evaluate politics and civic situations.
6. Off-beat editorials
    a. may be in essay form;
    b. may comment on literary, artistic, or cultural matters;
    c. may be designed to stimulate thinking, such as reflections on life and its philosophies;
    d. may be spoofs or human interest pieces.
7. Seasonal or anniversary editorials include
    a. meanings of holidays;
    b. patriotism in war and battles, and heroic actions;
    c. appreciation of events;
    d. commendations related to calendar.
8. Miscellaneous editorials include
    a. obituaries of persons recognized because of stature and achievements;
    b. exchange editorials taken from other publications;
    c. crusades for a cause, usually through a series;
    d. guest editorials from persons not on the newspaper staff.

How many editorials are needed for each issue? Dailies generally average four. The major one, called "the lead editorial" appears first and is often the longest. The others are usually much shorter. Some papers keep two of them very brief. Every paper should have at least one editorial. One is sufficient for most high-school papers unless there is a deluge of suitable serious subjects.

Editorials are not as timely as news. On many dailies, two or three or more days may pass before a given event is commented on editorially. The reason? Editorial writing is more than reporting. The writers need time to study and reflect before beginning the composition. The editorial page is a forum for expression and opinion.

The prime mission of the editorial in a democracy is to serve as a check on government. Watchdogging is its most important duty. This safeguarding of all citizens includes ferreting out graft and corruption in government on all levels. Editorials let the public fight—and often win against—city hall. They protect the public from the strangling bonds of bureaucracy. Editorials expose myths and kill illusions.

Editorials cultivate and mold public opinion. Editorial readership is somewhat low compared to the other sections of the newspaper. Readership response varies considerably depending on the education, occupation, and income of groups. The following survey from the American Newspaper Publishers Association tabulates the audiences of editorials.

Editorial Readership Percentages

	Male	Female
Prewar	41	25
During war	54	35
Postwar	37	25
Business-professional	55	41
Salaried	50	35
Skilled	42	26
Unskilled	36	22

Although editorials are read by less than half the population, their impact is nevertheless considerable. Editorials enjoy a large degree of oral transmission. People who read them often talk about them. Others are inspired to read particular editorials after hearing them discussed. As the table reveals, professional people are the most consistent editorial readers. Leaders of government, business, and community come from their ranks. Almost every person in a position of authority reads one or more editorials daily. They must be informed. Their interest may be personal as well as professional.

Congressmen, governors, large-city mayors, corporation presidents, and those prominent in almost all professions read two or more newspapers daily, including—and often especially—the editorials. Some read three and four newspapers daily. They must be aware of what some of the most respected editorial pages in the nation are saying. Thousands reach for *The New York Times* each morning more urgently than they do for breakfast. Their appetite may depend on the editorials.

Criticism of the mass media is widespread from time to time. The communications revolution has its little armies of critics. Television has had to cope at times with the most powerful condemnations. But many laymen do not know how to put the medium in perspective. Unfortunately, many people feel they are authorities on the media because they watch television and read newspapers. Consumption and conception are not necessarily synonymous. Television is a visual medium. Some editorializing will occur by word or by smile, leer, or other facial expression. As long as humans relay information to humans face to face, there will be the container—the human form—to consider. With the print media, it makes no difference if the reporters and writers speak in a drawl, are ugly or handsome, or have any pleasant characteristics. Only the product comes across. Seeing the producer of the product demands much of the viewer-receiver. He has to split his concentration and evaluations. He has to tolerate or absorb both the person and the product.

Famous Editorial Pages

In the last quarter-century four quality surveys of the top ten newspapers by the American Newspaper Publishers Association have been conducted. The most recent was made in 1970. The points considered included grading according to impartiality of news reporting, public welfare crusading, and meeting the goals and responsibilities of the free press.

The prestigious papers, according to the poll of newspaper publishers, in their order of distinction are:

1. *The New York Times*
2. *Los Angeles Times*
3. Louisville *Courier-Journal*
4. St. Louis *Post-Dispatch*
5. *Washington Post*
6. *The Christian Science Monitor*
7. *Miami Herald*
8. *Milwaukee Journal*
9. *Chicago Tribune*
10. *The Wall Street Journal*

The New York Times ranked first in all four surveys. Five other newspapers have made the list each time, although their ranking has varied: Louisville *Courier-Journal,* St. Louis *Post-Dispatch, Washington Post, The Christian Science Monitor,* and *Milwaukee Journal.*

Great editorial pages are essential for great newspapers. Some outstanding small dailies, and a few weeklies, do commendable editorial work. In the 1920's William Allen White made his small-town Emporia (Kansas) *Gazette* nationally important because of his brilliant editorials.

Very few magazines use editorials. With few exceptions, those that do use editorials tend to carry weak or almost pointless ones. Television editorial fare is limited and is usually restricted to topics that would not offend any major groups of society.

High-school and college newspapers should focus first on their own immediate environment. Serving local readership must be foremost. The commercial mass media serve everyone. But there must be balance. The high-school press, like some dailies, often lacks a variety of editorial topics. Variety is a part of stimulation.

After amassing the facts and allowing sufficient time to evaluate them, the writing must be done. On many newspapers, editorials constitute the only creative writings. The tone of the editorial page should be serious and dignified. When one flips through a newspaper, the editorial section is easily recognized because it looks different. Too many dailies have dull-looking editorial pages. And the editorials themselves will be dull today in many dailies.

Admittedly, dry-stuff editorials are not of the highest human interest. But good writing may be done on dull subjects. Some great literary works are about mundane topics And the really good editorial makes the poorer subject a little more palatable. But these types should not be used very often.

Propaganda

Editorial writers must be careful not to use any of the seven propaganda devices.

Name-calling is branding something or someone with terms that have bad connotations. Dubbing someone a hireling, dictator, copperhead, or Yankee, or as radical, conservative, liberal, or un-American is devious.

The transfer device calls on the authority, glory, or prestige of something or someone in an effort to associate only with the highest ideals. Use of mother, country, the flag, religion, Abe Lincoln, George Washington, and other symbols seeks to impress and to convey a good image of something or someone.

Testimonials, which cite authorities and celebrities for purposes of promotion, are standard in advertising. Examples are: Napoleon used this method of holding his spoon, and it was good enough for him. Famous football players attend this charity dinner. Thomas Jefferson said people should see the beauty of working with the soil, and this mayor toils in his garden when time permits.

The bandwagon device tries to capitalize on something—such as music, slogans, buttons, or stickers—to prove popularity. The appeal is made that since so many are doing it, why shouldn't everyone be doing it? The connotation is that it must be good because it is common.

Glittering generalities are words, phrases, or statements intended to adorn whatever the editorial or propaganda is promoting. Use of generalities is similar to the transfer device but tries to depend on the virtue of tradition. It is an effort to hide behind general rather than concrete terms.

Card-stacking is intentional, withholding of information for ulterior purposes. It is lying. Propagandists tell only what they feel will help their motives. They hope to sway the gullible to their view with only some of the facts.

Silent conspiracy may be the most vile of the devices. In this form of propaganda, something or someone is ignored or the existence of a situation is never formally admitted. Some aspiring politicians have had to abandon their plans because they were unable to get news coverage.

An editorial written in 1897 contributed an expression to the language that is still often used. "Yes, Virginia" is a saying that turns up in common conversation from time to time, is voiced by show business entertainers on occasion, and is printed periodically in newspapers and other media. The late Virginia O'Hanlon Douglas wrote the *New York Sun* from her home in Valatie, New York, when she was 8-years-old, asking if there really was a Santa Claus. Editorial writer Francis P. Church answered her with this editorial:

Virginia, your little friends are wrong. They have been affected by the scepticism of a sceptical age. They do not believe except [what] they see. They think that nothing can be which is not comprehensible by their little minds. All minds, Virginia, whether they be men's or children's, are little. In this great universe of ours man is a mere insect, an ant, in his intellect, as compared with the boundless world about him, as measured by the intelligence capable of grasping the whole truth and knowledge.

Yes, Virginia, there is a Santa Claus. He exists as certainly as love and generosity and devotion exist, and you know that they abound and give to your life its highest beauty and joy. Alas! how dreary would be the world if there were no Santa Claus! It would be as dreary as if there were no Virginias. There would be no childlike faith then, no poetry, no romance to make tolerable this existence. We would have no enjoyment, except in sense and sight. The eternal light with which childhood fills the world would be extinguished.

Not believe in Santa Claus! You might as well not believe in fairies! You might get your papa to hire men to watch in all the chimneys on Christmas Eve to catch Santa Claus, but even if they did not see Santa Claus coming down, what would that prove? Nobody sees Santa Claus, but that is no sign that there is no Santa Claus. The most real things in the world are those that neither children nor men can see. Did you ever see fairies dancing on the lawn? Of course not, but that's no proof that they are not there. Nobody can conceive or imagine all the wonders there are unseen and unseeable in the world.

You may tear apart the baby's rattle and see what makes the noise inside, but there is a veil covering the unseen world which not the strongest man, nor even the united strength of all the strongest men that ever lived, could tear apart. Only faith, fancy, poetry, love, romance, can push aside that curtain and view and picture the supernal beauty and glory beyond. Is it all real? Ah, Virginia, in all this world there is nothing else real and abiding.

No Santa Claus! Thank God! he lives, and he lives forever. A thousand years from now, Virginia, nay, ten times ten thousand years from now, he will continue to make glad the heart of childhood.

Until her death in 1971 at the age of 81, Mrs. Douglas was frequently asked at Christmas time to read Church's reply. She once remarked on her being immortalized by the little editorial, "I am anonymous from January to November."

Too many high-school newspapers end the academic year with editorials applauding the final issue, giving a flashback of some of the annual events, and praising the vacation season. One light or intellectually stimulating editorial is all right if there is another more serious one to accompany it. Constructive editorials on what students can do to better themselves and society during the summer should be considered. Safety and accident prevention are timely topics. Many students don't come back to school in the spring. Some die in auto wrecks, some drown in rivers and lakes, and some are claimed in freak accidents. The public consciousness has been numbed at times with accident prevention, but the end of the school year is a good occasion for such warning, presented with facts and figures.

When no suitable strong editorial topics are available, other types should be substituted. Informative or feature editorials on almost any subject may be used when there are no alternatives. The teaching function may be specifically exercised when the topics do not need editorial comment.

The following editorial from *The First Edition* of Memphis (Tennessee) Catholic High School endorses a piece of legislation. It has a good lead. Television and its powerful relationship to political campaigns are stressed. The editorial takes its stand in the last paragraph. Structurally, it outlines the influence of the medium, relates it to politics, and then brings up the proposed bill before bestowing editorial support for it. Note that the editorial is signed, even though the writer was a Page Editor of the newspaper.

Image-Maker Expounded
For Role in TV Advertising

Commercial television was just 15 years old when Marshall McLuhan introduced his theories on the effects of the audio-visual media on the modern American.

Now 25 years after the "tube" entered the American living room, the sponsor has a greater effect on the viewer than the show he is watching. What we eat, drink, and wash ourselves with is decided by a group of advertising agencies radiating from Madison Avenue, New York City. Citizens from all economic classes have insisted, however, that they they can still make up their own minds notwithstanding the living-color salesman that they watch and listen to an average of fifteen hours a week. Any sucessful corporation can disprove this belief in individual decision-making simply by presenting its record of sales before and after an extensive advertising campaign.

Although TV represents only a portion of the media scene, it is by far the most influential method of selling. The selling power of prime time has long been recognized in the business world by smart profiteers even if not by the consumer.

In recent years the politician's campaign manager has been replaced by the professional image-maker—a man who sells corn flakes in the off-years between elections. An examination of the image-maker's method reveals that statesmen are sold in the same way as a new [showbiz] cast: "With our product you get more for less than with the competitor's product." Thus, a candidate for public office need not be seen or heard in person as long as the television is saturated with his face and voice.

In America, where anyone can supposedly attain an elected position, the candidate lacking funds for his campaign exposure has no chance when the electorate consists of millions of people. For this reason we feel that the proposed bill of Senator Howard Baker of Tennessee to set limits on campaign expenditures in the television market should be given top priority in Congress and firm support at the grass roots.

—Jerry Herbers

To stimulate thinking and to be on guard against accepting the connotations of labels that people are prone to put on others are the motives of this next example. The editorial points out that people who are guilty of believing such terms are the true victims of labels. It was published in *Mustang Roundup* from East High School, Memphis, Tennessee.

LABELS ARE FOR CANS

Because we can never know everything, it is impossible to be completely sure—ever—that what we prefer is "right." If we are wise, then it seems we would strive to examine fully every viewpoint, every approach to an idea. When we refuse to do this, we cheat ourselves.

Many of us cheat ourselves daily for the sake of facility: it is so much easier to stereotype people than to take time to try to learn about them. Every day don't we really miss knowing people we have labeled or, worse, people we've allowed others to label for us? While generalization is a necessary tool of thought, being unaware of what is a generalization for the sake of necessity is surely the fault of the careless thinker.

It is unfortunate that nearly everyone prejudges others to some extent, categorizing people on the basis of first impressions and the attitudes of others who are important to us.

Just because a young man has a short haircut and likes R.O.T.C. does not mean that he is right wing or a "hick." A person who does not attend every sports event does not necessarily lack school spirit; maybe he prefers plays, musicals, art bazaars, or band concerts. On the other hand, people who ally themselves with particular interest groups in the school are often limited to their interest group because others reject that particular group.

The end product is that everyone is cheated. We gain little from labeling and jumping to conclusions and lose much. Our classmates have thoughts worth knowing, and by knowing their philosophy of life we gain self-knowledge and understanding of our peers.

The high-school press has the advantage of being published in an atmosphere of learning. The constant learning process can contribute measurably to the editorial quality of high-school papers. The following example of using literary reference to discuss liberty is good. It is a creative piece bringing up the responsibilities of the individual in "owning freedom." It appeared in *The Broadcaster* of Whitehaven High School, Memphis, Tennessee.

INDIVIDUAL LIBERTY

In the American classic, Moby Dick, Herman Melville devotes an entire chapter to a discussion of two simple statements that governed the once-glorious profession of whaling. Those two laws were so short and so simply stated that they seem almost insulting to the complex legal systems under which civilized man now governs himself and his actions.

Laws are supposedly made to protect man and then rights, but the brevity of the whaler's code makes it seem inadequate protection for a profession not hindered by boundaries. Melville stated the laws to live by:

"I. A fast fish belongs to the party fast to it.

II. A loose fish is fair game for anybody who can soonest catch it."

He then went on to explain that a fast fish was a whale that was somehow connected to those who caught it, or one that had been marked with some sign of possession that plainly evinced the owner's ability, as well as his intention, of taking the whale alongside his ship and into his possession. Thus, a loose fish was one not attached or marked in this manner.

Melville then made an interesting application of these whaling laws to the lives of men. He pointed out that many people believe that possession is half the law, regardless of how the possession came about. Sometimes, possession was the whole law, as in the case of slave ownership. Melville later supported this position by stating, "The right of man and the liberties of the world are loose fish." Therefore, if man could own liberty or rights, they would be his "fast fish."

The more one thinks about those simple, out-dated laws in relation to the concept of freedom, the easier it becomes for one to understand his individual responsibility in being free. For, if the rights and liberties of man are "loose fish," then all those who claim to possess freedom are marking it a fast fish. For a fish to remain fast, there is clearly the need for the owner to show not only his ability to protect his catch, but also his intention to do so. Failure to responsibly "own freedom" results in its becoming loose fish, free game for anyone who can take it.

It is very much an individual's responsibility to hold onto his fast fish. Today's fishermen did not harpoon this whale, but they do have the job of taking their fish alongside and continuing to protect it, while reaping the beneficial harvest to be derived from it. The law itself defends one's right to freedom, but the individual must protect his own liberty.

by VALERIE BREWSTER

Pointing out all kinds of danger is an important editorial duty. The following editorial from the newspaper of the University of Tennessee at Martin, *The Volette,* is an example of how editorials can often prevent bad news from happening. Three pictures were used with the editorial to show the lack of visibility at the intersection.

Editorial
Stop Light Could Prevent
Ambulance Flashing One

Editorial epitaphs just don't make it. Pointing out dangers after casualties result from them makes a hollow echo. Running blood always has more impact than jelled cells. Maybe the change in color lessens the lesson.

The Hannings Lane and Mt. Pelia Road intersection is probably the most deadly traffic hazard on campus. Although autos haven't collided there yet, the accident potential is overwhelming.

Turning onto Hannings from the southern side of Mt. Pelia Rd. is not so frightening. Making the turn from the north is a killer. Exiting either direction from Hannings onto the road elicits a variety of upsetting emotions when cars are coming.

Seeing the Mt. Pelia traffic from the north is almost impossible. The bank on the left is definitely opaque. Exiting drivers must pull their cosmetic bumpers dangerously close—many just jut the car nose into the lane—in order to get a little glimpse of Mt. Pelia heading north.

Drivers have to swerve to miss the front end of cars trying to get out. Jerking the wheel on a narrow road is not conducive to longevity.

Whacking off some of the enbankment would give more visibility. A caution light would be of no help in seeing. Anyone who has made the turn knows it to be very conservative. A trip stop light would be the best solution if the bank is not cut. The light would stay green and turn red only when cars on Mr. Pelia pulled onto the weight switch to change the light so they could exit.

The plea and alternatives are above. Either the campus or the city—or a joint effort—should remedy this before the sirens start after some human cargo or corpses.

Vandalism has plagued civilized societies for eons. The following editorial, also from the *The Volette,* probes vandalism in depth and then relates it to events that have happened on that paper's campus. Two pictures were used showing damage done by vandals. Pictures or other art help many editorials convey more impact. Too many newspapers, commercial, college, and high-school, neglect photography on the editorial page.

Editorial
Will Vandals Also Destroy Themselves?

Immaturity? Unconcern? Revenge? Hang-ups? What motivates one to destroy? The mind of the vandal is a maddening probe into some realm of insanity. If the word choice is too harsh, it is explosive instability.

WHAT IS THE mental condition of students when they kick in water coolers, rip telephones from walls, set fires in dorms, smash clocks, break lights, and damage ceilings, walls and doors?

Do the veins in their necks stand out? Is saliva spewing from their mouths? Does the fact they are upset over something get vented when they attack property? Is it a warped therapy which they feel compelled must happen?

"EMOTIONAL BEHAVIOR" is Professor Stanley Cohen's definition of vandalism. One of the world's foremost authorities on the subject, the British educator at the University of Durham says school-based vandals often steal nothing. Destroying is their only objective.

Last Fall quarter there was $1,554.68 damage done to Austin Peay Hall. Ellington Hall totaled $1,346.02 damage, presumably not just in the namesake of the governor, and Browning Hall had $262.44 during the same quarter. Multiply this by the length of the academic year, and the financial loss gets some emotional response when tax payers contemplate how much of their cash is wasted.

WHEN PEOPLE TEAR up parking meters, telephones, and vending machines, they do extensive damage for the little cash gain. They have no conscience concerning what they do to get a little. Vengeance vandalism is aimed directly at particular people whether they be viewed as individuals or a group. Wanton vandalism appears to be the most senseless.

Most wanton destruction is done to public rather than private property since ownership isn't considered. Excitement is the sole motivation of the hundreds of millions of dollars of vandalism done yearly.

VANDALS RARELY get caught. Most schools are somewhat isolated or are a complex of buildings offering an expanse in which to search and destroy. There were over 100,000 vandalism complaints in New York City last year. Only 3,000 arrests were made. Detroit had over 8,000 reports of wanton destruction, and some 900 arrests were made. In New York City it is 3 percent.

As gross and disturbing as campus vandalism is, the secondary level of education is abject terror.

AN ASSISTANT principal at Gwynn Park High School in Brandywine, Maryland, had his throat slashed by a dropout. A 12-year-old sixth-grader stabbed his teacher at Simon Elementary School in Washington, D.C., because of a spanking. He had attacked the man with a broken bottle. In East St. Louis, Illinois, three out of four teachers are carrying guns to class.

A vicious wave of violence is sweeping the nation's classrooms. Much of the terror is coming from junior high schools. The early teen years, particularly 13-16, have long been considered the most combustible period of adolescence.

On rare occasions, offbeat editorials may be excellent. The following example from *The Volette* shows how white space, sketches, and creativity may be combined for the optimum in effect and make a notable change-of-pace exception. This type must be done with care to avoid ambiguities.

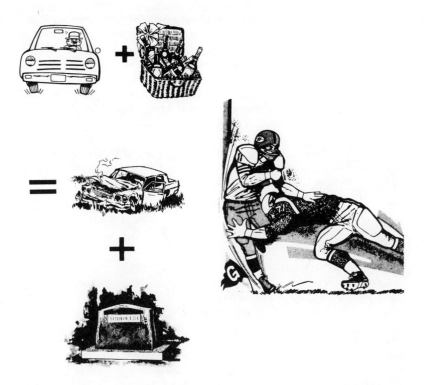

Letters to the Editor

Letters to the editor allow readers to comment on editorials, the news, and almost anything they desire. These letters are the public's only forum. Citizens can criticize or approve, offer suggestions, and even release frustrations through correspondence to newspapers.

Letters are unique in that they offer an intimacy that formal editorials cannot. It is not unusual for letters to be of more interest to readers than editorials. Letters follow no policies other than those of the individuals who write them. They entertain no taboos that editors might have for some particular reason. Newspapers that publish strong, crusading, conscientious editorials get many good replies from readers.

Readers who write letters are participating in freedom of the press. Probably over 10,000,000 men and women write letters to newspapers each year. Many more have good intentions about writing letters but never follow through.

Not all letters are printed, although some newspapers try to print every one they receive, excluding those that are libelous or in bad taste. Letters vary considerably in content and emotion from paper to paper and area to area. Letters are not accurately indicative of public opinion.

Many of the letters come from certain predictable groups or types of people. Men write about 45 percent of the letters; women pen 35 percent. The remaining 20 percent are anonymous. Some newspapers will not print anonymous letters. Others will do so if they regard them as significant. At times the safety of individuals depends on their not being identified.

Clergymen, civic leaders, public officials, and politicians account for many letters. Professional persons such as lawyers and doctors write several. Politicians who are disgruntled by news or editorials write retorts, whereas politicians who are seeking public approval use the columns for more constructive purposes. Secretaries of various clubs, groups, and organizations pen many letters fostering or protecting their causes. Then there are the publicity seekers, who may be responsible for one out of ten letters.

Educators, particularly female teachers, voice their comments through letters columns. But letters come from other sources representing virtually every segment of society.

There are also canned letters. Editors are alert for letters—particularly when they begin to appear in numbers—that sound as if they might have come from the same source, regardless of the names signed to them. At times certain groups or organizations send hundreds to many thousands of letters to various newspapers in the nation trying to promote some cause for their own benefit. When such a campaign is handled with finesse and subtlety, it is difficult to detect the propaganda or deception.

Most newspapers publish lettters from readers on the editorial page or the page adjoining it. A few collect letters they receive during the week and print them in the Sunday issue. They are displayed with heads, white space, and various typographical devices and given placement in makeup as the editors deem appropriate. The importance that a newspaper places on its letters can generally be determined by these factors.

Most newspapers publish a statement concerning letters to the editor in every issue. Sometimes it is placed in or near the masthead or elsewhere on the editorial page. It is generally set in boldface or italics and is often boxed.

The Tampa (Florida) *Tribune* always uses this declaration:

Letters must bear the writer's true name (signed in ink or pencil) and street address but, if specifically requested, only initials will be used in publication. *The Tribune* reserves the right to reject any letter or shorten it to meet space requirements. Normally, a letter may not exceed 500 words and must be written on only one side of the paper. Only original letters, written exclusively to *The Tribune,* will be considered. Poetry cannot be used.

Some college and high-school papers amend the statement. Many of them state:

Letters must be signed, typed, and submitted by [time and date]. The editors reserve the right to edit and abridge all submissions over 300 words when necessary. Opinions expressed in this newspaper are not necessarily those of the editors, adviser, staff, or the administration of this institution.

Every newspaper should carry an explanation of its policy regarding letters. Newpapers should keep the original letters for a time after publication. Proofreading errors occur in letters columns also. Leaving one letter off a word may completely reverse its intended meaning. If a person denies that he made a particular statement in a letter, the original is the newspaper's only way of determining the truth.

Published and unpublished letters should be kept confidential until they are destroyed. The editor- in- chief or the editorial page editor should restrict who may review the letters on file. High-school advisers should see that potentially libelous letters and those in bad taste are secured under lock and key. Anonymous letters may be just as bad or good as signed ones.

A few newspapers honor their most interesting letter writers. *The Nashville Tennessean* inspires its readers to write by grading their letters. It awards stars to the best letters it receives, and it gives $1 for what it considers the highest-quality letters. The small financial award may offer incentive to readers to write when normally they might not. The paper holds an annual banquet for its most distinguished letter writers.

High-school advisers and editors must be alert for letters from immature students who sometimes write out of emotion rather than logic, just as immature adults do. On occasion a letter writer is unaware that the only person likely to be harmed is himself. As tactfully as possible, someone of authority on the staff must warn unsuspecting writers that they may do themselves much harm if they demand that an unusual letter be published. Common sense and good taste are important guidelines in determining the worth of letters.

Letters to the editor are published under a variety of headlines. Some terms used are: Letters from the Readers, Letters from the People, The Mail Bag, Voice of the People, Public Opinion, Views of Our Readers, Speaking the Public Mind, Let the People Speak, What He Thinks, Mr. Citizen, and others. Some papers carry offbeat items to introduce their reader offerings. A few carry some famous lines. A couple introduce their mail with notable quotes.

One from Voltaire is, "Think for yourselves and let others enjoy the privilege to do so, too."

Letters columns should never be dominated by the same writers. Egomaniacs often try to claim the columns for their own.

Certain technical points on policy must be considered. Many letters have errors of fact, spelling, and grammar. Should the newspaper correct them? Each circumstance generally differs. If a newspaper receives a very condemning letter with a grammatical error from a professor, the newspaper may elect to leave in the error and indicate it with the word *sic.* The error, coupled with the letter's content, may say much more than the actual words. Policy on most newspapers is flexible concerning such instances. Almost all policies have exceptions or must submit to them at times. Never to question policy is to operate with a closed editorial mind. More care in regard to letters must be exercised by the high-school press than by the rest of the editorial world; the immaturity potential is higher in the lower grades because of a lack of education and experience, particularly among those in the early teens. Good guidance is necessary.

Editorial Cartoons

Editorial cartoons are an integral part of the editorial page. Cartoons with or without captions or cutlines may wield as much power and impact as any prose. They may graphically support an editorial, or they may be unrelated to an editorial. Visually, they editorialize on their own. Care must be exercised to avoid libel with cartoons, also. Depicting someone stabbing someone else in the back is likely to lead to lawsuits.

The editorial cartoon is the only feature of the editorial page that some readers notice. It takes only seconds to absorb the meaning of a cartoon. Some syndicates sell cartoons as well as news and feature services. The advantage of subscribing to one of the cartoon suppliers is that the art work is generally more professional than that of local talent, the quality is high, and the supply is dependable.

It is best to have a staff editorial cartoonist if a competent one is available. But they are rarely in abundance. Some editors assign their ideas to a staff artist. Some schools have a competent beginning artist who can be persuaded to do cartoons. He should be paid a modest fee, or his supplies should be furnished by the newspaper. Generally, a young artist finds the prestige of having his work published a sufficient reward.

Too many high-school newspapers use editorial cartoons that insult the intelligence of the students. The cartoons should be as intellectually demanding as the editorials. They should be slanted toward the average comprehension of the paper's readers.

Columnists are generally restricted to the editorial section. Their essays are signed features that may or may not editorialize. The writers must abide by the same editorial ethics and good taste that guide the news reporters, feature writers, and editorial writers. Many high-school

Editorial cartoonist Draper Hill of *The Commercial Appeal,* Memphis, Tennessee, achieved tremendous impact with this art. The governor had been using a plush penthouse apartment provided by a business firm. He promptly moved out when the press found out about the lavish quarters. The situation became so torrid that there was some talk by state politicians of impeachment of the governor.

One More Absentee

This cartoon by Hill boldly comments on the mayor of the city. Hill is nationally known for his work. *The Commercial Appeal* has had other outstanding editorial cartoonists, especially the late Cal Alley.

This excellent editorial cartoon was done by cartoonist Charles Bissell for *The Nashville Tennessean.* He is one of the most talented editorial cartoonists in the nation.

"A rags to riches saga! . . . The owner started out as just a poor boy throwing trash in his neighbor's yard."

This editorial cartoon by Bissell depicts the polluted waters of the world with great impact. The buoys carry the names of noted environmentalists who have warned man that he is killing the seas with contamination. This cartoon is also courtesy of *The Nashville Tennessean.*

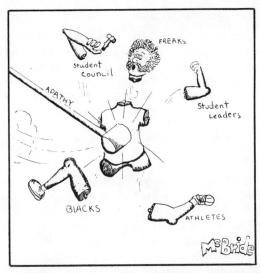

Editorial comments on apathy are standard. But few editorials or cartoons have ever had as much impact as this cartoon by Steve McBride for *The Oak Leaf,* paper of the Oak Ridge High School, Oak Ridge, Tennessee. Here, the hammer of apathy literally splinters the student body.

This editorial cartoon was done by McBride for *The Oak Leaf.* Student newspapers may comment on high-school political groups with as much impact as the commercial press does on other levels of government. This piece of art ably expresses an editorial opinion regarding the student council.

newspapers have too many columnists, some of whom are publicity seekers who want the prestige of being columnists. They can destroy the effectiveness of a newspaper. A paper with too many columnists can become a mere anthology of poor opinions. Good columnists are rare. They must be able to report, interpret, and write well.

Boards

Editorial boards are advisable. When editors confront controversial topics, they should seek assistance in making decisions. One of the nation's most noted editorial writers has a conference with select members of his staff before he writes any editorial involving his opinion. He calls the staffers together, presents his editorial argument, and then lets them consider it. Sometimes, he admits, they convince him that he is wrong, and he changes his editorial view. Putting one's opinion before a critical group before expressing it in an editorial demands courage. But that is just a basic characteristic of the good professional journalist.

An editorial council may be composed of select members of the staff plus some outsiders. High schools and colleges have the advantage of learned men and women being immediately available. Faculty members from various academic disciplines should be asked to sit on the board. Certainly, one would not want all political science teachers or just those from the biology department. A sound sampling of opinions and advice should be instrumental in reaching views on some editorials. Getting one or more professional newsmen to serve as consultants would be invaluable to any editorial operation.

Editorial councils composed of the press and the public are becoming more and more popular on major city newspapers. The press feels it can keep a much better sense of the wants and needs of the public by having citizens join in considering issues and problems.

"Let the people have the truth, and freedom to discuss it, and all will go well," Voltaire said.

The following five editorials all appeared in *The* (Memphis) *Commercial Appeal* on a Friday. "Limiting Secrecy," the lead editorial, is as long as the other four combined. It informs, interprets, and condemns governmental secrecy.

"Accord Needed on Mining Bill" is the second editorial. It calls for the resolution of political differences between the two houses of the state legislature. The aim of the legislation involved was to produce new laws governing strip mining of coal. The editorial is primarily critical and hopes to influence.

"Conflict of Interest" is the third editorial. It is a political duty type. The newspaper commends the timing of a conflict-of-interest law and calls for honesty among politicians. This is watchdogging for the public good.

"It Is a 'Public' Library," the fourth editorial, concerns the loss of library books. It is critical of a proposal to impose a 30-day jail sentence on book thieves and suggests alternative solutions and punishments. The final editorial, "Remember Horses?", is the shortest. It is an informative type. It makes its points in three short paragraphs, using a few statistics.

LIMITING SECRECY

A PROBLEM of confidence has assumed crisis proportions between the government and the American people with unsettling frequency during the last 10 years—unsettling to both sides in what should be a stable if not ecstatic affair of state. President Nixon, a victim of the so-called "credibility gap" and the shock effect of the Pentagon Papers, has moved to limit secrecy surrounding government documents.

In an executive order signed Wednesday, the President directed that greater restraint be used in classifying documents and that those already classified be made public on a quicker schedule than in the past.

Administration spokesmen acknowledged that the success of the order will depend largely on both the discretion and the commitment of many officials: The fine line between "national security" and the "public's right to know" still must be drawn by human beings, most of whom are bureaucrats. If they ignore the spirit of the President's order after June 1, when it goes into effect, its impact will be severely reduced.

AT THIS POINT, however, a measure of optimism is not unwarranted. The President sounded like he meant business. "The many abuses of the security system," he said, "can no longer be tolerated. Fundamental to our way of life is the belief that when information which properly belongs to the public is systematically withheld by those in power, the people soon become ignorant of their own affairs, distrustful of those who manage them, and—eventually —incapable of determining their own destinies."

These words apply not only to the federal government in Washington but also to every other government, whether at the state or local level. Members of the Memphis City Council and Board of Education, who haven't been able to shake off the crutch of closed meetings, should take note.

The problem of confidence is nothing new in American government or politics. George Washington is said to have hated the press until his death, although he vehemently espoused the need for an informed public. President Polk had his "Gulf of Tonkin" when he went to war with Mexico in 1846. Just before America entered World War II, Roosevelt declared for political reasons that it would never happen. Then there were flimsy coverups by Eisenhower over the U-2 flights and by John Kennedy over the Bay of Pigs, before Lyndon Johnson went what some consider the last mile of deceit over Vietnam.

Nixon's order may create an atmosphere more conducive to openness, even if it doesn't complement honesty with trust in one magic night under an election-year moon.

Had the order been in effect last summer, many of the documents in the Pentagon Papers would have been declassified when they were published.

Large numbers of documents from the Truman and Eisenhower administrations should become available. Papers dealing with the Bay of Pigs and the Cuban missile crisis will be eligible for inspection unless the government can prove that they would adversely affect the national interest.

Fewer departments and many fewer officials will be empowered to classify documents. In fact, the opportunity for the bureaucrats to make work with their red stamps will be reduced by more than 50 percent.

Some officials believe that national policies, especially in defense and foreign affairs, have become so complex that the public should be satisfied to let the experts take care of things without being asked a lot of ignorant and bothersome questions.

BUT WHEN the public's right to know becomes bad for national welfare, except in cases of national security, the kind of government in question ceases to be a democracy. And even cases of security offer room for argument. If rumors and half-complete reports about the Bay of Pigs had been published before the invasion, as they could have been by at least one major newspaper, the United States probably would have been spared an international embarrassment. Moreover, the very complexity of our society and world demands that greater efforts be made to inform the public before it becomes more difficult to do so. Information must flow freely if the nation is to maintain a system of freedom.

ACCORD NEEDED ON MINING BILL

EIGHT AMENDMENTS were added to the bill to tighten controls on strip mining in the Tennessee Senate this week. The result is a severe conflict with the less stringent measure passed by the House last week.

In both cases the votes indicate that the public and the legislators want to prevent the despoiling of Tennessee's landscape and environment, and at the same time make it possible for surface miners to continue to operate—for their products are needed. What bothers us is that there is now such a wide difference in the bills passed by the two chambers that reconciliation may be difficult.

We do not object to the Senate amendments, which make the bill stronger, but we hope the senators and House members will not allow their differences to lead to failure to pass any legislation during the current session.

The House debated amendments much like those accepted by the Senate, but put them aside with the idea of getting through a bill which at least will reduce soil erosion and stream pollution. The final House vote, with fewer amendments, was 77–3. The Senate vote, with more strictures on strip miners, was 30–0.

WITH INTENTION in both chambers clearly declaimed, let us hope they now resolve their differences promptly and give Tennessee a stiffer law which can be put into effect this year.

CONFLICT OF INTEREST

THE CITY COUNCIL has chosen a good time to push through a conflict-of-interest law for city councilmen and city appointees to the Memphis and Shelby County Planning Commission.

As passed on first reading, the measure would prohibit the specified officials from representing clients in zoning and property assessment cases before city boards.

No councilman or commissioner is involved in this kind of legal practice. So, since no one can feel he is being singled out, there should be little resistance to getting a good law on the books.

The County Court does have one member who handles zoning and assessment cases—Squire William Farris. But the court also should try to establish a clear-cut policy on conflict of interest. As a matter of principle, elected officials should make certain that public office cannot be used for private gain.

IT IS A 'PUBLIC' LIBRARY

LAMAR WALLIS, director of the Memphis and Shelby Public Libraries, is understandably upset about the disappearance of $45,000 worth of books last year. All of that could not have been caused by carelessness or forgetfulness.

But it does seem to us that the City Council's remedy, in the form of a threat of a 30-day jail sentence, goes too far.

If offenders can be identified and found, they should be fined in City Court as well as by the library. The return of the appropriated literature should be attempted. But it's a bit much to say the villain should go to the Penal Farm.

We would add that those who are offenders, who must be of high mind, would do well to remember that this is a "public" library, which means that when they borrow a book it should be returned so someone else can share it. Once read, a book decays on a bookshelf unless passed on through other hands. That's why we have "circulating" libraries.

REMEMBER HORSES?

Once in a long while we are told that modern highways are taking land needed for farming, forcing up rural land prices, contributing to the rising cost of food, and so on.

Of course, anyone can see it is the subdivision that is really cutting into the acres in fields, but in case the highway vs. crops argument ever pops up again it should be recalled that horses and mules once used a lot of space.

Before World War I we had 26.5 million farm horses and mules. It took about 90 million acres of oats, hay and pasture to feed them. But right-of-way for all the nation's public roads now use only 45 million acres.

This short editorial from *The Nashville Tennessean* is offbeat. Although it is somewhat light and entertaining, it has a serious motive beneath its humor. It is a lesson against deceit.

A GOOD TRY AT JUSTICE

A STEER NAMED Big Mac was crowned grand champion of the National Western Stock Show in Denver in January, nosing out Old Dakota in a close contest.

But immediately questions began to be raised about the purity of Big Mac's blood. Big Mac was entered as an Angus, but gossip spread that he had some Charolais in him.

A lengthy investigation followed during which black dye began to wear off Big Mac's whitish natural hair and un-Angusy horns sprouted from what should have been a smooth poll.

Last Friday Big Mac's title was taken away from him and Old Dakota was named the grand champion steer of the show.

The decision rekindled the sagging faith of some people that true justice does exist in the world. But these sentiments are weakened by the rest of the story.

Big Mac lived a life of ease and comfort in a Denver barn while the investigators waited for his horns to grow and the dye to rub off his deceitful hide. But immediately after the show in January, Old Dakota went to the slaughterhouse.

This obituary editorial, also from the *Tennessean,* is concise and well written. It is concrete and not flowery or stilted.

Mrs. Branham Will Be Missed

Mrs. John M. Branham of Gallatin, one of the nation's leading racehorse women and a vice president of the Nashville Tennessean, is dead after a lengthy illness.

Mrs. Branham was the former Laura Startton, member of an old Nashville family. Her husband, who started his career in the advertising department of the old Nashville American, predecessor of this newspaper, was the founder of one of the nation's largest advertising agencies—John M. Branham Co. of Chicago.

After he established the agency, Mr. and Mrs. Branham lived in Chicago. But they came back frequently to Sumner County where Mr. Branham bought a farm he had admired from childhood.

In the early 1920's, they moved back to the farm—which they named Foxland Hall—so that Mr. Branham could spend more time at his favorite pursuits, fox hunting and raising Thoroughbred horses.

Mr. Branham died in 1935, and Mrs. Branham determined that she would continue operating the racehorse farm. She became one of the most successful Thoroughbred breeders in this region and won the admiration of horsemen all over the nation. Horses from her stables became outstanding money winners and Foxland Hall became a well-known name in the Thoroughbred Industry.

The Kentucky Horse Breeders Association created a new award to honor Mrs. Branham in 1953. She was named Sportswoman of the Year, and Kentucky turf writers referred to her as "a leader in the revival of the breeding industry in Tennessee."

Mrs. Branham had been in failing health in recent years. But she had retained much of the vivacity and good humor coupled with keen wisdom which made her so popular with people everywhere. She will be missed.

High-school and college editorial pages are in essence no different from dailies. Each covers important items of local concern. Thus it must be dedicated to the area, state, nation, and world. For educational institutions to restrict their editorial coverage only to their immediate environment is short-sighted. They must have total vision instead of trying to write while wearing blinders.

These three editorials appeared in one issue of *The Axe,* the bi-monthly student newspaper of South Eugene High School, Eugene, Oregon. "Positive Sign," the lead editorial, asserts that school life today is in sharp contrast to that of 10 or 15 years ago. "Program Defended" is the second editorial, involving two deaths in a camping program. Significantly, the editorial points out that a city newspaper was editorially critical of the program. *The Axe* defends the program well.

In "Halt Mining," readers' support is asked in stopping an area from being mined. It is short and effective.

Positive Sign

High school life of ten or fifteen years ago differed greatly from that of today. At one time, a student's entire social and political life rested behind the ivy-covered walls of his or her own secure high school.

Along this same line, certain annual events highlighted the school year with a sort of spirited frenzy of high school nationalism. Happenings like the charity drive, the prom and the traditional basketball and football games would involve up to 75 percent of the entire student body.

But with the advent of student awareness toward local and national affairs, interest in these events has steadily decreased to a level of almost non-existence in the last few years.

Tradition states that every three years, each school will have a homecoming celebration. This year at South is a homecoming year, but no observance to speak of will be held. No parades, no car rallies, no bonfires, no school spirit. At one time, these occurrences had merit. They provided the main source of entertainment for students' social life.

But homecoming is out-of-date and obsolete. A student's social conscience today extends beyond rally girls and pompoms. The death of homecoming and other once-spirited functions is a prime example of a growing awareness toward more important affairs on the part of South students in particular. A positive sign.

—D.T.

Program Defended

The recent death of two teenaged girls participating in the Outward Bound program, although tragic, has been blown out of proportion.

The girls were skilled and knowledgeable in the field of mountaineering and wilderness survival, but when put in similar circumstances of rain, cold and fear, an almost normal reaction would be to break camp and flee.

In a recent editorial, the Oregonian, a newspaper in Portland, criticized the program for inefficiency and suggested that a public inquiry be made as to its operating procedures.

Since it formation almost 20 years ago, over 20,000 participants have successfully endured the three- to four-week excursions without as much as one death. This lays clear foundations for the program's defense.

During the same storm that the girls died in, 37 others escaped without so much as getting wet. The deaths resulted in human panic and over-reaction. They did not in any way reflect on the effectiveness of the program.

In suggesting a public inquiry into a privately funded program, the Oregonian verbally violated the right of private ownership. They might have been justified if due cause had been displayed on the part of the program, but the facts being as they are, the guilt rests with the paper, not the program.

HALT MINING

The granting of a permit to mine Rock Mesa, an area southwest of the South Sister in the Sisters Wilderness Area, would be a grave mistake.

The elected representatives of Oregon in the nation's capital realize this and are presently engaged in an attempt to block the mining. However, they are faced with a powerful lobby in the mining industry and will need all the support their state can give them.

To demonstrate your support, read the following carefully, sign it, then put it in the box in room 26 and we'll send it along to the representatives.

To the Representative of Oregon:

I hereby signify my support of your efforts to halt the mining of Rock Mesa in the Three Sisters Wilderness Area, and encourage you to take steps to prevent the recurrence of similar problems in other wilderness areas.

Sincerely, ─────────────────────

─────────────────────

P. S.

CHAPTER X

Syndicated and Local Columnists

Syndicated columnists are the most popular and powerful journalists. They are among the most widely read and influential newsmen. Not only are they unique in the editorial world, they are essential to the free flow of ideas—and sometimes, facts—in a democracy.

In the early 1800's, editors began voicing their editorial opinions in signed columns. The evolution of such columns was rather subtle. But some writers became renowned and increased the circulation of their papers. Throughout the century, the editor-journalist-columnist became an integral part of newspapers. Horace Greeley and James Gordon Bennett, Jr., became popular in their papers.

By the 1880's the work of a few famous reporters was being carried by several papers, but the syndicated column did not become a medium until the 1920's. Heywood Hale Broun joined the New York *Tribune* in 1912. He soon began writing his liberal and independent column titled "It Seems to Me," which shortly was syndicated. David Lawrence became syndicated in 1919 and was still very popular in the 1970's.

Syndicates are agencies that employ columnists and sell the columns to newspapers for a fee. Some columnists are carried by only a few dozen newspapers. A few popular ones are carried by almost 1,000 newspapers. It takes only 100 to 200 big-city newspapers to add up to a circulation of between 10,000,000 and 20,000,000 daily.

How often do they write columns? Some write once weekly, but most write three or five times weekly. Some write daily. They make from $50,000 to $250,000 or more per year if they are carried by several newspapers. Some have lower, others higher, incomes.

Local columnists write columns for their own newspapers. Producing columns may be their only duty, but some local columnists also do other reporting for their papers. They may be classified in essentially the same categories as syndicated columnists.

Types of Columns

1. Standard column. It is unsigned and appears primarily in magazines today. The content varies. It may be the work of one person, but usually it is not. Some better-known examples are "Talk of the Times,"

which appears in *The New York Times,* and "Talk of the Town," which appears in *The New Yorker* magazine. This type of column is not syndicated.

2. General signed editorial column. This is the most common type. It deals primarily with politics and personalities in the news. However, some general columnists write about any of society's ills. Some are liberal, others conservative. Some write with great impact, others with less. Some current popular syndicated columnists under this heading are William F. Buckley, Jr., John Chamberlain, James Reston, Joseph Kraft, Nick Thimmesch, Tom Wicker, Art Buchwald, and Russell Baker.

3. Dopester column. The dopester columnist tries to come up with exposés, the news behind the news, and stories having great force and consequence. Some general signed editorial columnists have uncovered major news stories, but the dopester seeks constantly to report any wrongdoing of scope. He is one of the greatest watchdogs against political and government corruption. The late Drew Pearson was the most notable such columnist.

Pearson, who wrote until his death in 1969, was responsible for a half dozen U.S. senators' going to jail or being censured by Congress. He obtained and published documentary evidence of their frauds or swindles of the American public. His column was inherited by Jack Anderson, who is the best-known dopester columnist today.

4. Gossip column. Celebrity and show-business gossip is the content of this type. One of the first and most famous gossip columnists was Walter Winchell. He retired in 1969 and died in 1972. During the 1950's Winchell's column was carried by some 800 newspapers. He was world-famous for his crusades against crime and communism, but his column was spiced with gossip from the entertainment world. Hedda Hopper and Louella Parsons were other famed gossip columnists. Almost every daily newspaper subscribes to at least one such column. The writers are either hated or idolized by entertainers. Most show-business people constantly try for mention in their columns. Whether the publicity is good, bad, or false, they know that even scandal stories help their popularity or notoriety.

5. Hodgepodge column. This is almost exclusively a local column. The writer rambles, expressing himself on literally anything. In one column of a few hundred words he may write about a dozen or more topics. He may write about oddities of nature, or about a housewife who has brought in a huge vegetable or flower she has grown. He is a sort of homespun storyteller of local events. This type of column is popular in papers of less than 100,000 circulation, although several bigger papers also carry them.

6. Contributor's column. This type tends to overlap with the hodgepodge column. It is rarely syndicated. Essentially, the contributor's col-

umn includes comments from people who send letters to the writer. The basic format is light and entertaining. It is like the hodgepodge in that it relates oddities. Variety is one of its aspects. Readers do most of the writing for these columnists.

7. Lovelorn column. People write to this type of column for advice about love, marriage, and related topics. Female journalists dominate this field. Ann Landers and her twin sister, Abigail Van Buren, are among the most famous lovelorn columnists. Each appears in some 700 newspapers. Between them they appear in almost every daily in the nation. Readers write them for their comments about some romantic problem, and their replies are often humorous. Although many people take the lovelorn column seriously, several newspapers cynically put it near the comic pages.

8. Specialty column. There are scores of highly specialized columns, mostly syndicated. They include columns on business, bridge, religion, medicine, sports, labor, how-to-do-it projects, and others.

A big-city daily has columns of almost every type. One or more columns are written for virtually every age group and most interests. College and high-school newspapers are too often overloaded with columnists. Some writers do a column—invariably, a bad one—just for the publicity it offers. They get a by-line. Occasionally, a college paper has a radical columnist who wants only a forum for himself, usually with no opposition.

Too many high-school papers have one or more columns per page. A quarter to a third of these papers' content is absorbed by columnists. This is bad. Many of the columns are pointless or in poor taste. Juvenile gossip, favoritism of a clique, and gibberish are the most common problems of high-school newspaper columns. The space they waste should be devoted to quality news features and pure features after all usable news has been inserted. Too many columns are devoted to the entertainment scene, music, and the arts. It is unnecessary to devote an entire column to each of such topics; generally, they can be grouped in one column. Gossip columns should never be used in the high-school press. Syndicated gossip columns are concerned only with show business.

Good columnists are reporters. They background their opinions with research and logic. Some columnists employ reporters who help them gather news and information. Good general columnists produce what amounts to an effective feature in each of their articles. Most columnists are also among the most effective writers. Some are popular more for their writing style than for their content. When a column loses its popularity with readers, it should be dropped. This is true of the press on all levels, from the daily to the secondary.

Signed editorial columnists with various political philosophies and attitudes toward life give the public evaluations and opinions on almost

all matters of importance. Readers who tend to be politically conservative will naturally be attracted to columnists who agree with their views.
The same is true for liberals and those who fall between the two concepts.

Often a newspaper is strongly opposed to the opinions espoused by
some of the syndicated columnists it carries. This is one of the best
expressions of freedom of the press, and freedom in a democracy. On
occasion a newspaper will find on a given issue that one of its columnists
is pro and one is con. Sometimes the editor will run the columns under
a single headline, emphasizing for readers that they may decide for
themselves which view they prefer. The success of a columnist depends
solely on whether readers like his work. This always should be the
deciding factor.

At times in history, a few newspapers have surrendered their editorial
powers to syndicated columnists. Rather than be bold and exercise their
responsibilities, some have elected columnists to do their editorializing.
This is dangerous. Syndicated columnists are remote. They are writing
primarily for the national scene. And the newspaper's first editorial duty
is to local readers. But good columnists are perhaps universal in interest.
They inform, entertain, guide, interpret, give their opinion, and often
communicate all life.

The following column appeared in the *Tiger Hi-Line* of the Cedar Falls
(Iowa) High School. "A-musing" is the kicker on the column, which is
very well written. Columnists must have something to say and be able
to present it well. This student columnist does a highly professional job
with this satire on raking leaves. And the headline is an effective play
on words.

A-musing

Would You Be-leaf?

by MARTHA FISCHER

One cool fall evening, a few days ago, I smelled the crisp smell of burning
leaves in the air, and decided that I would visit a friend of mine. Hard-luck
Hector, the community work-shirker, may have finally resolved to rake his·
leaves this year, I thought to myself.

I found him staring out the window at a yardful of leaves, terribly depressed.
"Hector," I started, "have you got a scheme for escaping leaf-raking this
year?"

"No," he muttered. "Didn't you hear of this summer's fiasco?"

"Well, what happened?," I asked after a respectful pause.

"I figured that leaves fell in the fall because Mother Nature ran out of
stick-um, so I decided to help out the poor old dame. I borrowed a small plane
from a friend, and mixed a solution of Elmer's glue and water to spray my
trees with. But that dern glop-dusting project didn't turn out too well (sigh)."

"Did you get someone mad at you?" I cautiously inquired.

"Man!" he exploded. "Why, I guess the whole dern community blew up!

You see, in the process of glop-dusting my trees, I accidentally got a few stray cats, dogs, and curious children. All the mothers in the neighborhood got riled . . .

"And 'cause I glop-dusted a few mangy birds and squirrels, the ecologists got upset. (Snixitfrixit dad-gummed eco freaks) . . .

"Some of the residents boiled over because it was football season, and I mangled a few antennas . . .

"The city officials got into the act, 'cause I didn't have a glop-dusting permit . . .

"Then my former friend, the owner of the plane, got mad at me too. It seems that everybody took down the number of the plane, and blamed everything on him . . .

"Two days later, we had a thunderstorm. I forgot about the glop, and hired somebody to mow my lawn. Six weeks later, I got my mower back, repaired at the exorbitant sum of $72.51!"

Poor Hector was so low that I could only leave him to his misery. I saw him again yesterday, and asked how things were going.

"I tell ya," he cried gleefully, "this year I really got it all figured out. Ole Ma Nature is riled at me fer tryin' to gum up the works this summer, and she's makin' the wind blow the leaves from the neighbor's yards into mine. I'll show her a thing or two! I got my snow-blower rigged up fer leaves, and come tonight, I'll put them dern critters back where they belong. I'm tellin' you—"

"But Hector," I interrupted, "won't that make the neighbors even madder?"

As I hurriedly departed, I heard him stewing and steaming about "dad-gummed pessimists."

Lydel Sims, a Memphis *Commercial Appeal* columnist, is well known for his wit. His column appears on page one below the fold. He is a humorist who blends the hodgepodge and contributors' column types. Some of his daily items come from his own experiences, but many readers tell him tales or send him letters concerning funny situations. Several commercial dailies have a front-page columnist who focuses on humor. The following column by Sims is rather typical of his work.

Assignment: Memphis—

Life Begins to Weigh on Young'uns

by LYDEL SIMS

Small children are beginning to share the national concern over having to pay more and more for less and less.

Seven-year-old Bobby Mayo, just to give you one example, sat down to supper the other night, took a look at the Brussels sprouts, and gasped.

"Gee," he cried, "they're even shrinking the cabbages now."

But bobby isn't the only youngster who is a bit confused by national affairs. Maggie Eikner, 6, has a thing or two to learn herself.

The family was discussing a proposed weekend in the country, and the question came up whether it would be more fun to stay in a tent, a cabin or a hotel.

"There might be spiders and snakes in a cabin," Maggie objected.

"Abraham Lincoln was born in a cabin," her daddy countered piously.

And Maggie, who knows little about Lincoln and even less about politicians, came back with a double-barreled blunder.

"Yes," she said wisely, "but everybody knows there are no snakes in Washington."

STILL, YOU CAN always count on the tiny tykes to put a lump in your throat when they offer simple homage to adults they love.

A Memphis schoolteacher had to keep a firm grip on her emotions as she read a note from one of her charges:

"Your just like a candy bar Sweet, Delisuse, chewy, wonderful, Gorgeas, lovely Melty, Sticky, chocklety Loveable, beautiful, Good as gold, Caramaly creamy . . ."

At this point, Teach brushed away a tear, turned the page, and read on: " . . . and ½ nuts."

QUICK NOW, WHAT do smart alecks usually write on dirty cars and trucks?

Exactly. Which is why one message fingered in the grime of a Memphis vehicle brought special attention this week.

"DO NOT REMOVE," it warned. "TEST DIRT."

"Home Grown" is the name of a column written by Patti Vincent for the South Eugene (Oregon) High School *The Axe*. The following is approximately one third of one of her offerings. It is light and entertaining.

Susie was last in line that day for show-and-tell at the Wunderbar Kindergarten, where the teacher was asking the kids what they wanted to be when they grew up. Most of the little boys wanted to be firemen and cowboys, with a few exceptions who wanted to be nuclear physicists and subsistence farmers. The girls wanted to be mommies, nurses, airline stewardesses and secretaries, with the exception of one short-order fry cook.

When it came to be Susie's turn to say what she wanted to become, she shuffled shyly to the front of the room and put her right hand in her mouth. (Almost.)

"What do you want to be, Susie?" the teacher asked as she had asked all the other pupils.

"A movie star," Susie said through her middle and index finger.

"How nice," the teacher said stifling a yawn. "Do you want all of the glamor, excitement, and fame that goes with the movie industry?"

"Nope," said Susie, "Governor Tom McCall says it's a non-polluting industry, which will offer employment, but will not endanger the state's natural environmental characteristics . . ."

"How nice," said the teacher . . .

Some high-school newspapers have good signed editorial columnists. They concern themselves with significant news stories and situations. They report and reflect on the problems of society. A newspaper must never have a columnist just for the sake of having one. The writer must be an asset. A poor columnist is a liability. Since space is at a premium in almost all newspapers, including the secondary press, columns should be tightly written. And all successful columns are.

CHAPTER XI

Sports Reporting

Hundreds of thousands of newspapers will be thrown away today, folded open to their sports pages. Thousands of people subscribe to a daily newspaper only for its sports section. They read it and nothing more.

America is one of the most leisure- and sports-conscious nations. Millions hunt, fish, boat, and go camping. Tens of millions attend all types of spectator sports. Tens of millions pitch horseshoes, play tennis, badminton, croquet, or Ping-Pong, bowl, and participate in dozens of other athletic endeavors. Golf, wrestling, archery, and racing are other sports in which people play and/or watch others take part.

Sports are lively, dramatic, entertaining. Sports editors and reporters must capture all those aspects. Atmosphere and emotion are always rampant in the major sports of football and baseball. Enthusiasm is synonymous with sports. Hobbies and sports are more important to some people than anything else, including their work and welfare in some instances. Dozens of fans take time off from their jobs each year or schedule their vacations so that they may attend the World Series.

Sports writing must capture the contest whatever it is, reflect the enthusiasm and emotions of the players and spectators, and do it vividly. Good sports writing has the impact of a smashing tackle, a ball sailing over the left-field wall, the sharp blow of a hockey stick, the screeching of the rear wheels going into a turn on the track at 190 m.p.h., all this and more.

[Author's note: The following section on sports was written by Professor Ira Baker of Eastern Carolina University, Greenville, N.C., a noted journalism educator and authority on the college press.]

Sports pages of leading high-school papers no longer concentrate on past sports events but rather emphasize coming events, the news of tomorrow.

Emphasis is on the future sports event rather than on long, boring, warmed-over recaps of last week's games and contests. Students read the sports pages in their local dailies and hear and view the electronic media. School papers are becoming more professional in their attitudes in re-

218

porting and writing sports. Past sports are being played down, and tomorrow's events are being featured.

Organization of Staff

An outstanding sports section invariably has an alert, dedicated, and talented staff. Sports editors and reporters must be familiar with all sports and be able to interpret and report on them. The sports editor must be a kind of team manager, able to coordinate and manage several writers and other staff members who work under him. The exact number of staff members varies according to the size of the school, the size of the paper or yearbook, and the number of teams representing the school, including intramural teams. The commercial press sports reporters are, ideally, in proportion to the amount and quality of local sports.

For example, a high-school newspaper published in a school of 2,000 students, with all major sports represented and belonging to a strong athletic conference, often has a sports staff consisting of a sports editor, assistant sports editor, and four reporters. More women are considering sports reporting. Some metropolitan dailies now have one or more female sports writers. One student usually serves as a sports copy editor. He edits all sports copy and helps make up the pages.

The sports editor is in complete charge of the sports department and sees to it that the overall desired level of performance is maintained. He critiques the sports pages following each issue and goes over the pages and various stories at staff meetings. One of his most exciting and challenging chores is to write a sports column for each issue, although some editors prefer to have a sports columnist whose sole duty is the column.

The assistant sports editor stands ready in an emergency to take over for the sports editor. His main job is to serve as a kind of news editor of the sports department, making assignments for specific coverage and meting out feature assignments. The assistant often is being groomed to assume the position of sports editor in some future time.

Sports reporters are mainly concerned with details of actual game coverage, attending and reporting practice and scrimmage sessions, and writing sports features.

On many high-school staffs the regular staff photographer serves the sports department when needed. Some larger high schools enjoy the luxury of a photographer who covers the sports beat only.

Precoverage

Much work in reporting a seasonal sport should be completed before the season begins. For example, before school starts in the fall, many progressive and aggressive sports staffs prepare for the coming season by writing to the coaches and athletic directors of opposing teams requesting brochures, pictures of coaches and captains, and perhaps a statement from each coach summarizing the team's hopes for the season. After this material is collected, the sports editor has a considerable morgue to work from each week. He collects similar materials from his own coaches. He will be on the lookout for local sports news in surrounding newspapers and magazines. All materials should be sorted, graded, catalogued, and filed in manila envelopes, one for each team, to be used at the appropriate time.

Most sports editors and reporters are concerned primarily with three types of sports stories: pre-game coverage, game coverage, and post-game coverage. Reporters assigned to actual coverage should have a genuine enthusiasm for sports as well as a better-than-average knowledge of the specialty they are assigned to cover. They must be conversant with rules, players, and coaches. They should know managers, trainers, grounds and gym keepers, ticket managers, and sports reporters for other newspapers and radio and television.

Pre-game Coverage

Pre-game coverage includes searching for good slants to hang stories on: old rivalries, championship implications, underdog role, unusual strategy, and records are examples. The files have information about the visiting team. The pre-game story should include the site and time.

The following is an advance or pre-game coverage story from *The Riparian,* the prize-winning newspaper of Broad Ripple High School in Indianapolis:

> The Ripple varsity basketball team, which finished the regular season last week with a 6–14 record, will meet Lawrence Central tonight at Hinkle Fieldhouse in the first round of the Sectional at 7 P.M.
>
> The Rockets defeated the 1–18 Bears in the opening game of the season, 79–73. Senior Greg Otey scored 23 points to lead the Ripple victory.
>
> The winner of tonight's game will play the winner of the Tech–North Central contest at Hinkle tomorrow night at 8:30 P.M. Ripple defeated Tech, 61–56, and lost to North Central, 87–70, in regular season play.
>
> In the 20 games played, Ripple averaged 63.25 points per game while its opposition averaged 70.05. Senior Rodney Cross was the leading Rocket scorer, with a 17.30 average. He was followed by junior Ronnie Scrivner, with a 11.25 average, senior Greg Otey, 9.75, and sophomore Jeff Gibson 8.05

Coverage

Actual game coverage chores may be divided. One reporter may do the action story, another the "color," which requires that he take note of the crowd, bands, dignitaries attending the game, and post-game visits to each dressing room for quotes from coaches and key players.

Where should the reporter assigned to actual game coverage sit?

Should he wander along the sidelines following the play up and down the field or the court? Should he mingle with the crowd? Sit in the press box? This decision may be a matter of preference after trying all plans and deciding which location or procedure suits best. Most reporters prefer to sit in the press box where seats have been reserved for them. For high-school and college sports reporters this arrangement lends dignity, not only to the individual but also respect for the papers and schools they represent. This provides a sense of personal satisfaction and probably will ensure more privacy and working conveniences.

Working reporters carry a score book and keep accurate and complete records. Game coverage should include participating teams, the winner, final score, site of contest, game highlights, and, if possible, the winning play. Not all these elements are needed in the lead, but they should appear at the top of the story.

The following basketball game coverage from the *Goldsboro Hi-News,* Goldsboro, N.C., has a terseness common in reporting past events:

> The GHS Cougars blistered the conference-leading Kinston Vikings 77–74 in a heart-stopping victory.
> The game was fast paced with a fairly good Kinston press in effect most of the night. Kinston's big gun, Doug Potter, fouled out with 4:00 minutes remaining, having collected 28 points. GHS had a sizable lead in the 3rd and 4th quarters but blew it close to the end.
> With one minute left, the score 69–68 GHS, Rozelle Barnes connected on two free throws. Play resumed and with 11 seconds left, Kinston was leading 74–73. With 4 seconds remaining, Larry Gooding popped a 10-footer to give GHS a one-point lead. Kinston called time out and tried to set up a last-second desperation play. On the inbounds throwing Larry Gooding deflected the ball to Mike Evans who swished a 12-footer at the buzz.

Post-game reporting can be the most exciting and most challenging because the emphasis may be on the Why? What happened? What went wrong? Tactfully worded questions about strategy may often provide answers to questions in the minds of fans.

Boring play-by-play reporting of old sports news in non-daily newspapers is very bad. When weekly, and less frequent, newspapers smother their sports columns with copy that is published long after the whistles have blown, they display their ignorance. Area sports fans have already read accounts of the games and contests in other newspapers and have heard or viewed the sports stories on radio and television. Many commercial weeklies and monthly high-school newspapers taint their columns with old sports coverage. If past sports activities must be reported, they should be short and evaluated very low in choice of placement on pages.

Coming sports contests should be featured prominently. Excellent pre-game reporting is vastly superior to ancient post-reporting.

Good action shots help tell the story. The photographer should be instructed to take action shots, scoring plays, and for a change in pace, he might take an occasional shot of fans reacting to a play, a goal-line stand, or a winning home run. Sometimes the faces of fans tell the story best. Sports pages should avoid mug shots of individuals if possible.

Sports Display

If today's papers are telling tomorrow's story first, in what fashion of makeup are these stories being displayed? The trend is toward more horizontal makeup and more stories set multicolumn across the page. And more high-school papers are using the banner head to announce the coming event.

Other popular trends, in keeping with the general streamlined tendency, include the one-up technique of putting a four-column story under a five-column head, giving the story extra white space. Sports editors are using large, attention-getting pictures carefully and dramatically cropped for added impact.

Cartoons and other illustrative art work are strongly recommended. Sports caricatures are popular, and lucky is the staff with a member who holds this talent.

Follow-up stories on alumni who are having successful careers in college and professional sports make good features.

The sports pages should be among the most widely read and most exciting sections of the entire school paper. Pages filled with stale, dully written post mortems of past events are happily disappearing. The better sports pages now emphasize the coming event, with the past event carefully toned down through a more subtly featurized treatment. The past event must certainly be recorded since the newspaper is, among other things, a history, but the past story is coming more and more to be reduced to pictures, sidebars, and column treatment.

High-school sports reporters have a tremendous social responsibility to their readers as well as to those athletes about whom they write. Because of the tremendous pressure and competition now characteristic of high-school athletes and because of their intense desire to excel, reporters must ever be on guard to be sincere, accurate, impartial, and objective. Because of rivalries and tough competition among individuals and groups, the sports writer of tomorrow must, as indeed must all writers, be ever guided by constant effort toward fairness—absence of prejudice because of color, religion, or any personal bias. High-school journalists of the future, especially those on sports staffs, are going to be increasingly held accountable for their journalistic stewardship. Some writers provide too much criticism, others too much praise. The case of the 18-year-old high-school football star of a few years back is a well-remembered example. He had been so lavishly praised both in his home-town and high-school papers as well as the media generally that college recruiters were intently after him. The pressure was too much. He disappeared and was later found in a state of nervous collapse.

This brings up an ethical concept that advisers, coaches, and sports writers may well ponder in these days of superstars. Would it not be better to "play up" the team and team play rather than overdramatizing in space and headline the heroics of one or two individuals? This keeps the glory spread out a bit and may otherwise shield the glory-grabber from getting a distorted sense of his own importance.

Other concepts are emerging that will have tremendous impact on the coverage and philosophy of high-school sports pages of the future: the emphasis on winning at any price; the athlete's privacy—does one report that the star quarterback was arrested for smashing a pinball machine?

Perhaps the crowning achievement for any sports staff is to feel that it is performing in the public interest, that it does have a social responsibility to its readers. In promoting racial harmony, in emphasizing sportsmanship, in praising team effort, in trying to be objective and fair in its own news reports—these achievements will be heralded on sports pages of the future in the high-school and the commercial press.

CHAPTER XII

Advertising: Madison Avenue in Hometown, U.S.A.

Red ink is the major business problem of the high-school press. Many schools cannot or will not provide adequate subsidies for a newspaper. Some simply cannot afford to contribute to the school press. Others could, but they are not enlightened enough to realize the tremendous potential benefits that could be derived from an effective school newspaper.

Advertising is the mainspring of the mass media economy. Even in the magazine world, it takes approximately three times the cover price of most publications to pay their printing costs. This is the reason that magazines with 5,000,000 or more circulation have died. Their great size was instrumental in their demise.

Circulation sales pay only a small portion of production costs. Advertising provides the profits. But the high-school press is not always entitled, or has access, to all the assets of capitalistic enterprise as does the commercial press. The high-school press, however, with rare exceptions, can compete profitably with all other mediums.

Unfortunately, some high-school advisers are not aware of the power and scope of their own papers. High-school students account for a major portion of the gross national product, directly and indirectly. Millions of students work part time. Many work full time during summers. And, like all consumers, they must buy things.

High-school newspaper advertising managers and salesmen must be educated as to the role of their medium in business and advertising in all society. Local business and industry must be enlightened as to the values and necessities of using the high-school press for its messages and advertising. Thousands of high-school newspapers solicit ads as if asking for charity. Many advisers are so inept and uneducated concerning high-school journalism and mass communications in general that they allow their high-school newspapers to run ads that say "Compliments of So-and-So."

High-school newspapers have excellent readership. The saturation of their audiences is higher in almost all cases than that achieved in any other medium, particularly all other newspapers. True, in many cases every student gets a copy of his school paper. This is often because the paper is one of the things he receives for his activities fees. The activities fee is also the primary source of income for most college papers. Many campus papers get a portion of the activities fee. The fee furnishes half the paper's budget, and advertising pays the remainder. Many college papers have become independent of their college and are free-enterprise operations.

Advertising should provide a source of income for the high-school newspaper as well. Ads enable local businessmen to market goods and services to the student population. Ads perform a service for readers. Buyers shop through the media before they go to stores. Ads are the way they find out what the stores are selling. And merchants should not be permitted to forget that most students take their high-school paper home. Millions of parents also read the school newspaper.

One important factor that business and industry must remember is that today's students are tomorrow's consumers, full-time citizens, and workers. It is the best of public relations for the business community to establish goodwill among students. Even though some merchants have low or no customer potential among students, they still should be permitted—as many are—to run ads that are in essence charitable contributions to the paper. Ads should be viewed by merchants, the newspaper, and its readers as good public relations. They may be considered as beneficial to business in general. Still, the merchant should have a selling ad, not one that shamefully says "Compliments of." Let a real-estate agency or a funeral home run ads. Students are not likely to add to their clientele immediately, but they are certainly going to be customers in the future. These are just long-range planning ads.

Most high-school advertising staffs are not properly trained in advertising. They do not know how to sell or prepare ads. Merchants are responsible for many poor ads; they are businessmen, not advertising personnel. Common sense, some study of advertising concepts, perhaps some instruction from journalism courses, and some pointers from working newspaper advertising people are some of the ways high-school students can become competent ad men and women.

Many high-school ad staffs could improve their incomes substantially by adopting a more professional approach. For modest cost, newspapers can provide their ad staffs with the standard business forms of the profession. Contracts, rate cards, statement forms, tear sheets, and such materials can be purchased. The investment will realize an increase in revenue in almost every instance.

Advertising is closely allied with various other activities. Sales promotion can include the use of samples, premiums or contests, and efforts to build enthusiasm and loyalty among dealers. The development of sales kits, sales literature, and sales training materials is also frequently considered as part of this function.

Publicity consists of impersonally communicated messages, which, like advertising, are designed to leave certain impressions upon the minds exposed to them. Unlike advertising, however, publicity is not openly paid for. It may be carried as part of the news or other editorial content of a newspaper or magazine, or as part of the news or entertainment broadcast on radio or television.

In order for publicity to be used by any of the media it must have news value or other inherent interest. Much publicity material does not appear in print or on the air because editors feel that it is merely disguised advertising. The source of publicity is not always identified.

Public relations is a broad concept referring to the total of all impressions made upon a given segment of the public by an individual or organization. Many tools are employed in an organized public relations program, including publicity, advertising, and company publications.

Many kinds of business organizations, institutions, governmental units, and individuals may make use of advertising at one time or another. Advertisers may be classed in four basic groups:

1. Manufacturers or other producers of goods
2. Dealers or resellers—retailers, wholesalers
3. Service businesses
4. Institutions and nonprofit organizations

Advertising agencies are frequently asked to provide various kinds of research services for their clients. At other times the agency may feel impelled to undertake certain research itself in order to make sound recommendations on media or copy policy.

Where do ad agencies get their ideas? Many writers have advanced many systems for originating ideas. One good five-step procedure is:

1. Gather information—the raw materials;
2. Organize the data within the mind;
3. Permit the materials to incubate in the subconscious;
4. Bring forth the germ of an idea;
5. Give the idea its final shaping for the job at hand.

Brainstorming brings to bear upon a topic the ideas of a number of persons in a group "think session."

In order for this system to work effectively, each person in the group must try to come up with as many ideas as possible pertaining to the subject or problem at hand. As fast as he thinks of an idea, the brainstormer must voice it to the group. Emphasis is upon creativity rather than evaluation. No criticism of any ideas is permitted during the session.

The think session is consequently most effective for producing a quantity—and a variety—of ideas.

Successful advertising is dependent upon repetition and continuity of ideas. A single ad may leave only a fleeting impression upon the reader or viewer. Messages must be reinforced.

The impact of a given ad is influenced by its size. The larger the ad the more likely it is to be seen and the stronger the impression that may be left on the reader. Ad researcher Daniel Starch studied the effect of size upon the readership of ads and also upon the number of inquiries received from direct-action ads. He found a similar pattern for both types of response in relation to ad size. If the number of readers attracted by full-page ads was given an index of 100, the number attracted by half-page ads was approximately 60.

Starch found in another study that attention value averaged 31 percent for double-page spreads as compared with single-page ads. The general rule with respect to the influence of size appears to be: Attention value increased with size but not in direct proportion; the attention value will tend to increase as the very large size units are reached.

The main objective of all ad activity is profits. AIDA is the goddess of advertising.

A—attention to an ad;
I—interest in the product or service;
D—desire (decision) to buy now or later;
A—action of buying.

The elements that grasp attention are: size, intensity, interest, isolation, repetition, and motion. The larger an ad is, the better chance it has of being seen. Using words like "impact" gives an ad intensity, especially if it graphically shows something like a smashing fist or a bulldozer. Interesting content commands concentration. Isolation is used effectively with white space. Many firms purchase a full page and then use only an inch or so of it. The ad may be in the middle or even in a corner of the page. As long as the eyes are led to the isolated message, it achieves its effect. Repetition has its effect. Many ads repeat key words several times. Motion can be conveyed with broken or curved lines. Arrows are good for representing motion.

The primary stimulants of interest are: editorial forms, comic strips, pictorial forms, primer or first reader approaches, stories, dialogue, poetry, handwriting, and music.

The primary functions of advertising are:

1. To increase sales;
2. To secure dealers;
3. To help the dealer;

4. To increase use per capita;
5. To relate new products to family;
6. To create insurance;
7. To create confidence in quality;
8. To eliminate seasonal fluctuations;
9. To keep the customer sold;
10. To create more business for all;
11. To raise standards of living.

The secondary functions of advertising are:

1. To encourage salesmen;
2. To furnish information to salesmen and dealers;
3. To impress executives;
4. To impress factory workers;
5. To secure better employees.

Three kinds of customers are:

1. Active—those who trade with the paper's advertisers;
2. Dormant—those who read the paper occasionally and buy only occasionally;
3. Potential.

How to write headlines

The following types of ad cover nearly the entire range of possibilities:

1. How
2. How to
3. Announcing
4. New
5. One-word
6. Now
7. Which
8. Money
9. Free
10. Amazing
11. Wanted
12. At last
13. This
14. To
15. They laughed
16. Advice

Examples:

1. "HOW your energy curve responds to the world's quickest hot breakfast."
   "HOW many a down-and-out kitchen has been reformed."
2. "HOW TO end money worries."
   "HOW TO get a better position."
   "HOW TO be generous to a man at Christmas."
3. "ANNOUNCING a three-quarter-ton truck."
   "ANNOUNCING a new help in solving the stained-sink problem."
4. "NEW deluxe Golden State Limited to California."

"NEW as tomorrow. Everyone is anxious for the new all-purpose
Scout."

5. ONE-WORD. "IMPACT." "REDUCE." "BASHFUL." "DIA-
MONDS."
6. "NOW comes the new shorthand."
"NOW in one volume, the world's best detective stories."
(There are a lot of cousins to Now: Good-bye, Presenting, Starting.)
7. "WHICH is the best battery for your car?"
"WHICH of these five skin troubles would you like to end?"
8. MONEY is receipt for labor.
"Make money at home. One cent a day brings $100 a month."
"Spare-time training that leads to better pay."
9. FREE. (Everybody wants something for nothing. It should be
used only with believable items; not money, for instance.)
"FREE plans for a clever Valentine party. Dennison Paper Co."
10. "AMAZING new taste sensation." (Must suggest something believable.)
"Get into electronics my amazingly easy way."
11. "WANTED—safe men for dangerous times."
"WANTED—man with car to run store on wheels."
(Curiosity makes this type of head very effective.)
12. "AT LAST, to take away frustrations there's a quick breakfast."
"AT LAST Kipling in one volume."
13. "THIS friendly sign is everywhere." (This ad is specific and draws
immediate attention.)
14. "TO the man who is making the old car do."
"TO the man who is 35 and dissatisfied."
"TO women whose husbands are wedded to their words."
("TO" lets you select your logical customer.)
15. (THEY LAUGHED was invented by John Caples, a member of
the Ruthroff and Ryan ad agency. He had to sell a course on
how to play the piano and developed a new formula. "THEY
LAUGHED when I sat down at the piano.")
(The headline is 50 to 75 percent of an entire ad. The illustration
is next in importance.)
"THEY LAUGHED when I sat down at the piano. But when I
started to play . . ."
(They laughed is flexible. "THEY gave me the ha-ha when I
asked for a dance." Subhead: "But when I stepped on the dance
floor they couldn't believe their eyes." This one is now outdated
and in social mothballs.)
"THEY GRINNED when the waiter spoke to me in French.
But their laughter changed to amazement at my reply."

"THEY LAUGHED when I spoke to the waiter in Italian, but he came right back with *Scotch.*"
(THEY LAUGHED when I X-ed, but when I Y-ed they Z-ed" is the formula for this type of ad.)
16. (ADVICE is a noun ad.)
"ADVICE to a young man starting out in business."
"ADVICE to wives whose husbands don't save money."

James Russell Lowell said you must get fired up to write. Just as the physician uses the same prescription many times with beneficial effects, and just as the civil engineer uses the same formula again and again in building a bridge, the copywriter can work successfully with tried and true methods relating to human behavior . . . methods proved by experience.

The writers work on the empirical method. They relate new ideas to past ones.

Of all areas of the verb world, the imperative mood is the strongest. The verb world is much stronger than the noun world. Many ads rely heavily on the command. Some imperative mood ideas are these commands:

1. Keep slender.	4. End household drudgery.
2. Increase your weight.	5. Retain your personal charm.
3. Increase your income.	6. Save money.

The anatomy of an ad includes the head, illustration, body copy, signature, trademark, slogan, and coupon.

Body Copy

AIDA is a large portion of the body copy. The function of the body copy is to interest the reader to the point that he will desire something.

The divisions of body copy are: description, narration, and exposition. The description pictures something. Narration tells a story. The exposition explains something. Exposition means the act of exposing.

1. *Descriptive*
   "How does it look?"
   "What will it do for me?"
2. *Narration*
   "What happened?"
3. *Exposition*
   "How?"
   "Why?"
   "How does the product operate?"
   "How is it made?"
   "Why is it good?"
   "Why is such and such a claim true?"

The signature is important because it tells "who said so." It gives the name of the manufacturer.

Trademarks are synonymous with values and quality. The eight forms of trademarks are:

1. Picture. Aunt Jemima's pancakes is a prime example. The Chiquita Banana girl is another. Prudential's Rock of Gibraltar is still another.
2. Design. The American Pacific R.R. uses the Yang and Yin symbol. Macy's uses the Red Star design and blends "Save Money" with the symbol. Nabisco uses the old symbol of church and state; it represented the divine right of kings.
3. Coined words. Uneeda Biscuit by National Biscuit Company is an example.
4. Fanciful sense words. Ivory soap, Arrow shirts, etc., are examples.
5. Names after famous persons. Lincoln Warehouse and Martha Washington Hotel are examples.
6. Articles named after proprietors of businesses. Walter Chrysler is a good example of a man attaching his name to a car.
7. Trademarks. Letters or figures—101 Ranch, Phillips "66," GE, ABC, and CBS are examples.
8. Color. Blue Coal Co. and Blue Sonoco Gas are examples.

The big 12 appeals in advertising are:

1. Health
2. Child appeal
3. Appetite
4. Sex
5. Economy
6. Comfort
7. Ambition
8. Beauty
9. Efficiency (quick and easy)
10. Safety
11. Vanity
12. Sympathy

Anatomy of an Ad:

1. Headline
2. Illustration or other art
3. Body copy (the core of advertising)
4. Signature
5. Coupon
6. Trademark
7. Slogan

The function of the headline is to get attention. The illustration sometimes does the attention-getting job. The function of body copy is to create desire. It is the sales talk. The signature demands attention to the brand. The trademark is the company's symbol. Slogans are often instrumental in fixing the product in the reader's mind. The coupon tells the advertiser how many people are reading his ads.

The Use of Typography

1. Type in headlines should be big enough and powerful enough to rivet the attention of the reader.
2. Type should be easy to read.

3. The easiest type for people to read is the type they read most. Ads that look like news stories are sneaky and deceiving if they are not clearly labeled.
4. Type used in magazines and papers is generally best for ads.
5. Avoid fancy type.
6. Avoid script.
7. Avoid italics.
8. Avoid type too faint or too bold.
9. If a headline is long, put the important word or words in larger type.
10. Don't be afraid to use off-balance headlines. They can often be unique and attractive.
11. Ads with photos in them should show people. The cemetery is a dead view. People like people.

High-school newspaper advertising rates should be equal or close to those of local papers, particularly weeklies. Certainly, most secondary school papers can't charge the same rates as the local dailies, but the school paper should receive fees at least near those charged by weeklies. In some situations, large high-school newspapers have double or more the circulation of some of the commercial weeklies. In such cases, their ad rates may well be considerably higher than those of the commercial weeklies.

Reprints

The following articles are reprinted with the permission of the Newspaper Fund, which is supported by *The Wall Street Journal.* Any financial figures should be adjusted to the most current prices.

ADVERTISERS LIKE 100% CIRCULATION
Dennis Leuchtenburg, Consultant
Cody High School
Detroit, Michigan

A good high-school newspaper sells itself, believes Dennis Leuchtenburg, adviser of *The Cody Star,* Cody High School, Detroit, Michigan.

The *Star* has nearly 100 percent patronage from its 4,000 students, which enables it to stay out of the red each year. "But you don't just get 100 percent patronage by publishing a school newspaper," writes Leuchtenburg. "You must make it valuable to the student."

1. The paper records all school functions and activities. A schedule of events for at least four weeks in advance appears on the front page of each issue. In addition, a complete schedule of classes is printed each semester so that students can make out their programs for the following term. And there are other features such as a "College Corner," a regular column that lists all college board exam dates, merit exams, state tests, and college and university requirements and application due dates.

2. The *Star* lists school policies, new rules, announcements, and regulations. It devotes space to club rosters, schedules for speed reading, chemistry, language, and writing clinics, all schedules, and all rules and regulations for lettermen.
3. Likewise, there are political columns, "Politician" and "The Patrician," that provide very mature thinking about national and international affairs.
4. "Sports Scene," a sports editorial column, moves away from school competition to analyze national sports and some of the finest players.

In order to include the above information in an issue, *The Cody Star* runs 12 to 16 pages.

After proving to the students that the paper is worthwhile, the staff must do the same to the community in order to secure advertising, according to Leuchtenburg. *The Cody Star's* advertising staff prepares a circular that includes the following ideas:

Mr. Advertiser:

Who reads *The Cody Star,* the student publication of Frank Cody High School and winner of several national awards? Recent tabulation indicates a readership of over 10,000 people including:

  4,000 students
  6,000 parents, relatives, and friends
    200 faculty and staff members
    200 exchanges with other schools

By placing your advertising message in the *Star,* you will be getting the most for your advertising dollar. Your ads will reach a group that has enormous purchasing power. We hope that you will find it worthwhile to place advertising with us.

The Cody Star

The paper runs features that might might promote a product, and tells the advertiser what the newspaper is doing. Here are some examples:

Motorcycles—run a feature about students in the school who own motorcycles; then sell ads to go along with the feature.

Or: Write a feature about students in the school who are members of a band; sell ads to the bands and to musical instrument stores.

Or: Run a feature about skiing; sell ads to ski shops, resorts in the area, apparel shops.

Or: Plan a feature about teen fashions. Get ads from clothing stores; include pictures of students from the school modeling the clothes. (This will increase the size of the ad and and, therefore, the cost of the ad.)

Build goodwill with the advertisers. Send them a card or letter at Christmas and again at the end of the semester. Tell them of the accomplishments of the newspaper and the school.

Here is a sample letter:

Dear Advertisers:

Another school year is coming to a close, and we on *The Cody Star* are glad to stop the presses for a summer break. We have enjoyed running your ad in the paper and trust that it brought you added business. Our advertisers have made possible this publication. *The Star* has had a successful year, receiving the All-American award twice from the National Scholastic Press Association and the International Honor Award and Gallup Award from Quill and Scroll. Also, our cartoonist received national recognition as the best of all high-school artists. Although we shall not publish a paper for three months, we are already making plans for our first issue of the fall semester. Have a pleasant summer. It has been a pleasure working with you this year. We hope that you will continue to find it worthwhile to advertise with us in the fall.

(Signed)
Business Manager

Cody is located in a middle-class neighborhood on the west side of Detroit. The enrollment varies from 3,600 to 4,000. The school provides precollege, business, and vocational programs. About 10 percent of the graduating class goes to college. With the exception of a few students who have brothers and sisters in the school, everyone purchases the paper for 50 cents a semester. In addition to the money from subscriptions, the paper charges $2 per column inch for advertising. In the 12-page paper it runs about $300 in ads. In 16-page issues it usually sells $400 worth of advertising space.

This seems like a lot of money coming in, but actually most of it is used for printing costs, photographs, zincs for pictures (about 16 in each issue), the newspaper office telephone, and general expenses.

DON'T BEG FOR ADVERTISING
Larry Christman, Consultant
Mt. Diablo High School
Concord, California

"Advertising is the key to a successful, student-operated newspaper," according to Larry Christman, Mt. Diablo High School, Concord, California.

"It provides a financial independence that weans it from administrative dictatorship of policy," writes Christman.

Christman was an adviser in the Portland, Oregon area before assuming a similar position in Concord. He was equally successful in both areas while using basically the same advertising plan.

"Most merchants want to reach the teenage market. What better way is there than the school newspaper?" asks Christman. "The paper has to call the shots, however. You set the rate. Decide how much space you can devote to advertising, how much income you need, and then set your ad rate accordingly. If the advertiser truly wants to use your media, he will pay your price."

In the two different areas he has been in, Christman has determined that his papers needed $2 a column inch. In the first area (Portland, Oregon) the going rate was $1. In Concord the established rate was $1.25.

After the rate was raised, Christman found that in both cities he had more than enough ads, and bigger ones than surrounding schools. There is one ad his school runs for $10 in each of 20 issues. Other schools get $7.50 for the same size ad.

Another provision that Christman stipulates is a minimum size display ad. This adds to the attractiveness of the page and eliminates the problem of having many tiny ads stacked on top of each other. If someone does not want to run the minimum ad, the ad is refused.

Advertising also is encouraged by these devices:

1. A 5 percent discount for contracting to run an ad five or more times is offered.
2. Riddles are run as fillers with the answers appearing in ads.
3. For eateries, coupons are sometimes run, giving a discount or a free soft drink with the purchase of some other item.
4. If an advertiser agrees to run an ad all year long, he is given "exclusive" rights to that area.

   Example: A barber shop, a beauty salon. They *do not* offer this in all areas, such as the bread-and-butter accounts (clothing stores, eateries).

In Metropolitan Portland, Christman's plan grossed $1,710 spread over 10 eight-page papers. This represented nearly 60 percent of the revenue and kept the paper in the black.

In Concord, a suburban, nonindustrial town, approximately $700 was taken in for the first 12 issues. This is in contrast with the $300 the year before.

"Financial independence of the newspaper is as important as good writing, clear pictures, proofreading, etc.," writes Christman. "Without its own income, the paper will never stray far from the administration . . . which can rightfully expect to call the shots if they are paying for it.

"My belief is that subscriptions (or a portion of an activity fee) and ads should support the paper.

"This year I inherited a network of fund-raising projects that netted about $500, and next year, by improving methods, will net closer to $800. These two gimmicks are football programs and student directories.

"The National Milk Council supplies the football program free.

"The student directory lists name, address, phone number and grade of each student, and it is a big seller in a coed high school. (Be careful you do not print any unlisted phone numbers.)"

Christman hopes the money made from the special gimmicks will be used for staffers to attend press conventions or summer institutes, since the staff earned it.

"When calling on an advertiser, don't go with your hand out. Be business-like, and give them a sales pitch," he concluded.

IT DOESN'T TAKE A LARGE STAFF
Miss Elizabeth Hurley, Consultant
Pampa Senior High School
Pampa, Texas

Does it take a large advertising staff to conduct a successful advertising campaign?

Not necessarily so, according to Miss Elizabeth Hurley, sponsor of the *Harvester,* Pampa Senior High School, Pampa, Texas.

"I am so pleased with my six-man advertising staff that I am still surprised at the good job they have done," writes Miss Hurley.

Advertising became an activity instead of a solid course about three years ago, and Pampa has not had the large numbers in the class that it once had. When school started she had no advertising salesmen returning from the previous year. Three prospective salesmen had signed up for the advertising staff during pre-enrollment the year before; one came in the first day of school and two more were recruited from a study hall.

Instead of individuals selling with individual account lists, Miss Hurley set up two-man teams (one girl and one boy on one team) because of the car situation. Each team had its own account list of about 20 firms.

After explaining the rate schedule, contract plan, how to measure newspaper display ads, and how to figure the costs according to size, salesmen were then taught the fundamentals of constructing ads.

They were taught how to make layouts, with the important elements for attractive and effective layouts—headline, illustration, copy, signature, white space, etc.

They started with rough layouts for firms with copy changes, etc.; then made layouts for all advertisers on their account lists to sell for the special Thanksgiving and Christmas editions. They had to have layouts made for prospective advertisers before they went "calling."

The advertising campaign was so successful that it pushed several of the regular eight-page issues up to 10 pages.

THREE KEYS TO NEWSPAPER SUCCESS
Mrs. Elizabeth Makinson, Consultant
Mission Bay High School
San Diego, California

How do you raise more than $3,500 to put out 15 issues ranging from four to ten pages in length? Mrs. Elizabeth Makinson of Mission Bay High School, San Diego, California (1,300 students), describes the program for the *Beachcomber*. The keys to success:

1. A strong advertising program.
2. An interesting student body and staff.
3. Good organization and planning.

Here is her story.

"The *Beachcomber* (circulation 1,000) has operated for ten years with income exceeding expenditures. Revenue comes from advertising, subscriptions, and single copy sales. Staff members are proud that they do not resort to cake sales, dances, and fund-raising devices. Instead, they operate the publication as a legitimate newspaper performing services for readers and advertisers.

"Each spring the business staff, along with the faculty business adviser and me, plans the budget for the coming year. Our budget changes little from year to year except when advertising rates are raised to meet higher printing and engraving costs. Ad rates for 20 or more inches are: single issue $1.50 per column inch; semester contract $1.40 per column inch; year contract $1.25 per column inch. Rates for less than 20 inches range up to $1.75 per column inch, depending on frequency of insertion."

Mrs. Makinson's budget for the school year called for 15 regular issues, as follows:

No. of Issues	No. of Pages	Printing Cost per Edition
2	4	$120
11	6	$180
1	8	$235
1	10	$290
1	Sports Special	$ 25

The staff for several years has secured enough advertising contracts in its first month of selling to guarantee 15 issues of a four-page newspaper. Special advertising drives bring in additional revenue for the larger issues.

Here is the actual cost lineup:

Income		Expenditures	
Advertising	$2,552	Printing	$2,793
Subscriptions	1,000	Photo Engravings	427
(Student body funds apportionment)		Postage	48
Quill and Scroll	69	Quill and Scroll	80
Senior Class	100	Film and Flash Bulbs	55
(Special pages in Senior issue)		Supplies	33
Miscellaneous	15	Miscellaneous	22
	$3,736		$3,458

All money from individual sales to students not holding student body cards automatically goes to the student body fund.

The advertising income is actually a "paper" estimate. The figure quoted is owed to the paper for advertising, but Mrs. Makinson estimates that approximately 10 percent, or $250, will not be collected. Thus, the actual profit is around $25.

Mrs. Makinson's report continues:

"The student business heads of the *Beachcomber* are the business manager, the account manager, and the advertising manager.

"The business manager keeps the cash journal, recording all expenditures and receipts, balancing books once a month with the financial secretary of the school. He also makes out the requisitions and keeps track of how closely the staff is keeping to the budget.

"The account manager posts the advertising charges from a list prepared after each issue by the advertising manager. The billings are put in a ledger which provides a separate sheet for each merchant (with name of firm, address, phone number, person to contact, date of issue of ad, size, cost and current balance). Also, they are put in a larger ledger where names of the merchants are recorded alphabetically on a large sheet with charges and current balance.

"At the end of each month the account manager sends itemized statements to the merchants. These have been prepared in duplicate and have been balanced with the entries in both ledgers.

"The advertising manager keeps the original copy of the contract. A duplicate goes to the merchant. In a notebook he keeps a form which lists the ads for the coming issue, size, price, and page on which it is to appear. From the amount of revenue recorded on this form the staff knows what size paper is possible for the coming issue.

"The ad manager assigns the ads to pages, types the copy, checks layouts and page proofs and makes sure no ads have been omitted. If an error appears in an ad, the advertising manager calls the merchant immediately, admitting the error and informing him that no charge will be made.

"All students in the first-year Journalism class are advertising salesmen as well as reporters. The first study unit is on advertising and covers psychology of advertising, methods of approaching the merchant and selling the ad.

"At the end of the school year a letter is sent to each advertiser thanking him for his business and expressing a desire to be of service to him the following year."

Mrs. Makinson concludes with this observation:

"Many parents express appreciation that their children were required to sell advertising. They feel that this activity did more to mature and develop the students than any other school activity. The financial side of high-school Journalism is important. Unfortunate is the school newspaper which is not forced to provide its financial sustenance. With this effort the newspaper loses half of its usefulness as a training device."

THE SEATTLE STORY OF A CO-OP PROGRAM
Elizabeth Yates, Consultant
Garfield High School
Seattle, Washington

The most unusual program we know about was started in 1938 by Howard M. Brier, now professor of Journalism at the University of Washington and founder of the Pacific School Slope Press Clinic.

It was directed by Warren M. Hazzard, Howard's successor at Garfield High School, in Seattle, Washington, until he retired in 1964.

It carries the label "Co-op All-City Advertising Sales" program and involves 11 public high schools in Seattle with a total enrollment of approximately 19,000 students. It works this way:

1. Any school newspaper advertising solicitor may sell space for all 11 publications. A standing agreement among advisers stipulates that each paper will always make room for an all-city ad. The school which made the sale sends an insertion order and a copy of the ad to all papers, bills and advertiser for space in all papers, and divides the money collected 11 ways.

2. If a merchant does not want his ad in all 11 newspapers, he may choose any five or more. This serves the merchant who wishes to advertise in a particular area.

3. All-city advertising rates start at $1.00 per inch per paper for the first 100 inches. The rate for more than 100 inches is 90 cents. "Local or community" rates also are available for one-paper insertions. Costs here vary, but go as high as $2.00 per inch.

In 1964–65 Mr. Hazzard (his school keeps all records) reported that close to 40,000 column inches of all-city advertising brought in approximately $30,000. This was over and above income from "local or community" advertising. Each of the 11 schools received more than $2,700 as its share of this cooperative venture.

An annual report is issued. It shows how much all-city advertising each newspaper carried, the total number of inches in advertising carried per paper, whether this represents a gain or loss from the year before, and the average number of inches carried per issue for each school.

For 1961–62 the report indicates that through the all-city program one school increased its advertising linage 34 percent; this was the smallest increase of the 11 schools. The biggest gain was 48 percent.

What advantages are there to a program like this? The *Pacific Slope Student and Publisher* summed them up:

There is no competition among the schools for advertising, no cut throat advertising rates, no special financial inducement to firms to advertise in any certain school paper. There is only cooperation and harmony among all papers and much thankfulness that the all-city advertising plan is a highly successful venture.

CHAPTER XIII

Makeup: The Face of the News

Makeup is the overall appearance of a publication. Layout is often used as a synonym for makeup. It is the completed package, all copy, art, heads, and graphics. It is the display of printed communication. Some newspapers and magazines are attractive; others are dull, bland, ugly.

Good makeup is dictated by principles. Blending creativity with the proper concepts produces distinction. It is possible to be both functional and attractive. Readability is one of the primary measures of makeup.

Besides providing a package or pattern for copy, makeup also grades the news and the features. Important stories are prominently displayed. The major news story today will be at the top of page one. Some days there are several stories of great national or international interest. Each editor must decide which story warrants the top of the front page. And editors differ quite often in their analysis. Sometimes they deem two or more stories to be of equal importance and try to give them equal display. But tradition generally considers the story in the top right columns to be the most important. Just because most newspapers have for generations put the major story of the day in the top right corner does not make it a requirement. Too many editors have considered this custom to be a rule. It is not. It is just as legitimate to put the major news story at the top left of the page. Besides placement, headline size also indicates the significance or interest of a story.

The average size—15" x 22"—eight-column newspaper format is difficult to read, compared to newspapers with fewer columns. Eight-column newspapers, whether separated by column rules or white alleys, are congested. Thin lines between columns do not allow enough room between them. Using white space to separate the eight-column arrangement is a slight improvement, but some journalists consider that the print is still too crowded. There is not enough air between the columns to allow them to breathe. They smother one another and the reader. The eyes have to thread out stories surrounded by others. Critics of eight-column papers have other valid points.

240

How Many Columns?

Eight-column makeup is considered traditional by those still using it. But authorities have learned that newspapers of fewer columns are much more readable. There is a direct relationship between line length and readability. Some editors, however, refuse to change from eight, at least for the present. They maintain that a newspaper isn't worthy of the title unless it has eight columns.

Historically, newspapers have chosen columns from one to ten, occasionally more. The first Colonial newspapers had two columns. Then three developed. But the first papers were of small dimensions. As the page size became larger, the number of columns increased. Four-, five-, six-, seven-, and eight-column newspapers appeared. During the early 1800's a few experimented with pages almost a yard wide and almost four feet long.

The first newspapers were not overly concerned with appearance. Very few towns had competitive newspapers in the 1700's. Competition inspired publications to be functional and attractive. Now, the aim is to be functional and attractive. Many newspapers—at least the more progressive ones in accord with the new knowledge on makeup—have converted to five, six, or seven columns. The most popular seems to be the six-column format. The streamlined format was inspired primarily by *The Christian Science Monitor,* which adopted five columns in 1965. The *Monitor* is one of the world's great newspapers. Since its founding in 1908, it has consistently been on every "Top Ten Newspapers" list. When it made the change, other newspapers noticed. Earlier, *The Wall Street Journal* had reduced its columns to six, but the general press largely ignored it, primarily because it is a specialized newspaper. The two dailies of Louisville, Kentucky—the *Courier-Journal* and the *Times*—were among the next notables to convert to this new, open, and airy makeup. They went to six columns. Scores of metropolitan newspapers now have five or six columns, and there are several modified versions of these formats. Any standard-size eight-column newspaper may improve its appearance and add to its ease of reading by converting to fewer columns. Some weeklies are impressive looking also. Many progressive publishers and editors in very conservative rural areas have changed to modern makeup.

Not all the five- and six-column newspapers have those formats on every page. Many have had to stay with the traditional eight columns on all pages that carry advertising. Advertising is still largely sold by the traditional measure of eight columns. Because it would not be possible to merge a less-than-eight-column format with ads designed for use in eight-column newspapers, many modernized papers have converted

This page one of The Nashville Tennessean *is quartered nicely. The boxed story at top uses columns one through five, the story set in two columns within them for good white space. A sidebar story is set inside the box. Note the feature photo in the lower right corner, boxed with heavier rules. The boxed story below the fold is displayed well. All elements are harmonious for effective horizontal makeup.*

Although The Tennessean *uses an eight-column format, it is rather open and airy, with white alleys instead of column rules between columns. Pictures are used well. This page devoted almost its entire lower half to four photos marking the beginning of spring. The five-column photo and the three-column story heading the page resulted in a row of tombstones. However, the markers are handled well. Two-column stories separate the single-column ones, adding the needed contrast.*

The Elmhurst Advance

Vol. 31—No. 31　　　Elmhurst High School, Fort Wayne, Indiana　Friday, May 21, 1971　　　Price Ten Cents

Program stays same

By Bob Redding

Districts alter varsity tryouts

Bulletin

Varsity cheerleaders for the 1971-72 school year are juniors Beth Hoag, Gwen Ranson, sophomores Sarah Campbell, Debbie Lichtsinn and South Side sophomore Gwen Burns. They were selected at Wednesday's tryouts in the gym.

By Linda Wight

Redistricting plans for next year caused several changes in Elmhurst's traditional varsity cheerleading tryout procedures. Problems arose recently concerning transportation, available scheduling, calendar conflicts and selecting judges since all five public high schools were involved.

Mrs. Mary Fast

Purdue director to address seniors at annual commencement exercises

Educators to sponsor workshops

Mr. Charles A. Henry

Adds peer influence

Teen Jury tries young violators

Spring Concert adds new production ideas

Just one more

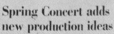

The Elmhurst Advance *of Elmhurst High School, Fort Wayne, Indiana, is sometimes a tabloid, but this is from one of its regular-size issues. The rectangles in each corner break up the six columns effectively.*

The Elmhurst Advance

Vol. 31—No. 4   Elmhurst High School, Fort Wayne, Indiana 46809, October 2, 1970   Price Ten Cents

Print change proclaims paper week

Cadent step

Keeping Marching Band members in step is part of the job junior Bob Taylor performs as this year's drum major. Bob organizes the band and helps add spirit as an example for the rest of the peppy football halftimes.

Grades, financial need, good character formulate requirements for scholarship

Students score high

Seniors receive Commendation

In Brief

* Afro-American Club
* Teacher smorgasboard
* High school days at college
* Booster Club uniforms

Outing replaces meeting

Hi-Y, Y-Teens plan picnic

Junior acquires position as drum major for band

DE, ICT aid laborers

Publications initiates new Governing Board

Cool, calm, collected?

Another regular-size Elmhurst Advance. In this case the six columns are tight with stories, but their arrangement and the art are effective. Some critics might say that more white space would have increased the quality.

The Courier-Journal, *Louisville, Ky., is one of the world's great newspapers, one of the most attractive six-column formats. Here, the page is dominated by the large picture. Every day the paper offers an excellent lesson in effective makeup.*

The Courier-Journal

VOL. 234, NO. 23 ······ LOUISVILLE, TUESDAY MORNING, JANUARY 25, 1972 48 PAGES 10 CENTS

$246.3 billion asked for fiscal 1973

The budget: A deficit to fuel the economy

By HOBART ROWEN

Highlights of the new federal budget

- As a warning to Soviets on arms control, the President asked Congress to approve $83.4 billion for defense.
- Nearly 40 per cent of the budget—even more than is requested for defense—will be spent on "income security" programs.
- The budget request for the Environmental Protection Agency is almost at the same level as last year.
- The FDA has been alloted $79 million more than last year to increase its inspection of food and drugs.
- One penny of every federal dime is earmarked for health in the President's budget.
- Major increases are sought in funds to catch narcotics violaters and help drug users.

Stories about the budget, Pages A 4, 5, 6.

Legislators oppose citizen panel probe of school systems

By RICHARD WILSON

Elsewhere...

Court adjusts operations

Judge Tucker arrested; starts six-month term

By JOHN FINLEY

I-64 section drops in Bath County

FTC seeks to break up cereal firms

By JOHN D. MORRIS

Cool move

Smaller Jefferson jail will suffice, its planner says

By JOHN FILSTRUP

Inserting some details in a sidebar to the lead story in the four center columns lends contrast and extra white space to break up the gray in this Courier-Journal *page one.*

only certain pages. These usually include the front, back, sports, editorial, inside front section, and the society pages. Newspapers that have converted all pages have had to make special arrangements for their advertising departments. Once advertising is able to create a flexibility that will accommodate the less-than-eight-column newspapers, the trend toward modernization will become dominant.

Regardless of the number of columns, makeup editors use the same tools and techniques. Basically, they have to paint with three colors. Copy is gray. Heads and photos are black, and there is white space. Other equipment includes lines, boxes, stars, arrows, and other graphic devices.

When one looks at a page, his eye path goes to the top left. Reading runs from left to right, starting at the top of the page. The termination point or destination area is the lower right corner of a page, where the page ends. When one starts to read a page, he pursues it line by line until he runs out at the last word on the last line at the bottom right of the page. This slash from left to right takes care of two corners. Something must be put in the other two corners of a newspaper page because they are not like book pages. A book page is just that. A newspaper page generally has more than one story on it. Each story is bidding for attention. Each is in competition with the others to be noticed and, hopefully, read.

Using many one-column heads in an eight-column newspaper results in vertical makeup. Readers must raise and lower their chins to course up and down the narrow bands of copy. Horizontal makeup is more desirable. Pages must be stripped into horizontal slices. Traditionally, as has been noted, the major story of the day goes in the upper right. One reason for putting it there is that it is a weak corner, as is the lower left. The aim of horizontal makeup is to produce highly readable and handsome rectangles. The four corners must have impact, and the areas between must be shaped into eye-attracting sections. Framing may be done with white space, which may also be used for contrast. White space used properly is cleansing. It washes the page, in a sense. But every element of makeup must be used in exacting proportions. Proportion is much of makeup. It is one of the variables.

Devices such as stars, asterisks, and lines must be used with great caution if at all. On rare occasions they may be permissible. Usually, they are gaudy, detracting, inky ornamentations. They hamper readability.

Setting a photo—even a mug shot—into a column of type adds appeal. Photographs and other artwork should be large enough to be emphatic. Not only has picture use increased tremendously during the past few years, but also much larger photos are being run. Large pictures distributed into five- or six-column formats with the proper amount of white space have great impact in makeup.

The Associated Press recommends using two-column pictures in a three-column slot, three-column pictures in four-column holes, and so on, for emphasis. This framing of white space may be very effective in some makeup patterns. White space may be used well with cutlines. Cutlines need not be flush left and flush right with the pictures. A one-and-one-half-column picture can use a one-column cutline. A two-column cutline may be put on a two-and-one-half picture, and so on.

Photographs dominate the makeup of almost all less-than-eight-column newspapers. They commonly run photos that cover the width of a page. Pictures in these sleek formats usually consume 25 to 50 percent of the front page, and sometimes of two or three other pages. It is highly desirable to have at least one picture on every page. Good photographers keep their newspapers supplied with a selection daily. A picture should never be used just because it is available. No picture at all is better than a weak one. A picture at the top of each page helps the makeup tremendously. The art prevents having to line up heads side by side like grave markers, which is called tombstoning. This is always deplorable; it is ugly makeup. Tombstoning can almost always be avoided. Makeup is flexible. Editors must never forget that pages are molded, not sawed or hacked. And the severity of the crime when it is seemingly unavoidable can invariably be lessened with a little more time applied to the situation.

Some authorities on typography—the total philosophy of makeup —also deplore the reverse device. Reversing is putting white type on a black background. Some surveys indicate that this reduces visibility by 11 percent. Many who deem this a bad device often have a tendency to avoid it altogether. They have had unpleasant experiences with it, or they have seen too many abuses of it. Reversing can be attractive and have impact when used properly. A few times a year certainly would not be too much. It should be considered as a tool in makeup.

One of the most hideous ornamentations is the flowery, curlicued, and sometimes almost unreadable type used for nameplates. Some newspapers are still using the same flag designed when they were founded. These overly inked, overly decorated monstrosities clash with the rest of the newspaper. Every newspaper using one should adopt a cleaner, more readable design, one that will complement its appearance.

A few commercial and other newspapers seem to have only half their attention on makeup, concentrating only on how the front page looks above the fold. This is doing only half a job, or less. The paper must be unfolded to turn each page. Some newspapers are so dull and gray that one almost needs a flashlight to read them below the fold. The page must be viewed as one unit, not two.

The commercial tabloid front page has traditionally followed poster makeup. In its pure form it usually consists of a large one- or two-line

The Courier-Journal

VOL. 234, NO. 59   LOUISVILLE, MONDAY MORNING, FEBRUARY 28, 1972   42 PAGES   10 CENTS

Communique hints Taiwan concessions

U.S., China plan trade, diplomatic ties

Hundreds missing in wake of flood in West Virginia

Survivors numbed

Lake spills death, chaos after unheeded warning

Preview of spring

WRECKED BUILDINGS and other debris are heaped high at a railroad bridge over Buffalo Creek in Latrobe, W. Va., the tourist town

Elsewhere...

Irish march peaceful

Lebanon fighting continues

On inside pages

Growers fear threat to leaf

Paper company buying burley stalks

For some, they're hell on wheels

Buyer complaints rise as mobile-home sales increase

Focus On
Mobile Homes

This Courier-Journal *was issued on the same day as the* Nashville Tennessean *on the following page. Both used the photo from the same catastrophe story. Both papers chose the story of the United States and China for their leads, the flood story taking second place in news valuation.*

The Nashville Tennessean *chose to run the picture of the flood damage—a catastrophe of great news magnitude—at the top of its page one. The three-column picture is boxed for effective contrast. The page is quartered well.*

The boxed story, bottom right, is a highlight of this inside front page from The Nashville Tennessean. *The head set in two open columns results in pleasant impact. The two-column story set in three columns at the top right is the second element making this an outstanding inside page.*

The National Observer *often uses the work of a talented artist to illustrate certain page one stories. The art merges well with its makeup.*

Although **The National Observer** *uses a six-column format for most of its pages, it usually runs five columns on page one. It uses subheads to break up the grayness of the long stories used on page one. The picture of the man in stride, Vice President Spiro T. Agnew, gives the page impact. At the bottom, a few inches of the page are devoted to small photos and blurbs about the contents of the inside pages.*

Constitution amendment proposes student-faculty council

If the proposed student-faculty committee is OK'd by student council, it will operate under the present constitution, heavily amended, Student Body President Rick Frey reported.

Wary of the hassles student councils of past years have encountered in ratifying a new constitution, Rick, along with Senior Representatives Steve Russo and Bob Fortuno, who drew up plans for the council, felt it would be wiser to amend the present constitution bit by bit.

The most vital amendment would be the establishing of the Council for United Student Action (Council USA), a 14-member committee.

Council USA would be made up of a student chairman and two student secretaries, all in a non-voting capacity.

Of the 11 voting members, eight would be students (two from each class), two would be faculty members, and one, a representative of the administration.

Acting as mediator between students and the committee would be the four class councils, comprised of the homeroom representatives.

Size offers advantage

Steve explained at the March 3 student council meeting that one advantage Council USA would have over student council is its size.

The largest group to meet at any one time would be the 14-member student-faculty committee as opposed to the 40-member student council which now meets.

A smaller group would mean better organized meetings and a freer flow of discussion, Steve explained.

One of the major aims of the Council for United Student Action would be to give the students more power by giving them a direct say in the decisions which affect them.

At the March 3 council meeting Student Body Treasurer Ron Cole pointed out that, in order to fulfill that aim, Council USA would have to have the power for decision-making in student matters.

Power not provided

Despite this, nowhere in the proposed amendments is this power delegated to the council.

Another amendment that will be voted on will be the addition of several written bylaws which include everything not judged important enough to be included in the articles.

Despite the proposed heavy amending, several sections, among them representative election procedures, qualifications to run for office, duties of the representative, and recall procedure,

See editorial page 4

among other sections will remain unchanged.

At last Wednesday's meeting, council began the process of preparing the amendments for presentation to the student body.

If the students approve, the amending of the existing constitution will begin, one section at a time.

THE CRUSADER

Vol. XXI No. 11   Salpointe High School, Tucson, Arizona 85719   Friday, March 12, 1971

Short 'Pointes

Drive rescheduled

Salpointe's annual chocolate drive has been rescheduled to begin on March 25. The individual student quota is 24 bars or half a case.

All American

"The Crusader" recently received an All American rating and four marks of distinction from the National Scholastic Press Association. It also received an "A" rating from the National Newspaper Service.

Walk to be held

The second annual Walk for Hunger will be Saturday, April 3. The walk will fund Los Amigos de las Americas and a local project which will aid the needy of Tucson.

Senior retreat

Seniors will have the opportunity to attend the yearly retreat, held on March 29 at Villa Carondelete. It will last from 10 a.m. to 8 p.m. All seniors will be excused from school on that day.

Committee to present conclusions

By Tom Arnold
Crusader Co-Editor

Final recommendations of the dress code committee were to be presented to Principal Fr. Vernon Mailley during the latter part of this week.

The committee voted on the recommendations at its fifth and final meeting Tuesday.

Conclusions of the committee were not made public by Co-Chairmen Mrs. Ann Goedeker and Junior Bill Thomasmeyer. The results were to be presented to Fr. Vernon in a sealed envelope.

Fr. Vernon's decision is expected to be announced sometime next week.

The committee's results were originally scheduled to be finished last week, but the two-week time limit had to be extended because only one student attended the fourth meeting.

There was a rule passed at the first meeting that only one student and one non-student could be absent from each meeting.

Committee members used dress codes from other schools plus parent, faculty, and student opinion polls taken by "The Crusader," along with information from last year's moratorium to help them make their recommendations.

School plans tuition hike for 1971 - '72

Despite the money raised during the 1970 magazine drive, a tuition increase of approximately 5 per cent is being tentatively planned for next year, according to Fr. David Engle, school treasurer.

The exact amount of the increase will not be known until next year's budget is approved at the end of this month.

"Some increase is needed because of the inflationary economic period we are now in," commented Fr. David.

The amount of tuition increase also depends on how much the parishes in the diocese contribute to Salpointe this coming school year.

Key Club clean-up

KEY CLUB MEMBERS Tony Olfer, Don Smith, and Bob Gaston pick up litter in Sabino Canyon during the club's service project last Saturday. The Key club also painted the park's garbage cans. King Photo

Councilman Kennedy reports on law

Opposition fails to get anti-loitering law repealed

By Gary Kimble
Crusader Co-Editor

Although a number of individuals and several citizen-oriented groups have questioned the constitutionality of the anti-loitering law adopted several weeks ago by city council, opposition has not been strong enough to get the law repealed.

"The Crusader" recently interviewed Councilman Richard Kennedy, who introduced the law to council.

"In passing the ordinance, the city council felt that it was entirely within the United States constitution," Mr. Kennedy said.

"The law is patterned after similar laws in New Jersey

See editorial page 4

which have withstood the test of constitutionality," he continued.

It is generally believed that the anti-loitering ordinance was a spur-of-the-moment law passed as a direct result of the riots on the University of Arizona campus. Not so.

"The ordinance was asked for at an October 26 city council meeting. It was thoroughly researched by City Attorney Lewis Murphy to make sure it was entirely within the constitution before being presented," Mr. Kennedy said.

Legality questioned

Why, then, have informed individuals and organizations questioned the ordinance's constitutionality?

"They seem to feel it infringes on an individual's personal freedoms," Mr. Kennedy answered.

The February 24 issue of "The Crusader," reported that the Arizona Civil Liberties Union (ACLU) is one group which feels this way. The report said that ACLU was waiting for a case to come up in court which would prove the law to be unconstitutional.

To this date, however, only one person has been arrested for loitering and the police department reported that he pleaded guilty to the charge.

This raises still another

question. Why has a law which has so aroused public opinion been exercised only once since its adoption?

Other intention

Mr. Kennedy explained that the anti-loitering ordinance was not actually proposed to stop people from standing on a street corner.

Its real intention is to break up gangs and dispel crowds which might be the spark of a riot.

In other words, had the law been in effect during the January riots at the U of A, it would probably have been strictly enforced.

It will be used primarily when crowd control is necessary to maintain peace, Mr. Kennedy said.

Speakers' corner delay blamed on lack of student participation

After undergoing countless modifications, the student body failed to respond favorably to speakers' corner. Consequently, it has been temporarily discontinued.

A Monday 20-minute study period at the end of the day was set aside by council as the time for this corner. Students wishing to speak were to contact an executive board member prior to this time.

Not one student asked to speak at the initial speakers' corner held February 22.

On the following Monday, March 1, the speakers' corner was cancelled because students showed no interest in it.

"No one asked any member of the executive board if they could speak," Student Body President Rick Frey said.

"If students have nothing to say, we're not going to waste our time," he added.

He explained that should any student show interest and ask to speak, the corner would be temporarily reinstated.

The tabloid Crusader *of Salpointe High School, Tucson, Ariz., often floats its flag. This page one is typical of its quality makeup. The "Short 'Pointes" column is a standard feature; setting the head inside a gray strip adds effective contrast to the black and white.*

headline and a photo covering the rest of the page. One of the minor liabilities of the tabloid is that many people still consider it synonymous with sensationalism because of its somewhat lurid past. But this is ridiculous. Being the same size of some newspapers that were once largely sensational does not taint the present. Some eight-column newspapers have been just as sensational, if not more so. Tabs may have a few other disadvantages compared to the bigger newspaper page. But these are technical and also rather moot.

The assets of the tab stem from its size. The paper is easier to read because of the ease of handling. It is easier to create sections that may easily be pulled out. A tab is really a sort of loose-leaf magazine. The tab is usually thicker than its larger counterpart. Perhaps this bulk subliminally suggests that the reader is getting more for his money. Ads can be so arranged as to have more pages free of them if desired. High-school, college, and other newspapers find the tab ideal.

Most tabs have five columns, but some commercial and institutional ones have gone to four columns, picking up more white space and setting the columns wider. This gives them much of the flexibility of the larger streamlined papers. The horizontal makeup of larger-page papers is often called "magazine makeup." Since the tab is almost magazine size, it is easier for it to assume this look. Not many school or other noncommercial tabs use poster makeup for page one. Space is at a premium, and they can't afford to use one page for just a head and a photo. Thus most tabs are merely smaller versions of the regular size in all respects.

Although the makeup of every page is important, more stress is given to page one. It is the face of the paper. People see it first. The first item to consider is the nameplate. Does it always go at the top of the page, or does it float? Floating the flag is the term used to define the nameplate's being dropped to the upper third of the page. Some papers keep the flag in this area all the time. Some papers move it around every issue, sometimes putting it at the top, or floated to the left, or floated to the right. Naturally, a floating flag has to be smaller than one that courses almost all the way across the page.

The first step after determining the position of the flag is to decide if the day's lead story is going to be put at the upper left or the upper right. As noted earlier, traditionally it is the latter. But it may be placed just as effectively in the left corner with a photo or other art occupying the right. But since this is by habit a strong focal point, the photo must be of high interest. Makeup is not inspired by any financial competition from other local papers. Over 90 percent of the more than 60,000,000 newspapers sold today were by subscription. Street sales exist only in major cities. Even then competition is almost negligible. Most readers buy the same paper every day.

Each day's news, features, and photos dictate makeup. One does not adopt a pattern and try to cram the contents inside. This is one of the variables of makeup. There will be a basic repertoire of makeup guidelines. But there will be variations in each presentation. Not all stories are the same length or type. To use only one method of display would also be monotonous.

Five- and six-column regular-size papers obviously cannot use as many stories on page one as the eights. The former average six to eight stories, the latter usually have ten to twelve. One factor in not using a banner or streamer head in every edition is that it allows the editor to display other stories of equal or almost equal news value above the fold. This means little to some editors, but more to others. It is a matter of individual taste.

In order to ensure there will be no gray blobs of copy in makeup, some editors use money as a measure. They take a dollar bill and lay it horizontally at one end of a focal point—a bold area, such as a head, photo, box—and it must touch another contrast area. Some makeup editors have a piece of wood or cardboard cut to the size of paper currency to use as a gauge. This is useful for tabloids also. Some makeup editors insist that the same measurement be applied vertically. This limits two-column stories to the length of a dollar bill and guards against vertical bands of gray. The gauge should be applied in both directions.

Classes of Makeup

As noted, makeup consists of two general types, vertical and horizontal. Some shortcomings of vertical makeup have been cited. It is top-heavy, relying on one heavy headling or several one-column heads at the top. Heads in vertical makeup are supposed to be progressively smaller from the top down. This makes the page grayer as it courses to the bottom. Fortunately, pure vertical makeup is almost extinct.

Balance—formal and informal—contrast and balance, brace, and broken are the four basic types of vertical makeup. Often it is difficult to classify some pages. It is possible to include more than one type of makeup on a page. Makeup types often overlap. With formal balance, copy, art, photos, and heads are arranged in a precise geometrical pattern. Informal balance deviates from the formal in that it does not balance equal weights.

Contrast and balance is a modification of balance. One side of a page is contrasted with the other. Attention is called to the page since there is often a picture in the bottom left corner and in the upper right corner, or vice versa.

Brace makeup focuses the major emphasis of a page to the left or the right. The brace can go in either direction. This gives a definite concentration. If the rest of the page is not handled adequately, the result is too much black in one area and too much gray in others.

Township High school

Vol. 62, No. 11
March 9, 1972

the Lion

La Grange & Western Springs, Ill. 60525

Exclusive —

'Assistance key to murderers' arrest'

by Judy Piper
Gary Posselt
Terry Schmitt

Authorities say they know who murdered Alan Fredian, '74 but are not ready to make arrests.

Two Cook county state's attorney's investigators told Lion reporters last week they are interested mainly in four south campus students. Two of these are believed to know who killed Alan and two allegedly witnessed or committed the act.

ALAN'S BODY was discovered Oct. 17 in the 'hole,' a wooded area opposite south campus that since has been cleared. He had been hit with a piece of concrete and, although he would have died from the wounds, he was asphyxiated when buried alive.

The investigators, who wish to remain unidentified, are sure at least four boys know what happened.

"Of the four youths who have the necessary information, we feel that at least two committed the act," said one of the investigators. "The others had to have prior knowledge of what might happen, because they were busy outside Fredian's house that night.

"ONE WAS SO concerned that he made four or five calls because he was 'super-scared'

about what might happen to Alan. He was mad at the person who was going to the 'hole' with Alan to allegedly get dynamite."

The investigators said "dynamite" could refer to explosives or a high grade of marijuana; but laboratory reports indicate that Alan was not on drugs.

THE LIVES OF students who have knowledge of the case, especially those who know who committed the murder, are in danger, according to investigators.

"Whoever killed Alan Fredian knows that somebody knows he did it," said one. "Sooner or later the killer is going to think. 'He poses a threat to me. He can put me in a penitentiary. I've got to get rid of him.'"

THE INVESTIGATORS have much physical and circumstantial evidence. They say they can prove who dug the grave. The investigators said they know where the shovel is that was used to dig it. They can link the suspect to a burned LT swim team T-shirt found in Waiola park. They can also link the victim to the same burned clothing and the suspect to the victim.

The investigators said there are students who know something of the murder but have remained silent. "We have lacked cooperation from students and parents," said one.

"THE MINUTE THE spotlight focuses on a student as a target suspect, his parents obtain an attorney for him. This cuts off communication because the attorney has advised the students to say nothing.

"Some of the kids we felt might have had knowledge of the case have been cleared through a voluntary polygraph (lie detector) test with parental permission. Others have refused.

"THE PARENTS OF the boys who have taken the polygraph test have cooperated fully. They believe in their children and believe their children are not involved in any way.

"A few parents are afraid of getting involved and feel that the police will dig up information without their kids testifying."

The investigators feel that someone had to see something related to the murder.

"AT THAT TIME of the evening with that many people around that area, with the dance going and the party at a sophomore's house, somebody must have seen something," said one.

"We've got a list of 15-20 kids who were going back and forth through the 'hole' that night. Maybe whoever they saw they know and they don't make any connection.

"THE AREA ISN'T that big and there are only a few paths through it. Alan was buried on one of the primary paths."

Although the police are sure they know who murdered Alan, they do not know the motive. They have constructed possibilities from circumstantial evidence.

Of these, it is most likely that Alan was killed by students he knew were trafficking in "dynamite."

"When Alan Fredian went into the 'hole,' he must have considered those with him friends," said one investigator. "I don't think he'd go there with a stranger or somebody he didn't like."

The case has taken so long to solve because of the lack of cooperation from the students, parents and community, said the investigators. "A case that could have been and should have been cleared up in a week is now five months old."

This front page from The Lion *of LaGrange & Western Springs High School, Illinois, is dominated by the reversed head, white type on black. The usual five columns of the tabloid were reduced to four for this page one exclusive on a crime story. The contrast of the white space in the first column contributes heavily to the effectiveness of the page.*

Capture 5th in state

Swimmers' outlook bright

Completing their best season, the Sealions roared to a fifth place finish in the state meet at New Trier East Feb. 25-26.

THE TEAM amassed 80 points, placing behind Hinsdale Central, Peoria Richwoods, New Trier East and Evanston.

The Lions sent ten swimmers to state, and only two, Chris Polzin and Greg Shannon, are seniors. Coach John Weber said he is extremely hopeful for next year.

"We can place higher in the state meet next year," he said. "We should be stronger in almost every event."

ONE EVENT in which the Sealions will not be as strong is breaststroke. Shannon broke the LT record for breaststroke at state with a time of 1:02.8, which makes him eligible for all-american honors.

Polzin, who along with Shannon was a state finalist last season, broke a varsity record as he placed sixth in the 100-yd. backstroke.

Other LT swimmers who will return next year placed high. Brad Vear '73 broke his own record in the 100-yd. butterfly, taking seventh place with a time of 55.0. Bill Johnston '73 took eighth place in the 200-yd. freestyle.

Mark Wintercorn '74 placed seventh in the 100-yd. backstroke, his time not far behind Polzin's. Larry O'Connor, one of two LT freshmen to qualify for the meet, finished twelfth in the 200-yd. individual medley.

BOTH LT relay teams did well. The medley relay team, with Bob Easter, Polzin, Shannon and Vear, took second place with a time of 1:40.4, qualifying for all-american and placing them on the all-state team.

The freestyle relay team, consisting of Easter, Johnston, Tom McGarrity '73 and Polzin, wound up tenth and merited all-american honors.

Diver Jim Lyon '73 finished fifth, one-quarter point behind Mark Antinoff of Downers Grove South. After the preliminary dives Lyon was eighth, but diving coach Tom Johnson was confident he would move up.

"Jim and I knew he could improve his position in the finals," said Coach Johnson. "Most of the other finalists had to throw their good dives to make it to the finals, but Jim still had his left."

The entire LT team has many things left, and they will be out to prove that next year. If things continue on schedule, Hinsdale's current domination of the state meet may not last much longer.

Sophs show balance

Sophomore basketball coach Roger Johnson must have been a happy man.

He was standing in the locker room after his team's final game of the season Feb. 25, savoring his fourth conference championship in nine years of coaching LT sophs.

But this championship probably meant more than others, because it was a team effort. Last year as freshmen these players tied for first in conference, but they had Rex Blackwell, who is now a starter on the j-v team.

"I didn't expect to have him (Blackwell)," said Coach Johnson. "Not to take anything away from Rex, but we've got eight or nine guys who can do the job."

Coach Johnson has had many "guys who can do the job," and has never had a team that finished lower than third. He has had three second-place teams and two thirds to go along with four firsts. "We've always had good kids," he said.

There must be many "good kids" in LT's basketball program. LT killed R-B on all five levels in the final regular season games Feb. 25-26.

The j-v team stomped R-B 72-45. Jim Banks led LT with 19 points, while Jim Kolar had 18 and Blackwell added 15.

While Coach Johnson's sophs were winning 73-42 led by Ed Steinman's 19 points, both frosh teams stretched their conference records to 10-1 with easy wins over R-B.

The A team led 29-9 at halftime and coasted to a 48-25 decision, while Coach Harold Erickson's B team won 65-38. Starters on this year's B team were Scott Burson, John Larkin, Joe Miller, John Strnad and Curtis Topps.

Sports wrap-up

Trackmen cop 2nd in WSC

LT's varsity trackmen won seven out of the 13 events in the conference meet March 4 at Proviso West, but still finished second to Proviso.

LT's Dave Allen won the mile run in 4:24.4, his best time ever. Other winners for LT were Gary Bowbin, Jim McMath, Scott Racine (2) and both relay teams.

The varsity gymnasts will send John Arends, who quali-

fied in all-around, and Neil McDermott, in side horse, to state as a result of Saturday's sectional meet.

The gymnasts qualified seven men in the district meet at Proviso West Feb. 26. LT took second place with 85 points.

Three LT gymnasts, Arends, Larry Buck and Paul Lat, qualified in all-around. Arends also qualified in free exercise, side horse, rings and high bar, and

Buck in free exercise.

Other LT qualifiers were Tony Balbetti, high bar and rings, McDermott, side horse, Bruce Palese, parallel bars and Steve Johnson, trampoline.

Dave Battaglia, the only LT wrestler to go to the state meet at Normal Feb. 25-26, was beaten in his second match by Tom Arliss of Montini. In his first match Battaglia beat Sycamore's Kevin Mathey 3-2.

This inside page from The Lion *offers good contrast with its reverse head over a story set on a gray background. Setting the top of the page in three columns also helps to make this an effective display.*

League victors
Salpointe,
Tucson High
meet tonight
in rematch

THE CRUSADER
Divisional Special

A tabloid sports special edition of The Crusader. *The dominant photo was purposely screened very coarsely; this roughly textured photo* makes *the effectiveness of the page. A typical well-defined photo would have minimized the impact; this device enhances viewer appeal.*

Dropouts often find new freedom boring

by Wendy Myers

Don's parents bothered him about his poor grades and ditching. He had no job or money. He wanted to get away. "I blew everything out of proportion," Don said. "I blamed everybody but myself.

Mr. Carl Herren, counselor-at-large, and Mr. Clay Pheasant, a YMCA social worker, explained to him the drawbacks of dropping out.

Don was not going to come back after Christmas vacation his junior year. During vacation, however, he talked with his older brother and sister. They said the same things Mr. Herren had said, but they were easier to relate to, said Don. "What they said made sense." He came back after vacation.

Don plans to attend college and become a parole officer and court worker.

About 150 students (2.7 per cent of the student body) dropped out of LT last year. Mr. Thomas Hansen, director of pupil services, explained that this figure includes students who have decided to end their formal education.

"MANY STUDENTS have met with limited success in school," explained Mr. Carl Herren, counselor-at-large "Many cannot read well, many are not bright."

"Some students want to escape from unpleasant home situations, while some are just bored," said Mr. Hansen. "Some of our dropouts are so emotionally disturbed that confinement for six hours a day on a regular basis is more than they can cope with."

Mr. Herren explained that LT's major advantage is its excellent counseling staff. "There are many people who work with students to prevent them from dropping out," he said.

The counselors-at-large discuss with students problems they have with teachers, classes, home or anything that might keep them from doing their best in school.

MR. RICHARD Yena, prevocational counselor, and Mr.

Robert Neuneker, vocational counselor, help students with pre-vocational courses and help them find jobs.

When a counselor is alerted that a student is considering dropping out, he calls him for a conference. If they are able to pinpoint reasons for unhappiness, they can try to work out the problems.

Sometimes schedule changes are necessary. Social studies and humanities courses offer some students the long needed chance to say what they want and thus build up confidence.

FOR FRESHMEN and sophomores there are special English and social studies classes. Juniors and seniors may enter the cooperative vocational education program which provides preliminary job training for students not planning to attend college.

Counselors do what they can

to keep a student in school. But if he decides to leave, they help him adjust to his new environment.

Boys are informed of the armed service programs that enable them to receive the equivalent of a high school diploma. LT also provides a night refresher course for the General Educational Development test, which is equal to a high school diploma for the student who passes it.

"WE HAVE a deep concern for the kids who are dropping out," said Mr. Hansen. "When a student drops out we don't want him to feel that communication is cut."

Because he doesn't want communication to end, Mr. Hansen is sending a letter to students who have not completed their high school education. The letter informs them of possibilities to further their education.

School bored Gary. He ditched classes and was late for school, and as a result, flunked many courses. He was in a constant hassle with the dean.

Finally Gary decided to drop out. He left during the first semester of his junior year.

By working full time as a stock boy in a drug store, he could have worked his way up to store manager. But working was not what Gary thought it would be. "It was boring because all my friends were in school and I wasn't," he said. After six weeks Gary came back to LT.

Gary stayed in school because he got into a work-study program, he said. He is now president of the local and state distributive education clubs.

Now Gary wants to go to college to teach distributive education.

The first time Peter dropped out, he told his parents he had been suspended. He frequently got into trouble with his teachers because he could never keep track of his books. His courses seemed irrelevant and a waste of time, so he left in the middle of his junior year.

Peter began working, but found it as boring as school. He just stayed home and watched television.

The next year Peter came back to school but was suspended after two weeks and never returned.

Since, Peter has been kicked out of his house, and is now staying at a friend's house, watching television and doing dishes.

Peter has no plans for the future.

Peter is a dropout.

Boxing and setting the copy on a gray background can add much to effective makeup, as in this inside page from the tabloid Lion.

Isolated and dilapidated buildings occupy Pearce, Arizona

Unkempt graveyard

Forsaken storage shed

Romantic legends surround history of Arizona ghost towns

By Maureen King and Tony Offret
Crusader Staff Reporters

In the town of Total Wreck, Arizona, a man named Salsig got into an argument with another man who drew his gun and fired.

Salsig would have been killed except that he had a large pack of love letters in his vest pocket. The bullet lodged in the letters, saving his life. Later Salsig married the lady who had written the letters.

Whether fact or fiction, the vast variety of stories connected with Arizona ghost towns have prompted many people to visit them.

The ghost towns of today originated as mining camps. These were a backlash of the California Gold Rush.

Most of them boasted a post office, saloon, hotel (in many cases only a tent with cots), a general store, and a schoolhouse.

In a camp, the mining company, for whom the inhabitants worked, owned everything.

Life was simple. For amusement there were baseball games between camps. In some places where women were scarce, there were stag dances and drinking contests.

Vigilante groups

Common to most towns were vigilante groups, citizens who took the law into their own hands. This practice led to many lynchings; one of which took place in Tombstone.

In December of 1883, five armed men robbed Goldwater and Castaneda General Store in Bisbee and escaped leaving four people dead.

A posse was formed with the help of John Heath, a saloonkeeper. In his desperate attempt to lead the posse away from the obvious trail he brought suspicion on himself.

Saloonkeeper arrested

He was arrested, tried, and found guilty of being an accessory to the crime. He was sentenced to life imprisonment and taken to the jail in Tombstone.

The citizens of Bisbee and Tombstone were angered, feeling Heath deserved to die.

On February 22, 1884, a raging mob stormed the jail, dragged Heath to a telephone pole, and lynched him.

The other five members of the gang had been captured in the meantime, and their execution date set for March 8.

Invitations to the hanging were issued and some citizens built a tier of seats around the scaffold.

They intended to charge 50 cents admission. But a sympathetic group tore down the bleachers the night before the execution.

The hanging took place as scheduled, two weeks after Heath was lynched.

Such are the stories that make ghost towns places of intrigue. The towns are dead; the legends live on.

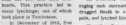

Deteriorated house in Mowry, Arizona   Abandoned mining machinery

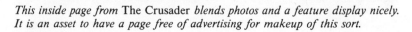

This inside page from The Crusader *blends photos and a feature display nicely. It is an asset to have a page free of advertising for makeup of this sort.*

TIGER Hi-Line

Vol. 22 No. 15   Cedar Falls (Iowa) High School   Friday, January 22, 1971

New school addition proposed by board

BY RAE RIEBE

The Board of Education has begun paving the way for a third school bond issue by proposing plans for additions to the high school.

Plans were suggested after school administrators and a citizens' committee spent several months studying the needs of the school. Proposed plans, calling for additional classrooms and a new gymnasium area, would cost approximately $870,000.

The first part of the proposal calls for a 20,000-square-foot instructional area to be built west of the west wing, possibly as a separate building. This addition would cost approximately $400,000.

A second part of the proposal suggests a 100 x 100 foot girls gymnasium to extend north of the existing gym. The bottom floor would house locker rooms and a 45 x 75 foot regulation size competitive swimming pool. Above would be the gymnasium. Cost of the addition would be about $400,000.

The two gymnasiums would be separated by folding bleachers. By folding back the bleachers, additional seating space would be gained for indoor athletic events.

Principal Norman Jespersen says the proposed plans would fit together well with the existing building. "What we are trying to do is to utilize the ground space we don't use and not have to give up any outdoor athletic activity area," he said.

Remaining money would be used to construct a corridor extending from the west door of the main building to the west wing and the new addition. "The existing corridor system is L-shaped," states Jespersen. "All traffic has to go and return the same way." A connecting corridor would achieve a circular traffic flow.

Subject areas to be housed in the new west addition would be the business, art, math and foreign languages. Plans are not definite at this time.

A number of departments would be expanded in the present structure. Industrial arts would expand into the present arts area. Journalism and yearbook classes would move to the existing business section.

Home economics, guidance library and English departments would expand, and some rooms in the present English section would be converted into an English resource center. Additional custodial space for the receiving of materials would also be provided.

The proposed plan would "give an opportunity for organizing additions in the present building while keeping the departments together," says Jespersen. The plan also puts departments that do the most library work near the library.

"Each year becomes more critical for us," says Jespersen. "We are housing 1,450 students in a school built for 1,200 to 1,350 students. This really puts a lot of pressure on coordinating and scheduling."

"We can see about 1,600 to 1,700 students that will be in high school in coming years. This is not considering city growth," adds Jespersen.

Two school bond issues, one in November 1969 and one in September 1970, failed to get the 60 per cent majority required for passage. This was the first time that school bond issues were ever defeated in Cedar Falls. The needs are the same now, but the proposed buildings have changed.

The suggested plan should appear as part of a new school bond issue this spring.

Jespersen has faith in the citizens of Cedar Falls. "I am hoping that the general public will realize the need and necessities of the school, and have the desire to keep the standard of education up in Cedar Falls" he says.

'Give me a T'

Junior Karen Miller, left, and senior Marsha Porter lead cheers during a recent Cedar Falls-Columbus basketball game. (Dan Johnson photo)

Night classes to begin for adults, students

Beginning this month and continuing through April, Hawkeye Institute of Technology will be sponsoring night classes in the Cedar Falls Community School district.

The night classes are mostly for adults. High school students who wish to enroll in a night course must have permission from their school principal.

Classes that are open are General Typing, Secretarial Workshop, Photography, Bookkeeping I, Great Books, Tailoring, Advanced Sewing, Ceramics, Beginning Sewing, Intermediate Sewing, "Keeper-Finders" (Antiques), Handling Your Dollars With Sense, Enrichment Sewing, Stocks, Bonds & Investments, Drapery Construction, Sewing for Your Children and Environmental Pollution—Crisis in the '70's.

To register for classes or to obtain further information, call Miss Blumhagen at 266-7940, Ext. 25, after 1 p.m.

Abuse of safety law can result in class expulsion

Refusing to wear safety glasses in industrial arts classes may result in expulsion from class, according to department head Bill Paup.

"Not all students know about the Iowa eye safety law, first passed in 1965, says Paup. "We have been telling them the consequences of not following the law and making them aware of the potential dangers to themselves," Paup adds.

The law requires that all students in industrial art shops or chemical laboratories wear quality protective eye devices at all times while participating in activities hazardous to the eyes or while in an area where such activities are being performed. These activities include servicing a vehicle, welding, sawing, grinding, cutting or working with hot molten metals and caustic or explosive materials and chemicals.

The law further states that it is the teacher's responsibility to see that the requirements are complied with. If any student does not wear the safety glasses, he may be temporarily suspended from class. If after suspension the student refuses to wear the safety glasses, he may be expelled from the course.

The effort to acquaint students with eye safety laws has been strengthened due to the "increasing number of court cases against schools and teachers because of eye accidents," says Paup.

"Over 155,000 eye accidents occur in schools each year. A large share of these could have been prevented. There has not been a serious eye injury in the Cedar Falls schools in the last six years. There have been near misses, where glasses definitely saved lives," Paup says.

Semester ends today

First semester ends today. Teachers must record grades by Wednesday. Report cards will be mailed to parents later.

Homerooms meeting

Homerooms will be held today so students can see their schedules card for the upcoming semester. Homeroom will begin after second period.

Prom May 1

Prom will be held May 1 at the UNI Commons Ballroom with the Inner Light playing. The group was booked through Crown Productions of Des Moines. The dance is semi-formal and will be held from 9-12 p.m.

Y-Teens to organize

All high school girls are invited to a Y-Teen discussion meeting Monday. The Y-Teens' first project will be to set up a style show for February. Sponsors from the Young Women's Christian Association (YWCA) will meet with interested girls at 3:15 p.m. in Room 172.

Extramurals planned

Recently the extramural basketball team was formed under the guidance of Phyllis Ver Ploeg, physical education teacher.

Members of the team are seniors Carol Cook, Sandy Fait, Jean Heisterkamp, Sue Mehaffy, Billie Dee Ryberd and Jennifer Shreve and juniors Marsha Furguson, Sue Kemp, Debra Ramsted and Ann Spinell and sophomores Janae Fuller and Cindy Hogeland.

This front page from the tabloid Tiger Hi-Line *at Cedar Falls (Iowa) High School utilizes its five columns superbly. The three stories make good rectangles. The middle story, set wider than two columns in the three columns, offers pleasing contrast. The effective photo concentrates on just two cheerleaders rather than the usual group shot. The boxed column of shorts has good white space and contrast.*

Vol. 23 No. 24   Cedar Falls (Iowa) High School   Friday, March 10, 1972

Simulating emergency situations
Students use new driving range

BY DEBBY WARD

Driver education students have begun driving on a new driving range located on a nine and a half acre tract at University and South Main streets, behind Nazareth Lutheran Church.

Cedar Falls Community Schools and UNI share the new range. "We are now using the range for a regular program of driver education," says Keith Young, CF driver education instructor.

On Mondays and Tuesdays, half the class drives at the driving range and the other half has car simulation in the classroom. The remainder of the week classes have regular driver education instruction.

The range was built with federal and state funds. UNI uses the range to train adult dri. er education students and future driver education teachers.

"The range is used to create emergency situations," Young says. "We create our own traffic with about 10-12 cars on the range at the same time." Students drive alone in each car.

A control box and portable

Motorized maneuver

Soloing on the new driving range, a student driver takes a corner. Students hear the instructor's directions on the car radios. Cedar Falls High School driver education students use the range, located near University and 27th streets, on Mondays and Tuesdays. (Mark McGraw photo)

microphone permit the instructor to communicate with students through car radios. "In the

future, we hope to have a small tower so the instructors can see everything more closely," Young said.

Young said the range is more realistic to use. On the range,

students properly learn how to deal with different types of intersections, one-way street situations, interstate and merging traffic patterns, angle and parallel parking, traffic lights and curves.

"The biggest thing students are able to learn is how to handle emergencies such as brake failure, accelerator jamming, skid recovery and basic maneuvers," Young said. "Maybe someday it could save their lives."

Students also learn how to brake, how to pass another car and what to do in case of a motor mishap.

"Future plans are to bring elementary children to the range to teach pedestrian safety and create pedestrian traffic for student drivers," Young said.

The driving range is blacktopped with concrete curbs.

Ranges are quite new in Iowa. Davenport, Sioux City and Waterloo also have ranges.

The Cedar Falls fire department, police and school transportation system might be using the range in the future, according to Young.

Teen center draws big crowds Sunday

BY KEVIN SCOBEE

Cedar Falls' new teen center, Freedom House, which had its grand opening Sunday, receiving a booming response, plans its next senior high school dance March 18.

"I'm very, very happy. A lot of people have come out and used the new center," said Recreation Department Director Harry Venik. "The kids put a great deal of time and labor into the building and have done a great job."

Dances will be held every Saturday, and two police officers will always be hired to monitor dances. "This is a must and sort of a safeguard for parents," says Venik.

Students must present their school ID cards to be admitted to dances. This requirement was made to prevent junior high students from getting into senior high dances and vice versa, Venik said.

The building may be rented out from 9 a.m.-noon to various groups other than teens, according to Venik. But its primary use is "for the kids," he said.

Facilities currently in the use at Freedom House are two pool tables and checker, domino and chess games. Items still expected are two ping pong tables, one bumper pool table, 12 colored lounge chairs, a fireplace screen, restroom doors and a number of

novelty games.

"Another thing we would like to get is a color television set," Venik said.

"I've heard nothing but compliments about the building, and the kids have told me that the dance last Saturday went a lot smoother than any dance ever held at the Utilities Building," he said.

Although the Recreation Department can only hire college students to supervise the center, teens may be hired for custodial work. Venik said this matter is still under consideration.

Spring and summer teen center schedules are being planned by various committees of teen board

members.

Teen board members from Cedar Falls High School include seniors Pam Lee, president, and Debbie Boarman, junior Tom Geessman and sophomores Doug Chandler, Nancy Davis, Denis Knupple, Robin Newill and Diane Porter.

Peet Junior High School representatives are Dave Sloan, vice president, and Todd Ellison, Debbie Munkres and Lori Trotter. Holmes Junior High School representatives are Claudia Corning, secretary, and Terry Chamness, Kathy Pope and Duane Visser.

Northern University High

School and St. Patrick's Elementary School have not selected teen board members.

Freedom House hours follow. Open for high school students during open lunch, 11 a.m.-1 p.m. weekdays, reopening 3 p.m. everyone 3 p.m.-9:30 p.m. Monday-Friday.

First and third Saturday of every month, open to everyone 1 p.m.-8 p.m. High school dance 9 p.m.-midnight.

Second and fourth Saturday of the month open to everyone 1 p.m.-6:30 p.m. Junior high school dances 7:30-10:30 p.m.

Sunday the center is open to everyone 1 p.m.-9:30 p.m.

'Dark at the Top of the Stairs'
High school to present serious play in April

Cast members for "Dark at the Top of the Stairs," to be presented April 21-22, have been announced by Merle Picht, director.

Sophomore Kathy King will be Cora Flood, junior Clark Rickard is Rubin Flood, sophomore Mark McGraw is Sonny Flood; sophomore Rosie Conrado is Reenie Flood; senior Tammy Parker is Flirt Conroy; junior Doug Jones is Morris Lacey; Teresa Keys is Lottie Lacey; senior Dave Hosteller is Sammy Goodenhaum, and junior Jeff Berg is Punky Givens.

Picht said that he chose the William Inge play because the students asked for a serious show.

"It gives them a real idea to sink their teeth into," Picht continued. "We haven't done a show by Inge before. He's got an exciting theme."

Charles Koch is technical director and Karen Carroll, who teaches at Holmes Junior High, has charge of costumes.

Crew chairmen are lights, junior Jon Hesse; sound, junior Kathie Wolff; costumes, sophomore Anne Hathaway; makeup, junior

Kevan Chamness; ticket sales, seniors Teri Bauer and Paige Shreve, properties, senior Kristi Brom, and house manager, senior Becky Duffy.

Senior Joni Gray is student director. "The stage manager will be announced at a later date," stated Picht.

"There won't be any afternoon sessions," Picht continued. "This is a serious play just to be presented Friday and Saturday nights. It isn't a comedy children's play as 'Sleeping Beauty' was.

According to Picht, the theme of the play is that "life's fear and insecurity can be dissipated by understanding, by tolerance, by compassion and by a bond of companionship that demands not conformity, but love.

"If this could be in reality, it would be a far better world," Picht said.

Activity and season tickets will be honored. "The show will run about an hour and a half," said Picht. "We haven't started rehearsals yet."

Curtain time is 8 p.m.

Actors audition

Ward Faust, junior, and sophomores Kathy King, Forrest Rindels and Carol Corning (from left) read parts for the upcoming play, "Dark at the Top of the Stairs." Cast members were chosen last week. (Greg Jensen photo)

This five-column page one of the tabloid from Cedar Falls (Iowa) High School is divided into three equal bands. Boxing the middle story gives the proper contrast.

Broken-column makeup breaks every column; no column runs unbroken from north to south. Some multicolumn heads or art cut across all columns. This forces dispersal of units. An extreme example of this type is called circus makeup. It avoids any semblance of a pattern.

Horizontal makeup explains itself. The sweep is west to east. It utilizes a lot of horizontal rectangles and pictures. Horizontal may accurately be called magazine or tabloid makeup. Focus makeup is more applicable to the horizontal than to the vertical. The layout editor views each page as quartered and places good-size pictures or heavy heads in each of the four quarters. A variation of this is to fill both quarters above the fold and put something that has much eye appeal in the center of the page below the fold.

Except for the variation and combinations, there are just four types of makeup:

1. Balance:
   a. Formal
   b. Informal
   c. Contrast and balance

2. Broken
3. Focus
4. Horizontal

These types may be used on any pages free of advertising. But on inside pages advertising governs makeup. Ads may be placed in the inner or outer columns, and they must be placed on the page first. Some experts say that no ad should be buried. Every ad must be allowed to breathe. It cannot be smothered with other ads. Stacking ads like crates is very bad. Competitive ads should never be placed side by side and should not appear on the same or facing page if possible.

Should copy touch all ads? The answers or alternatives are controversial. Almost all advertisers are aware that if their ads are near copy, they have a much higher potential of being read. Most newspapers try to have all ads adjoin copy. If an ad has enough pulling power, it will be seen regardless of its location. Some advertisers ask for a particular place on a certain page. And some newspapers have a policy prohibiting smaller than one-page ads from running the width of a page.

So that ads will not clamp down on copy, they should be put below the fold. Copy below the fold on inside pages has much less pulling power than that in the top half. Some authorities maintain that copy below the fold on inside pages has 50 percent less attention arrest. Ads tend to run larger than most stories, so ads below the fold have more prominent display than copy. It is not a matter of discriminating against ads. It is the most efficient and best order.

Ads may be placed in a half-triangle on inside pages. These are stair-stepped from the foot of a page. Technically, the half-pyramid should go to the right because the top left quarter of a page is the primary viewing area. Ads that reach too high when marching to the left could invade this prime space. Some newspapers form a complete pyramid by building half on the right side of one page and half on the left side of the facing page. And a smaller pyramid may be built on one page by constructing a triangle with various size ads. The triangle can also be reversed. Half goes to one side, half to the other, and the two do not touch. If only one column separates the pieces, this create a well. This deep, narrow hole has very little pulling power; any story placed in it is squeezed out of much attention.

One important aspect of makeup to remember is the lack of continuity of interest in daily newspapers of fifty pages and up. In most dailies, the reader starts with the most significant news and ends with the classified section. For this reason, some newspapers have a back page of some consequence. Some use the last page for all jump stories. Others use it for a picture page, a montage of the selection for the day. A few progressive papers use the final page as the editorial page. Every newspaper should consider utilizing its back page in one of these three ways. If jump stories are used and the page is not filled by them, the remainder of the space should be used for pictures or an interesting story. A newspaper should open with impact. It should close with some finesse.

Traditional big-city tabloids often use the last page for pictures. The center spread, the two pages in the middle—called a double truck in the jargon—generally is used for a two-page picture spread. However, some tabs sell these prime pages for advertising.

Chapter XIV

Staff Organization for the High-School Paper

Adviser
1. Oversees entire production.
2. Responsible to principal.

Editorial Staff
Editor-in-Chief
1. Oversees staff so that it works as a group.
2. Calls meetings.
3. Plans editorial page.
4. Supervises editorial writers and columnists.
5. May write editorials.
6. Responsible to adviser and principal.
Managing Editor
1. Supervises the work of the news and feature editors.
2. Responsible for makeup on first page.
3. Sees that copy gets to printer, artwork and photographs to engraver.
News Editor
1. Has direct supervision of the work of reporters, seeing to it that entire school is covered.
2. Prepares assignment sheet for reporters.
3. Responsible to Managing Editor.
Club Editor
1. Supervises coverage of club activities.
2. Responsible to News Editor.
Feature Editor
1. Assigns feature articles.
2. Sees that feature articles are in on time.
3. Makes sure that feature stories are covered.
4. Responsible for makeup of feature page.
5. Responsible to Managing Editor.
Sports Editor
1. Has overall responsibility for sports coverage.
2. Makes assignments.

3. Responsible for makeup of sports page.
4. Responsible to Editor-in-Chief.

Exchange Editor

1. Responsible for sending out and receiving exchanges.
2. Clips items of interest from exchange papers and reprints or rewrites them, giving credit to the publication from which they came.
3. Searches for new ideas and points them out to the respective editors.

Editorial Writers

1. Write editorials.
2. Responsible to Editor-in-Chief or editorial board.

Feature Writers

1. Cover features assigned.
2. Responsible to Feature Editor.

Sports Writers

1. Cover sports assigned.
2. Responsible to Sports Editor.

Reporters

1. Cover assignments.
2. Responsible to News Editor.

Columnists

1. Allowed a certain amount of freedom of style and content in assigned columns.
2. Responsible to Editor-in-Chief.

Copy Chief

1. Oversees copyreaders.
2. Responsible for seeing that the copy is read and corrected.
3. Sees that all factual, grammatical, writing, and spelling mistakes are corrected, rewriting where necessary.
4. Writes and checks headlines for accuracy and count.
5. Sees that headlines are properly marked for printer.
6. Responsible for seeing that all copy is properly prepared for printer.
7. Responsible to Managing Editor.

Copyreaders

1. Check copy for incorrect facts, mistakes in mechanics, faulty composition, and poor leads.
2. Write and mark heads.
3. Responsible to Copy Chief.

Proofreaders

1. Check galleys for printer's errors.
2. Responsible to Copy Chief.

Picture Editor

   1. Supervises photographs and artwork.
   2. Responsible to Picture Editor.
Photographer
   1. Takes pictures assigned.
   2. Responsible to Picture Editor.
Cartoonist
   1. Responsible for editorial cartoon and/or cartoon strip; other artwork.
   2. Responsible to Picture Editor.
Librarian
   1. Responsible for filing of clippings and cuts.
   2. Responsible to Editor-in-Chief.

Business Department
Business Manager
   1. Supervises work of advertising and circulation managers.
   2. Keeps records of financial transactions.
   3. Bills advertisers.
   4. Responsible to adviser.
Advertising Manager
   1. Directs the soliciting and advertising production staffs.
   2. Sees that ads are properly marked and sent to the printer.
   3. Proofreads the ad galleys.
   4. Responsible for makeup of ads on pages.
   5. Responsible to Business Manager.
Circulation Manager
   1. Plans a circulation campaign for the paper.
   2. Responsible for delivery of the papers.
   3. Keeps a written record of the number of subscribers and the amount collected.
   4. Responsible to Business Manager.
Ad Solicitors
   1. Obtain ads.
   2. See that contracts are properly filled in.
   3. Responsible to Advertising Manager.
Advertising Production Staff
   1. Responsible for ad makeup.
   2. Responsible to Advertising Manager.

Note: In organizing the staff, advisers may prefer page editors who are responsible for the work of the page assigned. Page editors are responsible to the News Editor or the Managing Editor. A Makeup Editor may be assigned the responsibility of making up all pages.

The following chart, prepared by the *San Francisco Chronicle*, illustrates the chain of command on a modern newspaper.

WORKING

EDITOR
responsible fo
fecting both t
conduct

EXECU
responsible to
news operat

MANAGING EDITOR
the liaison between the executive editor and all news departments

CITY EDITOR
coordinates the work of all general
assignment reporters

NEWS EDITOR
oversees editing and makeup of all
news pages

REPORTERS
report and write local news

COPY EDITORS
responsible for the editing and writing
of headlines for all news stories

REWRITE MEN
turn facts (usually phoned in) into
finished news stories

WIRE EDITORS
responsible for editing all news which
comes over the news service teletypes

PHOTOGRAPHERS
assigned to cover spot news, society,
sports and features pictorially

COPY BOYS
low men on the journalistic totem pole
—serving their news apprenticeships

COLUMNISTS
specialized writers who cover special
fields, writing under their own by-lines

PRESS

PUBLISHER
olicy decisions af-
torial and financial
e newspaper

E EDITOR
publisher for the
the daily paper

EDITORIAL PAGE DIRECTOR
responsible for determining and writing Chronicle editorial opinion

SUNDAY EDITOR
oversees all Sunday feature sections,
buys all syndicated features and supervises special sections

SPORTS EDITOR
responsible for the Sporting Green
which functions as a newspaper within
a newspaper

WOMEN'S WORLD EDITOR
coordinates the work of the fashion,
society, food and club editors

FINANCIAL EDITOR
covers all financial news and writes
daily column interpreting business
trends

LIBRARY STAFF
responsible for keeping all background and reference materials
available

ARTISTS
responsible for all graphic material—
drawings, maps, charts, and retouch-
ing photographs for reproduction

LITERARY EDITOR
reviews books for the daily and edits
Sunday Book Section

Chapter XV

Appraisal of Mass Media

[Author's note: This chapter was written by one of the nation's most noted journalism educators, Professor J. W. Click of the School of Journalism, Ohio University.]

Americans, always critical of their mass media, began taking the First Amendment more seriously in the 1970's. The severest critics of the media are the practitioners within them, but activities of the late 1960's showed much greater interest in the media among the general public.

Looking at the media as a whole and the tendency to praise outstanding examples of work by newspapers and broadcast stations, noted critic Ben H. Bagdikian suggested:

> It is not enough to point to the best work of the best newspapers and broadcast stations. A better test is to take a 300-mile drive in any part of the country. Pick up every newspaper published within ten miles of the highway. Listen to every radio station receivable along the way. Then characterize their average contribution to the well-being of their communities. I do not recommend this for anyone susceptible to extreme depression.

Several criticisms apply to media in general or to a given function within several media. Discussing news judgment, Irving Kristol notes that a central failing of the media is that most news organizations confuse judgment with prejudice and decide not to get involved in making judgments about the news because they fear the result of personal prejudice by the reporter or editor. Kristol has written, "The commitment to so-called 'objective' and impersonal reporting of 'spot news' is, in practice, a rationalization for 'safe' and mindless reporting. To keep a reporter's prejudices out of a story is commendable; to keep his judgment out of a story is to guarantee that truth will be emasculated."

The media have a distinctive function in American society if only they will accept it, according to Bagdikian's analysis. He says the "system" so often attacked by rebels "is not usually wicked. It is usually sluggish. It has to serve too many people in too many ways, and the servers and the servees have trouble talking to each other." A successful system, he says, "ought to know what its people need and want, and if they are not getting what they need and want, the system ought to have a quick way to detect it."

The role of the press in such a system, Bagdikian says, is obvious. "It is a natural vehicle for the expression of local needs. And it is a natural instrument for the detection of breakdowns in the social system. On the whole, the press has not been doing either of these tasks very well.

"For one thing, too many news organizations see their job as doing no more than transmitting information that comes most easily over the transom. Few have the competence to understand the systems of government and business they should monitor. And lastly, too many are so close to officialdom that they are defensive about its performance. News organizations too devoted to the status quo resist evidence that the status quo isn't working. For too many news operations in too many communities the official, bureaucratic view of the world is the press view of the world."

With the loss of the small community and the school in the small community, where all sorts of backgrounds, races, income levels, and occupations were represented, Bagdikian suggests that only the mass media remain to give people a common view of each other, to show and report how people of other neighborhoods and schools live, act, and think. He also suggests that media should concentrate more on presenting proposed solutions to leading problems by thoughtful men outside of journalism. "Once a social problem has reached crisis proportions, we begin to discover that thoughtful men had earlier figured out some answers," he says.

Pseudo-World

Another charge against the media in general is that they create a pseudo or a synthetic world that gives the reader a distorted view of reality. When there is too much emphasis on crime, war, social problems, violence, unusual human interest events, and prominent persons by the media, it does not add up to a balanced presentation of the real world. The very definition of news says that something must be unusual to be reported, and therefore that news reporting will not recreate reality but rather be a fairly balanced report of the aberrations from the status quo.

Entertainment content of the media encounters the same situation. Viewers and readers want conflict, action, and unusual stories, not plots just like their own daily lives.

People depend on the mass media for almost all knowledge and entertainment. Because they are not interested in routine re-creations of experiences they have already encountered, or facts they already know, they are willing to accept a slightly distorted world synthesized through mass communication. Criticism of the media for the pseudo-world stems from a matter of degree and a simple question: Should the media give the public what it wants or what it needs?

The reader, listener, or viewer—called "consumer" for simplicity—has great effect on the media. Research has shown that much exposure to media is based on previous reward—favorite television programs, columnists, magazines, disc jockeys. Also, consumers filter communication through a set of attitudes they have built up over the years. They interpret a message in terms of responses they have learned and in ways that fit previous experiences and accepted values. Consequently, messages often are distorted to fit comfortably with beliefs and attitudes.

Media professionals write news broadcasts, entertaining features, and television shows to appeal to consumers' attitudes and inclinations, although the emphasis in news writing is toward being understood rather than having an argument or point of view accepted. Looking at it the other way, some important news stories have been read by very small numbers of people because they did not appeal to readers at the time they were published. So how far does one go in appealing to a mass audience?

Beyond merely appealing to large segments of the total audience, though, is a more serious pseudo-world. Part is created by newsmen, part by public relations men. Douglass Cater in his *Fourth Branch of Government* relates a typical case. A fairly routine treaty with Austria came up for Senate debate. One reporter went to the committee chairman and got a statement that Austria would receive no money or military aid under the treaty, only long-term credits. That was his lead. The next day's debate was dull, but one senator made a crack about President Dwight D. Eisenhower, which the reporter dispatched as an insert. The treaty's adoption just after 3:30 P.M. was handled as a bulletin. Although too late for most afternoon newspapers, a new lead would be needed for the morning papers. So the reporter got another senator to say that the first senator was weakening the president's authority. This charge was originated by the reporter, not the senator, and further, the reporter had called seven other senators before he got someone to make such a charge. Cater writes, "The reporter's imagination brought the Senator's thinking to bear on alternatives that he might not have thought of by himself. . . . The 'overnight' is the greatest single field for exploratory reporting for the wire services. It is what might be called 'milking the news'."

Besides newsmen's participation in creating news, public relations practitioners stage events ranging from hospital dedications to beauty pageants to get publicity for their clients.

Social Responsibility

The prevailing concept of mass communication in the United States through the first half of the twentieth century was the "libertarian" concept. It assumes that everyone has a right to express his opinion, even if he is the only person who holds that opinion. The idea goes back to John Milton and his *Areopagitica,* which was a reaction to the authoritarian practice of his time. Milton said, "Let her [truth] and Falsehood grapple: who ever knew Truth put to the worse in a free and open encounter?"

Milton based his statement on the premise that men have reason and wisdom to distinguish between right and wrong, good and bad, and therefore should be given a free choice. The thesis had little effect in Milton's eighteenth century but gradually became accepted after John Stuart Mill's *On Liberty* in the nineteenth century.

The libertarian concept implies that each idea must have an equal chance and everyone must have access to the channels of communication. As media of communication have grown more complex, with huge audiences and circulations, and so much more costly, it is virtually impossible for citizens to start their own newspapers, magazines, or stations. And even if they do, they are not guaranteed that their ideas will reach as large a number of persons as existing media. There also is a suggestion that man often cannot distinguish between truth and skillful propaganda and that a *laissez-faire* approach to the battle between ideas will not necessarily result in the common good.

From the libertarian concept has evolved a "social responsibility" concept of mass communication. It dates approximately from the publication in 1947 of the report of the Commission on Freedom of the Press, which suggested that the press, including electronic media, has a responsibility to provide "a truthful, comprehensive, and intelligent account of the day's events in context which gives them meaning," to be a "forum for the exchange of comment and criticism," to give a "representative picture of the constituent groups in society," to help in the "presentation and clarification of goals and values in society," and to "provide full access to the day's intelligence." The major mission of mass communications, according to the commission, is to raise social conflict "from the plane of violence to the plane of discussion."

This social responsibility concept goes beyond the First Amendment, which says nothing of balanced coverage in context, impartiality, or mentioning opposing views.

Social responsibility is not easily defined and cannot be enforced. Part of the difference between it and libertarianism is easy to see. Under libertarianism, with free combat among ideas, each owner advanced his own position, even if it meant distorting the truth, because truth would win in the minds of rational men. Under social responsibility, the media have an obligation to report truth in context—to present truth or reality, not advance a cause or position at the expense of truth. Truth is to be sorted out, as much as it can be, by the media rather than the consumer.

Access to Media

Ideas and philosophies still will come into conflict, of course, and the media will have their editorial positions. When there are conflicts, who has the upper hand? Doesn't a syndicated columnist obviously have a distinct advantage over an hourly wage earner? The wage earner may get a letter to the editor published, but the columnist has a built-in audience for his ideas. How can any individual get his ideas advanced in conflict with a network commentator?

Today's critics argue that access is a problem, that ideas don't have an equal chance nor do the people who express them. Jerome Barron in the June 1967 *Harvard Law Review* asserts that the press stifles unpopular and unorthodox views by closing them out. He argues that merely restraining the government does not assure freedom of speech "if a restraint on access is effectively secured by private groups."

The idea of guaranteeing everyone access to the media of his choice is appealing, but it also is unworkable. For local issues, local media are relatively accessible, but broader issues involving networks, magazines, and large numbers of newspapers are difficult to impossible to reach. And guaranteed access to the consumer of course would take away freedom from the media themselves. Encroaching upon one person's freedom to grant another's is a questionable solution.

Other Challenges to Media

Many other issues face the press. The heat of the controversy rises and falls, but the topics remain relatively constant: the conflict between a free press (and the public's right to know about crime) and the fair trial of the alleged criminal; the effects of violence in the media on children and other consumers; government management of news; neglect of minority viewpoints and activities in news reports; and distorted reporting of riots or "civil disorders." Obscenity and pornography also come in for discussion, but more in motion pictures and books than in other media. Extensive discussions of these topics appear in many other places, such as the quality or idea magazines, and need not be repeated here.

An overall appraisal of mass media is nearly impossible. As one looks at individual media, he tends toward appraisals based on the chief functions of each medium.

Newspapers

The chief function of newspapers is to inform readers of what is going on in the world they live in and particularly in their local community. Newspapers are judged mainly in a journalistic context—their effectiveness at gathering, processing, and disseminating information. The entertainment function of newspapers seldom receives much attention, and the expression of editorial opinion receives some but not a great deal.

Criteria of a Good Newspaper

A good newspaper prints the important news and provides the information, comment, and guidance that is most useful to its readers.

It reports fully and explains the meaning of local, national, and international events that are of major significance in its own community. Its editorial comment provides an informed opinion on matters of vital concern to its readers.

By reflecting the total image of its own community in its news coverage and by providing wise counsel in its editorials, a good newspaper becomes a public conscience. It must also be lively, imaginative, and original; it must have a sense of humor, and the power to arouse keen interest.

The implementation of these principles of good editing requires a skilled staff, an attractive format, adequate space for news and comment, and a sound business foundation.

The staff must possess the professional pride and competence necessary to breathe life and meaning into the daily record of history. Good writing must be combined with an effective typographical display of copy and pictures to capture the full drama and excitement of the day's news. Good printing is essential. News and comment of most immediate interest and importance to the local community must have priority for the available space, which will depend on the size and resources of the newspaper.

To assure a financially strong and independent publication, and one that is competitive with other media, a good newspaper must maintain effective circulation, advertising, and promotion departments.

Finally, a good newspaper should be guided in the publication of all material by a concern for truth, the hallmark of freedom, by a concern for human decency and human betterment, and by a respect for the accepted standards of its own community.

A good newspaper may judge its own performance—and be judged —by the criteria that follow.

Integrity

The newspaper shall:

Maintain vigorous standards of honesty and fair play in the selection and editing of its content as well as in all relations with news sources and the public.

Deal dispassionately with controversial subjects and treat disputed issues with impartiality.

Practice humility and tolerance in the face of honest conflicting opinions or disagreement.

Provide a forum for the exchange of pertinent comment and criticism, especially if it is in conflict with the newspaper's editorial point of view.

Label its own editorial views or expressions of opinion.

Accuracy

The newspaper shall:

Exert maximum effort to print the truth in all news situations.

Strive for completeness and objectivity.

Guard against carelessness, bias, or distortion by either emphasis or omission.

Correct promptly errors of fact for which the newspaper is responsible.

Responsibility

The newspaper shall:

Use mature and considered judgment in the public interest at all times.

Select, edit, and display news on the basis of its significance and its genuine usefulness to the public.

Edit news affecting public morals with candor and good taste and avoid an imbalance of sensational, preponderantly negative, or merely trivial news.

Accent when possible a reasonable amount of news that illustrates the values of compassion, self-sacrifice, heroism, good citizenship, and patriotism.

Clearly define sources of news, and tell the reader when competent sources cannot be identified.

Respect rights of privacy.

Instruct its staff members to conduct themselves with dignity and decorum.

Leadership

The newspaper shall:

Act with courage in serving the public.

Stimulate and vigorously support public officials, private groups, and individuals in crusades and campaigns to increase the good works and eliminate the bad in the community.

Help to protect all rights and privileges guaranteed by law.

Serve as a constructive critic of government at all levels, provide leadership for necessary reforms or innovations, and expose any misfeasance in office or any misuse of public power.

Oppose demagogues and other selfish and unwholesome interests, regardless of their size or influence.

Radio and Television

The electronic media are and always have been primarily entertainment media. But the Communications Act of 1934 calls for them to be operated in the "public interest, convenience, and necessity." News, although expensive to program, traditionally has been the principal public-interest programming. Although some news reports, documentaries, and special broadcasts have been criticized, over the long-term history of broadcasting the most critical comments have been aimed at the entertainment programming.

Although the limited spectrum space available for broadcast stations requires them to be controlled by the government through the Federal Communications Commission, once a station gets a license it almost can count on renewal every three years. Federal regulation of broadcasting limits freedom somewhat, primarily in requiring stations to serve their listeners and viewers and to meet community needs.

Radio does not receive a lot of critical attention. Networks supply many stations with newscasts and special events packages, but most programming is locally originated for local audiences.

The National Association of Broadcasters has a code, originally adopted in 1937 and revised periodically. It suggests standards of practice for dramatic programs, news, political broadcasts, advertising, acceptability of advertisers and products, and time standards for advertising.

The Radio Code can provide the basis for discussions about radio's performance as a medium of communication. The code is available in many standard reference works and from the National Association of Broadcasters, 1771 N Street, N.W., Washington, D.C. 20036.

After a preamble, the Radio Code opens with this section:

Advancement of Education and Culture

Because radio is an integral part of American life, there is inherent in radio broadcasting a continuing opportunity to enrich the experience of living through the advancement of education and culture. The radio broadcaster is augmenting the educational and cultural influences of the home, the Church, schools, institutions of higher learning, and other entities devoted to education and culture:

Should be thoroughly conversant with the educational and cultural needs and aspirations of the community served.

Should cooperate with the responsible and accountable educational and cultural entities of the community to provide enlightenment of listeners.

Should engage in experimental efforts designed to advance the community's cultural and educational interests.

One should be able to think of a radio station in terms of that statement.

It is fashionable at almost any time to criticize American television. Whether critics are satirical or serious, they pounce on programming that seeks the "lowest common denominator"—or the largest possible audience—and that gives the public "what it wants" instead of "what it needs." These criticisms are generally harmonious with the social responsibility concept. If man were truly rational, he would select the content he needs. Since he doesn't, the critics argue, the media have a responsibility to give him what he needs.

Pointing out that people can be free from media as well as free to use them, Stan Freberg discussed both advertising and "the programming that interrupts it" at the University of Kansas in 1968. He contended that "the average viewer, treated as though he had some degree of intelligence, would, out of gratitude if nothing else, go out and buy the product."

Freburg cited a *Christian Science Monitor* poll that found that of 1,000 responses, 72 percent said commercials were annoying, 64 percent found them not tasteful, 49 percent found them unacceptable, and 46 percent found them intolerable. He referred to a 1965 survey conducted by the American Association of Advertising Agencies that found the public able to categorize, either favorably or unfavorably, only 16 percent of all ads it is conscious of being exposed to. In other words, 84 percent did not evoke enough response to let the consumer categorize them either way. One advertising man remarked that agency management faces a "tremendous problem, the monumental indifference of consumers toward most advertising." The situation hasn't improved much since then.

A problem of television often mentioned by industry spokesmen is a talent gap, particularly that there simply are not enough writers to produce enough quality material to fill all the time available on the tube. Freberg reacts:

> So tell me this: Where is it written in blood that all waking hours of every single day must be filled up to the orthicon with television programming? . . . If television is spreading its programming too thin, and its commercials too thick, while our minds slowly turn into rutabagas from trying to find some meaning in it all, let us reason together. The Freberg Plan would call for an immediate de-escalation of programming and commercials. Henceforth, America could watch television only three nights a week. That way the networks could weed out the deadwood and consolidate just the cream of their programs into Monday, Wednesday, and Friday. (It is just possible, of course, that when they finished weeding out the deadwood, they would end up staring at a test pattern. But I'll let that pass for the moment.)

Freberg says that television would continue as usual on Monday, Wednesday, and Friday. Tuesday? He'd let the stations telecast one word: *Read!* Thursday: *Talk!* Saturday: *Unsupervised Activity!*

What happens to Sunday? You may well ask. We have to have somewhere to lump all those leftover commercials, don't we? Think of it! Twenty-four glorious, uninterrupted hours of advertising! A veritable cavalcade of all they hold dear at the Harvard Business School! A salute to the mouthwashes, dog foods, aspirins, and deodorants that have helped to give us "the good life"!

Television has broadcast superb documentaries, taken viewers to the moon and the political conventions, shown them the assassination of Lee Harvey Oswald and other events that were undreamed of a generation ago. But the bulk of TV programming is entertainment, and usually not challenging or informative entertainment at that. Most of it is provided by networks and syndicates. Local programs are minimal in most cities, and much of that local programming is begun only after a minority or pressure group threatens to challenge a license renewal.

A medium that uses an electromagnetic spectrum that belongs to all the people has some obligation to those people. The NAB Television Code is harmonious with the social responsibility concept of mass communication, but it is a voluntary code and is not effectively enforced.

The Television Code begins with a preamble and a section very much like that of the Radio Code on "Advancement of Education and Culture." It then continues into a section on "Acceptability of Program Material" that begins:

> Program materials should enlarge the horizons of the viewer, provide him with wholesome entertainment, afford helpful stimulation, and remind him of the responsibilities which the citizen has towards his society.

It continues with a long list of items that are acceptable or not acceptable on television.

Besides the broadcasters, of course, one must consider the behavior of the consumers. Viewers have shown preferences for an afternoon soap opera over a Senate committee hearing, for a prime-time variety show over a moon shot or a statement by the President. If the electromagnetic field really belongs to the people, how does one determine what should be broadcast to satisfy them and any concept of broadcasting responsibility?

Magazines

There is so much more diversity in the magazine field than in the other media that have been discussed that it is nearly impossible to outline a way to appraise this medium. Magazines appeal to people of vastly different interests and enthusiasms with content on widely varying topics. Compare even the 600 consumer magazines to just four national television networks, including PBS, and the number of daily newspapers available in your city. Many more ideas, voices, opinions, and helpful articles are available through magazines as an aggregate, but of course each appeals to a relatively small readership.

Generally, magazines could be appraised by the social responsibility concept of whether they are placing truth in context, offering a forum for ideas and opinions to their readers, and generally helping both individual readers and society with their content.

Theodore Peterson, in his book *Magazines in the Twentieth Century,* distinguished between one group of magazine publishers he calls "missionaries," because they had a mission for their magazines, and a larger group he calls "merchants," because they were businessmen interested primarily in making money from their magazines, which did not champion causes. Study of the magazine field suggests the merchant type of magazine generally reaches a larger audience and is financially more successful than the missionary type, although Peterson includes *Time* and *Reader's Digest* in his missionary group.

Magazines certainly need to be appraised on more than their circulations and profit margins. If compared with one another, the comparison should be made between similar magazines. How could one, for example, judge the comparative social responsibility of *The New Republic,* circulation 135,000, and *TV Guide,* circulation 15,400,000? It is almost absurd to try.

Financial success in magazines depends on balance between circulation and the size of the group or market logically interested in the content of the magazine, not merely in the largest circulation obtainable. Because advertising pays most of the costs of magazines, staying in business requires attracting enough of the right kind of readers to sell to the advertisers. The advertisers' decisions about whether the audience has good enough potential as customers is as great a key to success as the editorial content of the magazine. It might be better some other way, but few magazines can succeed without a large amount of advertising. A few magazines charge their readers the full cost, as *American Heritage, Consumer's Reports, Horizon,* and *Mad.* Others operate all or partly on a subsidy from an organization or institution, often a portion of annual dues.

There is no truly national magazine that binds America's people together. The national medium is television. A special-interest magazine such as *TV Guide,* with more than 15,400,000 circulation, or *Better Homes & Gardens,* with nearly 8,000,000, has an impressive audience but hardly a nationalizing influence. Each offers readers interested in a particular subject content about that subject. The community of interest is a topic rather than a geographic region or locality.

Magazines, then, may be judged on their usefulness to society at large, to the intended readers of the specific magazine being appraised, and to the advertisers who wish to reach the readers. Because of the great diversity in the field, some magazines mainly entertain, others primarily inform, and others attempt to influence or persuade. Each can be judged on its own terms, but always with a view to whether it is useful to society as a whole.

CHAPTER XVI

Libel and Other Legalities

Libel is visual defamation of a person. Some of the formal definitions from lawbooks and other sources are long, minutely detailed, and sometimes difficult to comprehend if one is not a lawyer or well acquainted with the jargon of the profession.

Slander is oral defamation. Libel is visual, concrete. Scratching a libelous statement or comment about a person in the wet cement of a sidewalk may get one sued, fined, or both, and involved to the extent of the possibility of going to prison for the action. The *American and English Encyclopedia of Law* states:

> A libel is a malicious defamation expressed either by writing or printing or by signs, pictures, effigies or the like; tending to blacken the memory of one who is dead, or to impeach the honesty, integrity, virtue or reputation, or to publish the natural or alleged defects of one who is alive and thereby expose him to public hatred, contempt, ridicule or obloquy; or to cause him to be shunned or avoided, or to injure him in his office, business or occupation.

Words may be libelous, but photographs, cartoons, sketches, or other art may also be defaming.

It is extremely rare that a commercial newspaper intentionally libels a person. An occasional exception occurs, unfortunately, when an unethical person intentionally lies or distorts the truth. But beginning journalists must be well informed on the ethics and need for accuracy of the press. Many words in the dictionary are libelous per se. Several of them have been responsible for libel suits that cost publications vast sums of money and have weakened or ruined the once good reputations of reporters, as well as causing them in some cases to lose their jobs and be subjected to fines and other punishments.

Reporters rarely have to use the following words, but when they do they must use them with extreme caution:

anarchist	confidence man	evil	gambler
arsonist	conspirator	extortionist	goon
bigamist	deadbeat	forger	hoodlum
blackmailer	drunk	fugitive	hooligan

283

idiot	moron	rapist	villain
incompetent	murderer	robber	violent
kidnapper	nut	shyster	wanton
killer	nitwit	sinner	wife beater
lunatic	perjurer	thief	
libeler	prostitute	turncoat	

One need not use any specific words to defame. If one merely imputes incorrectly, inaccurately, illegally, or in any erroneous way that defames, it may result in a libel suit. The implication that a person has leprosy has caused libel suits. The disease has a social stigma today as it did thousands of years ago. Such an implication could cause a person, his friends, and his family much harm. He could lose his job, see his friends and kin subjected to abuses, lose his social standing by being ostracized by the community. To call a person something he is not may be the vilest of crimes, depending on the case.

Many libel cases are caused by getting the wrong address, the wrong name—an initial may be all-important—or by misspelling a word. Many people have the same names. Saying that Mr. ABC was arrested for drunken driving and putting down the wrong figure in his street address may be libelous if another Mr. ABC down the block has the address that was printed. He is innocent, the other man guilty. And the error leads to a libel suit.

Recently, a newspaper was involved in a libel suit because headlines were accidentally switched on two stories. A head may be libelous if it doesn't belong to the story. As a lesson in watching superlatives in news stories, one newspaper editor pointed out that he once had "lovely Jane" turn out as "lousy Jane." The error got past the proofreader after the printer had set it.

The Supreme Court has ruled that famous people must sacrifice some of their liberty concerning libel. It has noted that to some degree "public people become public property" and that one may say or write almost anything defamatory about them. This especially applies to politicians. Ethics, accuracy, and good taste should always be applicable, however. The Supreme Court has stated that the press may say almost anything about politicians if it is done without malice.

Truth, privilege, fair comment, absence of malice, and retraction are the five defenses against libel. None of them is absolute.

Truth is the best defense, and it is all-encompassing in civil actions. But having printed the truth maliciously may not be a proper defense against a libel charge.

Privilege means that the press may or may not have the privilege to print something. Some records, files, documents, and papers may be published for proper purposes even though they may contain libel. This comes under freedom-of-the-press guarantees. However, the press must abide by the law as to when privileged items may be printed.

Fair comment covers the Supreme Court rulings regarding public figures whether they be politicians, public servants, writers, artists, entertainers, or otherwise in positions of national exposure. The working press may ethically comment, including condemnations, on the work or performances of such persons. This does not apply to their private lives. And prying press reporters have on occasion been charged with invasion of privacy and/or harassment.

Absence of malice may be the only defense in some libel cases involving misspelled words and ironies of that nature. There are two types of malice in libel situations. Malice *in fact* means that the malice was flagrant, inspired by some feeling ranging from mild ill will to intense hatred and a desire to defame. Malice *in law* means that the malicious act was done with the motivation of violating an individual's legal rights.

Retraction means that the publication that commits the libel must publish a retraction of the statement. This withdrawal and apology story must be displayed and run in a special way. When a potentially libelous situation is set up by a misspelled word, this defense is adequate in some states.

Libel laws vary from state to state. Some are more rigid and complex than others. All mean much trouble for journalists. Reporters must be careful even in quotes.

A reporter does not say that a person "was arrested for murder" or some other crime. He "was charged with" some crime. Attributions must be used often and with care in most crime stories.

Accuracy is the best way to avoid libel. When one is in doubt about a fact, statement, or word, he should always leave it out. If he cannot verify it by contacting the persons involved, it must not be used.

When a journalist refers to brand names of goods and services, he must abide by certain laws. Some corporations have brought suits against publications that spelled the names of their products with a lower case rather than a capital letter. Certain products have become so imbedded in the public mind that people refer to them by the name of the leading manufacturer. Shoppers often ask for a tissue by giving a brand name.

Refrigerator salesmen know that millions of people refer to their applicance as a "Frigidaire." This is the trade name of the refrigerators made by the General Motors Corporation. Many people refer to their food freezer as a "Deepfreeze." But the Amana Corporation dislikes having its "Deepfreeze" spelled with a small letter. The name is copyrighted.

When one mentions brand names, he should be accurate. All of the words must be accurate at all times.

Bibliography

ADVERTISING

Nelson, Roy P. *The Design of Advertising*. New York: Wm. C. Brown Company, 1967.

BOOKS ON WRITING

Cosbey, Robert C. *The Writer's Job*. Glenview, Ill.: Scott, Foresman and Company, 1966.
Gunning, Robert. *How to Take the Fog Out of Writing*. Washington, D.C.: U.S. Department of Health, Education, and Welfare, 1950.
Mathieu, Aron, ed. "The Creative Writer," Cincinnati, Ohio: *Writer's Digest,* 1961.
O'Hayre, John. *Gobbledygook Has Gotta Go*. Washington, D.C.: U.S. Government Printing Office, 1960.
U.S. Department of Health, Education, and Welfare. *Getting Your Ideas Across Through Writing*. Washington, D.C.: U.S. Government Printing Office, 1960.

EDITING

Crowell, Alfred A. *Creative News Editing*. New York: Wm. C. Brown Company, 1969.
Westley, Bruce H. *News Editing,* 2nd ed. New York: Houghton Mifflin Company, 1972.
Wimer, Arthur and Dale Brix, eds. *Workbook for Head Writing and News Editing*. New York: Wm. C. Brown Company, 1966.

FEATURE WRITING

Giles, Carl H. *The Student Journalist and Feature Writing*. New York: Richards Rosen Press, Inc., 1969.
——————. *Writing Right—To Sell*. Cranbury, N.J.: A. S. Barnes & Company, 1970.
Mathieu, Aron M., ed. "The Creative Writer." Cincinnati, Ohio: *Writer's Digest,* 1968.

HISTORY

Emery, Edwin. *The Press and America,* 3rd ed. Englewood Cliffs, N.J.: Prentice-Hall, Inc., 1972.
Giles, Carl H. *1927: The Picture Story of a Wonderful Year*. New Rochelle, N.Y.: Arlington House, 1971.
Kobre, Sidney. *Development of American Journalism*. New York: Wm. C. Brown Company, 1969.

Mott, Frank L. *American Journalism*. New York: The Macmillan Company, 1965.

LITERARY LAWS

Ashley, Paul P. *Say It Safely*. Seattle: University of Washington Press, 1966.
Pilpel, Harriet and Theodore Zavin. *Rights and Writers*. New York: E. P. Dutton & Co., Inc., 1960.
Wittenberg, Philip. *The Law of Literary Property*. Cleveland, Ohio: World Publishing Co., 1957.

MAKEUP

Arnold, Edmund C. *Modern Newspaper Design*. New York: Harper & Row Publishers, Inc., 1969.
Nelson, Roy P. *Publication Design*. New York: Wm. C. Brown Company, 1972.
Turnbull, Arthur T. and Russell N. Baird. *The Graphics of Communication*. New York: Holt, Rinehart & Winston, 1964.

MARKET GUIDES

Christian Writer's Handbook. Wheaton, Ill.: Christian Writers Institute, 1961.
Polking, Kirk and Natalie Hagen, eds. *Writer's Market* (yearly). *Writer's Digest*.

MASS COMMUNICATIONS

Clark, Ramsey. *Crime in America*. New York: Pocket Books, 1971.
Edwards, Verne E., Jr. *Journalism in a Free Society*. New York: Wm. C. Brown Company, 1970.
Rivers, William L. and Wilbur Schramm. *Responsibility in Mass Communication,* 2nd ed. New York: Harper & Row, 1969.
Rucker, Frank W. and Herbert L. Williams. *Newspaper Organization and Management,* 3rd ed. Ames: The Iowa State University Press, 1969.
Sandman, Peter M. *et al. Media, an Introductory Analysis of American Mass Communications*. Englewood Cliffs, N.J.: Prentice-Hall Inc., 1972.
Siebert, Fredrick S. *et al. Four Theories of the Press*. Urbana & Chicago: University of Illinois Press, 1956.
Wells, Alan, ed. *Mass Media & Society*. Palo Alto, Calif.: National Press Books, 1972.

PERIODICALS

"Columbia Journalism Review," bimonthly, $9 a year (700 Journalism Building, Columbia University, New York, N.Y. 10027).
"Editor & Publisher," weekly, $10 a year (850 Third Ave., New York, N.Y. 10022).
"Masthead," quarterly, $6 a year (1725 N Street, N.W., Washington, D.C. 20036).
"Quill," monthly, $5 a year (35 East Wacker Drive, Chicago, Ill. 60601).
"Quill and Scroll," monthly (School of Journalism, University of Iowa, Iowa City, Iowa).
"Scholastic Editor Graphics/Communications," monthly during school year,

$5.75 a year (18 Journalism Building, University of Minnesota, Minneapolis, Minn. 55455).

"The Writer," monthly, $4 a year (8 Arlington St., Boston, Mass. 02111).

"The Writer's Digest," $3.50 a year (22 E. 12th St., Cincinnati, Ohio 45210).

PHOTOGRAPHY

Ahlers, Arvel W. *Where and How to Sell Your Pictures.* New York: Amphoto, 1962.

Arnold, Edmund C. *Feature Photographs That Sell.* Hastings-on-Hudson, N.Y.: Morgan & Morgan, Inc., 1960.

Davis, Phil. *Photography.* New York: Wm. C. Brown Company, 1972.

Hurley, Gerald D. and Angus McDougall. *Visual Impact in Print.* American Publishers Press, 1971.

MacDougall, Curtis D. *News Pictures Fit to Print . . . Or Are They?* Curtis D. MacDougall, 1971.

Rhode, Robert B. and Floyd H. McCall. *Press Photography.* New York: The Macmillan Company, 1961.

PUBLIC RELATIONS

Kelley, Stanley, Jr. *Professional Public Relations and Political Power.* Baltimore, Md.: The Johns Hopkins University Press, 1956.

Kobre, Sidney. *Dynamic Force of Public Relations Today.* New York: Wm. C. Brown Company, 1964.

Schwartz, James W., ed. *The Publicity Process.* Ames: The Iowa State University Press, 1966.

SPORTS

Daley, Arthur. *Sports of the Times.* New York: E. P. Dutton & Co., Inc., 1959.

Heath, Harry and Lou Gelfand. *How to Cover, Write and Edit Sports.* Ames: The Iowa State University Press, 1969.

Murray, James. *The Best of Jim Murray.* New York: Doubleday & Co., Inc., 1968.

Stapler, Harry. *Sports Reporting.* New York: Richards Rosen Press, Inc., 1967.

Ward, Bill. *Reporting and Writing Sports* (NSPA, University of Minnesota, 1971).

STYLE

Strunk, William, Jr., and E. B. White. *The Elements of Style,* 2nd ed. New York: The Macmillan Company, 1972.